T0324929

Workstations and Publication Systems

Rae A. Earnshaw
Editor

Workstations and Publication Systems

With 50 Illustrations

Springer-Verlag
New York Berlin Heidelberg
London Paris Tokyo

Rae A. Earnshaw
University of Leeds
LEEDS LS2 9JT
Great Britain

Library of Congress Cataloging in Publication Data
Workstations and publication systems.
    1. Electronic publishing.   2. Microcomputers.
I. Earnshaw, R. A. (Rae A.), 1944–
Z286.E43W67   1987   070.5′028′5   87-9683

Printed and bound by R.R. Donnelley & Sons, Harrisonburg, Virginia.
Printed in the United States of America.

9 8 7 6 5 4 3 2 1

ISBN 0-387-96527-0 Springer-Verlag New York Berlin Heidelberg
ISBN 3-540-96527-0 Springer-Verlag Berlin Heidelberg New York

Editor's Introduction

Review

Office automation and associated hardware and software technologies are producing significant changes in traditional typing, printing, and publishing techniques and strategies. The long term impact of current developments is likely to be even more far reaching as reducing hardware costs, improved human-computer interfacing, uniformity through standardization, and sophisticated software facilities will all combine together to provide systems of power, capability and flexibility. The configuration of the system can be matched to the requirements of the user, whether typist, clerk, secretary, scientist, manager, director, or publisher.

Enormous advances are currently being made in the areas of publication systems in the bringing together of text and pictures, and the aggregation of a greater variety of multi-media documents. Advances in technology and reductions in cost and size have produced many 'desk-top' publishing systems in the market place. More sophisticated systems are targeted at the high end of the market for newspaper production and quality color output.

Outstanding issues in desk-top publishing systems include interactive editing of structured documents, integration of text and graphics, page description languages, standards, and the human-computer interface to documentation systems. The latter area is becoming increasingly important: usability by non-specialists and flexibility across application areas are two current concerns. One of the objectives of current work is to bring the production of high quality documents within the capability of naive users as well as experts.

Recent developments in the area of computer graphics have emphasized the advantages of formulating standard definitions (e.g. GKS, PHIGS) for producing recommended interfaces to devices and application programs and for greater transportability of information (e.g. across networks). In addition, the formulation and acceptance of standards result in further significant benefits such as aiding the understanding and use of graphics methods, uniformity of documentation, common methodologies and working practices, and conformance and validation tests. The latter are proving to be of great value to the customer when assessing commercial systems, in that they provide quantitative yardstick metrics by which systems can be compared. In the area of documents, the Standard Generalized Markup Language (SGML) has reached the final stages in its preparation as an ISO international standard. The Office Document Architecture (ODA) standard is also reaching the final stages of being an ISO standard, and also a European Computer Manufacturers' Association (ECMA) standard. ODA is concerned with the underlying architectural and processing model for documents and provides a hierarchical, object-oriented view. Although these are useful standards in their own right, neither handles graphics or pictures in a flexible manner. SGML allows the incorporation of system-dependent graphics and ODA supports the exchange of graphics metafile information. What is really needed is an effective mechanism for incorporating graphics from a variety of sources such as CAD and drafting systems, business graphics, bitmapped images, painting systems, geometric illustration systems, digital prepress and video.

Topics Covered in the Present Volume

This volume presents contributions on a number of topics in the general areas of page description and graphics, document structures and editing, workstations and human-interface aspects and languages and implementations. The material is divided into these corresponding four sections following a general survey and introduction. The allocation of a contribution to a particular section was not always clear-cut; numerous authors touch on matters outside the principal domain of their paper. To come extent this is inevitable as electronic publishing is a strongly interrelated field where there is much overlap. For example, text merges with graphics, workstations interface to networks, pages within documents are parts of the document structure and editing facilities are required for all components of multi-media documents.

Although these papers cover mainly European work, they are not unrepresentative of similar developments worldwide. In view of the diverse nature of some of the topics covered, there is no intended unifying theme running through the book except that covered by the overall title. The aggregation of this material is thus heterogeneous rather than homogeneous, and ranges from introductory and review (e.g. the paper on SGML), through strategy and overview (e.g. the first paper on the five-year publishing forecast), to detailed implementation case studies (e.g. PLEIADE, POSTSCRIPT) and studies of theoretical aspects (e.g. grammar formalisms). This combination of tutorial review and detailed examination of selected areas should enable most readers to derive maximum benefit from the volume.

It should be emphasized that the material in this volume describes developments and systems in the public domain. Company confidential information has obviously not been included. Thus some significant current activities in research and development laboratories are not covered, but it may be some time before such designs and products see the light of day in fully supported commercial systems.

The contributions in this volume may be taken as illustrative of some of the techniques they set out. Some papers have been prepared using the systems they describe. Some have been transmitted from the author, received by the publisher, and integrated and combined into this book all using electronic techniques. Readers are invited to assess the success of this in the appearance of the final product. The lessons learned from this experience by authors, editor and publisher may well be the subject of a further paper (but not in this volume!)

The general introduction consists of an invited paper by Sandy Campbell, Vice-President of Xerox Corporation, and reviews anticipated developments in publishing technologies over the next five years. These include a 'publishing workstation' of 5 Mips and 8 Mbytes primary storage; increasing use of high-speed scanning input; improved communications technologies and storage/filing capabilities; development of document base management systems; quality raster printers (including color); and the definition of document structures,

In the second section on Page Description and Graphics, the invited paper by Nenad Marovac of San Diego State University and Composition Software Systems - Xerox, surveys concepts and implementations of page description languages. These are programming languages used to describe the structure and appearance of a document page in a device-independent way. Implementation experiences from two projects related to Interpress, a Xerox document description language, are used to illustrate how to make the transition from theory to practice.

This is followed by three contributions. The first, by Stephane Querel, Bruno Borghi and Daniel de Rauglaudre, describes the implementation of SMSCRIPT - an interpretor for the POSTSCRIPT (+) page description language under UNIX (++). The second, by Crispin Goswell, discusses some novel features of implementing POSTSCRIPT for high-resolution bitmapped displays (for previewing pages prior to output). The third by Nigel Hall, Sue Laflin and W. Dodd, describes the approach adopted in the Birmingham and Loughborough Electronic Network Development (BLEND) project for combining graphics and text within an electronic journal document.

The third section on Document Structures and Editing commences with an invited contribution from John Honeywell, Assistant Editor of TODAY - a quality color newspaper in the United Kingdom. He describes the systems currently in use at TODAY and the computerized procedures used to produce 365 newspapers per year. The emphasis is on the pragmatics of the commercial world rather than the abstractions and theoretics of academia.

This is followed by a description of PLEIADE by J. Nanard, M. Nanard and G. Cottin, an interactive document manipulation system for texts, graphics, formulae, tables and other structured documents defined by the user. It uses an iconic language and objects to interact with visual representations on the workstation screen.

+ POSTSCRIPT is a trademark of Adobe Systems Inc.
++ UNIX is a trademark of AT & T Bell Laboratories

The next paper by Ulrike Harke, Manfred Burger and Ruppert Gall, describes a graphics editor for the creation and manipulation of graphics and their incorporation into documents. This is followed by a theoretical paper describing a picture grammar formalism developed to drive a syntax-directed editor for graphical notations, by Mark Woodman, Darrel Ince, Jenny Preece and Gordon Davies. It is thus exploring the possibility that picture grammars can be used to describe software engineering notations. The editor forms part of a set of software tools for the Open University Syntactic Graphics Project. Finally in this section, Bruce Spicer describes a system designed and used at the British Petroleum Group Research Center - the Sunbury Integrated Technical Publishing System - and outlines the improvements in document production and communication brought about by the methods used.

In the fourth section on Workstations and HCI aspects, the invited paper by Peter Brown describes a methodology for presenting and interacting with on-line documents on workstation display screens. This approach enables readers to adapt the displayed document to their own needs, and utilizes the interactive facilities of the workstation to the full.

This is followed by a description of GENIE-M - a generator for multi-media information environments by Ian Angell, Yuen Ping Low and Adrian Warman. This enables the mixing, integration and interaction with static media types (such as text and graphics) and dynamic types (such as sound, video, film and animation).

The next contribution is a further paper by Jenny Preece, Gordon Davies, Mark Woodman and Darrel Ince on a methodology for specifying the design of the user interface to documentation systems. This design also provides an opportunity for developing a conceptual model which more closely correlates with the users' requirements of the system.

This is followed by a further HCI paper describing a model for an interactive graphic interface to an electronic office system by Michael Butcher. Utilities within the system allow a range of users of varied ability and experience from novice to expert to be equally catered to. It is thus an example of an adaptive system.

The next paper by Lesley Beddie and Pat Napier examines a method for accessing information via an Electronic Document Delivery/Exchange Service (EDDS) supported on a wide area network within the context of academic institutions.

In the final section on Languages and Implementations, Robert Stutely presents a survey and review paper on the Standard Generalized Markup Language (SGML). This will be of special interest to all those who have no knowledge of, or connection with, the various processes that have led to the formulation, development, refinement and formalisation of the current standard. This paper also includes a useful biography and list of associated organisations and contacts.

This is followed by a description of the Chelgraph SGML structured editor by Peter Cadogan. This is a set of software tools for facilitating document design and creation in the personal computer environment.

The next paper on personal publishing by Richard Whitaker and Lindsay Robertson outlines the various components required in a personal system and their interrelationship. This is a rapid growth area; many more systems are expected in the market place within the next few years. Potential users without experience will be overwhelmed by the variety and will not know which to select for their purpose. This paper gives some quantitative guidance on criteria to be used in assessing the components of a system.

A paper by Mike Clarke describes a simple pagination system for high quality text documents. It is argued that a system designed specifically to cater to this task will be more appropriate than a generalized page make-up system. The system is designed for a range of users from authors to typographers and will run on personal computers.

Finally, on a subject orthogonal to all the other contributions in this volume (but included for reasons of diversity), Barry Ashdown surveys the current achievements and future prospects for videotex.

The Future

This volume has highlighted a number of significant areas of interest and importance in electronic publishing. This includes combining text and graphics, document structures, page description, multi-media documents, standardization and human-computer interface issues.

Additional research issues of current importance are color reproduction (and matching hard-copy pictures to screen pictures); graphics design tools; digital typography; imaging; distributed system architectures; multi-processor architectures; automated presentation techniques; and illustration interchange. It is anticipated that significant progress will be made on these topics in the next year or so.

Further areas of interest are those to do with the quality and visual appearance of the text (and pictures) in the document, whether on screen or on paper. This involves the following aspects and topics: jaggies; fonts; line weights, contrast, color, style, spacing, dynamic range and white space.

Current standardization efforts will have a wide-ranging impact on the methods of document preparation and interchange. Joan Smith examines the implications of SGML for scientific publications in a recent article in the Computer Journal (1).

In a recent book on *"Designing Integrated Systems for the Office Environment"* (2), William Newman summarizes the anticipated developments over the next few years. These include: more rationalized user-interface design; increasing power and reducing costs of workstations; greater resolution of display screens; easier networking; typeset-quality printers; integration of text and graphics; increase in the use of electronic mail; and sophisticated information management systems. It is clear that most of these anticipated developments are technology driven. Software systems, HCI and successful integration of the technology all tend to lag behind such developments, as do evaluation measurements of the effectiveness of the systems currently designed for existing technology. If we have no quantitative measures for current systems and technology, the anticipated rapid developments on the technological front will leave us even more in the dark concerning how to exploit them.

What is needed above all is detailed and quantitative studies of interface characteristics in order to produce optimum and effective man-machine communication. This interface may incorporate a number of software layers beneath which appropriate hardware can be utilized. The systems are thus designed top-down and automatically tailored and integrated into the real needs, requirements and application of the users, rather than as a system driving the user. Producing systems that are user-driven rather than technology-driven is one of the major challenges for the future.

Rae A. Earnshaw
University of Leeds
United Kingdom

January 1987

1. J.M. Smith *"The Implications of SGML for the Preparation of Scientific Publications"*, Computer Journal, Vol 29, No 3, pp 193-200, 1986.

2. W.M. Newman *"Designing Integrated Systems for the Office Environment"*, McGraw-Hill, pp 446, 1987 (ISBN: 0-07-046332-8).

Acknowledgments

Thanks and appreciation are expressed to all the contributors to this volume and to Gerhard Rossbach of Springer-Verlag, Computer Science Editorial, USA West Coast Office, Santa Barbara, who organized the incorporation of electronic versions of the papers into this volume.

These papers formed the basis of an International Conference and Exhibition held in London and we are very grateful to our sponsors; the British Computer Society, the Computer Graphics and Displays Group, the Electronic Publishing Group, and the Computer Graphics Society. Our thanks and appreciation go to Mrs. Frances Johnson, Conference Officer at the University of Leeds, and Brian Booker, for all their help and support, and to all those delegates who attended from numerous countries and contributed by their discussion and interaction.

A volume such as this is not possible without planning and preparation and we thank all those who assisted us in this process. We thank especially the authors who kept to the deadlines for their contributions and also Springer-Verlag for invaluable help, guidance and assistance.

Rae A. Earnshaw
University of Leeds
United Kingdom

January 1987

Contents

A Five Year Publishing Technologies Forecast

Dr. Ronald B. Campbell, Jr.
Xerox Corporation, Connecticut, USA

Abstract   Recent rapid advances in electronic technologies, especially those associated with powerful bit mapped workstations and raster printers, have enabled corporate electronic publishing as an effective and efficient process. Advances in the key technologies supporting electronic publishing are forecast for the next five years. The effect of these advances upon electronic publishing is assessed.

Introduction   Electronic publishing may be regarded as a subset of document processing. This phrase is used to emphasize the contrast between data processing and document processing. Data processing operates upon data in the form of fields, records, files, and data bases. By contrast in document processing the atomic elements are words, paragraphs, pages, documents, etc. It is convenient to define a document simply as information structured for human comprehension. Electronic publishing then denotes that subset of document processing where the output is emphasized, i.e., the document is an end in its own right, but also connotes an emphasis upon quality and some degree of permanence for the document.

Historically, the earliest form of document processing was word processing, although text processing is a better term. Electronic publishing can be viewed as an evolution of word processing. To the capabilities of processing text are added capabilities for graphics, for greatly enriched formats, and for much richer styles.

One way to better understand electronic publishing is to look at its applications in various areas, for example, personal publishing, work group or departmental publishing, and enterprise wide publishing. From a technological point of view, however, electronic publishing is best regarded as the process integration of six functional technologies as they are applied to the publishing task. (Fig. 1) These are the functional technologies for creation and manipulation, scanning and recognition, storage and retrieval, communications, printing, and copying and reproduction. These six functions fit naturally into three groups: input, management of the publishing process, and output. These groups will be reviewed in turn. (Fig. 2)

Input technologies   There are two input technologies: creation and processing, and scanning and recognition (or capture). Some batch publishing tasks which are highly repetitive and utilize data already stored in a computer are best done on a computer, but in applications where there is any significant degree of interaction, powerful publishing workstations are employed. These desktop units provide the usual functions for keyboarding and temporary storage and display, but emphasize the graphics capability and the manipulation of electronic documents. Workstation technology is the first major enabler of corporate electronic publishing.

"3-M" Workstation   The state-of-the-art in publishing workstation technology is characterized by the so-called "3-M" workstation. The 3-M technology offers about one million pixels (or dots) on the screen, processing power of about one MIP (one million instructions per second), and one million bytes or one megabyte of primary or working storage. Such a workstation supports the display of two full pages side-by-side. (Fig. 4)

Publishing Workstation in 5 Years

Over the next five years, the trends in the underlying semiconductor technology will continue to drive a year-to-year improvement in processing power and speed of approximately 20 to 25 percent, with memory growing somewhat faster. That will lead to capabilities of some five MIPS, and eight megabytes of primary storage very early in the nineties. (Fig. 5)

During the same period, the cathode ray tube will continue as the dominant display technology. No other technologies come close to meeting the CRT's combination of resolution, brightness, speed, display area, contrast, and so forth. One million pixel displays will proliferate; higher resolution displays will find special application.

The major benefits from this plenitude of powerful workstations will be more rapid and comprehensive editing and formatting capabilities. An example of enhanced capability will be seen in the advent of the "digital darkroom", which will permit users to represent, display, and manipulate pictures. For instance, different screens and tone reproduction curves can be experimented with prior to printing.

Another major benefit will be dramatic improvement in ease of use, made possible by advanced software and display controllers. Advancements to enhance ease of use will include wider use of pop-down menus, windows, and diagnostic and help facilities to provide electronic equivalents of publishing activities.

What is called intelligent support software should become widely available either on workstations or knowledge servers. A current example of such intelligent support is the spelling-checker software presently available on typewriters and word processors. In five years expert systems for editing, composition, and even authoring should be available. There will be a move toward systems that can check not just spelling but syntax ... and even semantics. Even today, the first packages that help to organize thinking are available. Language translation aids will be generally available.

One key thrust of this intelligent support software will be to improve the quality of documents by improving their content -- that is, the information they contain. Most of our current computer-based tools have seduced their users into becoming more preoccupied with the form, as opposed to the content, since the tools have focussed on providing access to fonts, formatting, etc. However, "idea processing" environments, such as Xerox' NoteCards, are beginning to emerge that help an author (a) to collect and organize information, (b) to discover the structure of the information by browsing over it and establishing relationships, (c) to reason about the logical coherence of the information, (d) and to build persuasive rhetorical arguments for certain points of view. Sophisticated authoring environments like NoteCards will contain intelligent tools, such as (a) content analysis for associative retrieval and clustering of related ideas, (b) advanced visual browsers (color, animated, 3-D), (c) "truth-maintenance" tools for supporting multiple, inconsistent points of view, and (d) rhetorical representations based on recent theories of the nature of argumentation.

Linguistic tools can help the author craft the language of the document. Spelling and punctuation can be automatically corrected; we are beginning to even deal with words in their grammatical context (e.g., distinguishing "there" from "their"). Thesaurus and dictionary lookup services will give us the ability to start to deal with the meaning of the test, such as synonymy. And grammar checking will help us identify pronominal referents.

The second key thrust of quality improvement is how the content of the document is presented. There is a great deal of expertise in designing graphical diagrams and in the page layout of a document. Research is beginning to unearth the tacit abstractions that human have developed with centuries of use of paper documents, and some of this knowledge is just beginning to be incorporated into intelligent systems. Thus, we can begin to see the basis of sophisticated interactive systems for aiding graphics design by maintaining the underlying constraint relations that must hold between the elements of a page layout. We can see the possibility of advising on and even automating much of this graphic design activity.

Tomorrow's expert systems will, in effect, bring the expertise of a seasoned professional editor or graphics designer to the end user. Color may be cited as another area for the application of expert systems. In the hands of an inexperienced user, color capability can produce garish results, instead of enabling more effective communication. The net result will be that tomorrow's workstation will allow a moderately experienced user to produce a professional quality of work, and enable professionals to work more rapidly and effectively.

The workstation of tomorrow will offer powerful capabilities for creating and processing documents, but it needs to be closely integrated with the capability to capture and to process existing documents in paper form and photographs. There is a large existing base of paper documents, created without the use of electronic publishing technologies. There are also cases in which documents have been created electronically, but where the electronic master is not available or is not compatible. This is where scanning comes in - as a means of capturing this existing material - and bringing it into the electronic world. (Fig. 6)

Conversion Bridges

Scanning is the bridge between two domains - from the domain of the paper document to the domain of the electronic document, just as printing is the bridge in the other direction. Dramatic advancements are being made in scanning and recognition - advancements that will result in qualitative changes in electronic publishing.

Scan Processing

There are several levels of scanning, starting with raw scanning and compression, as represented by facsimile. The CCITT algorithms used for facsimile transmission produce compressions that reduce storage and transmission requirements by typical factors of 10 to 20, but do not recognize the scanned material. Thus it cannot be edited. The next level of scanning involves simple recognition, as in optical character recognition (OCR).

OCR scanning is limited to one font, but does provide greater compression, typically 30 times that of facsimile. This provides a net compression of a factor of 300 or so with alphanumeric text. That factor dramatically reduces storage and transmission requirements for electronic documents. (Fig. 7)

More recently, there has been the introduction of intelligent scanning or ICR. This technology, which is advancing very rapidly, allows the capture of documents with multiple fonts, a much broader range of documents. An example is the Kurzweil 4000 intelligent scanning system.

Great progress is being made in raster to vector conversion, which allows conversion of vectors in raster form - lines in charts and drawings, for instance - to a much more compact form that can be edited. Multiple-font recognition and vector to raster conversion are a step in the direction of the ideal scanner. That scanner will not be confined to just numbers and alphabetic characters.

The ideal document recognizer will be able to simultaneously recognize vectors and graphics. It will be able to handle pictorial matter, without special instructions. The output of this device will be encoded into a very compact representation for editing, storage, and transmission. The document recognizer is the inverse of a printer. A (raster) printer converts an electronic master into a paper master; the recognizer does the inverse function. (Fig. 8)

High-speed array scanners the width of a page, the base component of the ideal scanner of the future, are now becoming available. Recognition algorithms will be facilitated by powerful new processors because the processing requirements of these algorithms are considerable.

These trends will greatly reduce the size and costs of intelligent scanners. Thus, scanners will no longer be high cost, limited use devices, but will become widely available as components of integrated systems.

Management Technologies

The two basic management technologies are communications, and storage and filing. (Fig. 9) For all but the very simplest personal publishing, communications are critical. That is because publishing typically involves a very interactive process among a number of people, and between the various technologies used at different stages of the publishing process. The needs for effective communications are compounded as publishing moves in the direction of decentralized and demand publishing. The work of multiple authors must be coordinated, approval and revision processes handled, production scheduled, and archiving managed.

Electronic tools, distributed over an electronic network, are a key to improving the process of document production. The publication process is extremely complex, involving many people, simultaneous jobs, and intricate scheduling and coordination of many specialized functions. Communication, coordination, and scheduling tools can improve quality, as well as reduce errors. Advanced user interface tools, such as multiple window environments, can help individuals in the complex mental task of switching between jobs and "getting back into context".

Coordination tools will not only be isolated within publishing departments, but will be integrated with the sources of information that the documents convey. For example, maintenance documentation for machines needs to be tied to the engineering CAD tools, so that engineering changes can be propagated to the appropriate service documentation. Coordination tools are especially critical when multiple documents must be coordinated. For example, school texts must be coordinated with workbooks and teachers' manuals, and the text for any grade level must obey mandated "complexity metrics".

Electronic publishing, because of its quality standards and the growing use of pictorial materials, is "bandwidth-intensive". Bandwidth-intensive implies that electronic publishing requires broader communications pathways than typical data processing applications. These broad paths are needed for the rapid transmission of digital data representing pictorial and graphic material and also to support color, animation, integrated voice, and linked computational processes.

There are two levels of publishing communications, departmental or intra-plant and inter-plant. Departmental publishing activities are well served today by local area networks. For instance, the 10-megabit local area network, as defined by the IEEE 802.3 standard, meets departmental publishing needs well. However, at Xerox we have predicted that intra-plant or departmental bandwidths will have to increase by a factor of 5 to 10 to support the publishing of tomorrow's more advanced and complex documents. Fiber optics will be the best medium for this requirement.

There are rapid advances in the communications technologies needed for inter-plant publishing applications. These advances are being fueled by two factors. The first is the deregulation of the communications industry, which has lit the fires of competition. For instance, depreciation periods have been greatly shortened, which permits much more rapid introduction of new technology.

The other factor is the rapid installation of fiber optics, which will make long distance high bandwidth services much cheaper. The integrated services digital network (ISDN) is an example of the new type of services that will be available to support inter-plant or distributed electronic publishing. This trend toward distributed electronic publishing is discussed later on in this paper.

The ISDN, with its 2 B + D format, will increase by approximately 15 times the bandwidth of the typical channel offering 9600 bits per second. The two B channels provide digital end-to-end throughput of 128 kilobits per second. Coupled with this greater bandwidth will be the ability to establish a connection in milliseconds, rather than in seconds.

The net result will be significantly reduced communications costs and response times. These will encourage and facilitate remote document entry and demand printing. Thus, a user at a workstation on the other side of the country will be able to make use of centralized publishing facilities, or other distributed facilities (such as printers), with great ease, and with little perception of distance. Network architectures based on remote procedure calls will be facilitated.

**Storage/Filing
Technology Trends**

Advances in storage technology are essential to electronic publishing. This is because of the trend toward higher quality and longer documents. Especially when documents contain bit maps, storage requirements are greatly increased. This section focuses primarily on the technologies needed for secondary storage, rather than on the semiconductor storage technology of primary memory. (Fig. 11)

There are several secondary storage technologies, but those of primary interest to electronic publishing today are magnetic storage, including floppy and hard disks, as well as tape, and optical storage. It is interesting to note that magnetic recording, which has been evolving steadily now for 30 years, has a longer track record of continuous progress than that of semiconductor random access storage technology. The key figure of merit in magnetic recording is areal density, the number of magnetic bits per square inch. The number of bits per square centimeter has doubled about every two and a half years.

Since no short term barriers to progress are evident, we can foresee a quadrupling of capacity for a particular format within five years. This implies that secondary storage at workstations could typically be around 500 megabytes, with multi-gigabyte storage available on even small departmental systems. One gigabyte equals 1,000 megabytes, or one billion bytes. That offers a capacity, even without compression, for about 1,000 pages of text and graphics, at 300 dots per inch.

One billion bytes sounds like a great deal of memory, but electronic publishing will want more. More is on the way in the form of optical storage. Optical storage is available now in read-only and write-once. Later, read-write capability will be available. Read-only technology can play a major role in the distribution of documents that are fairly static. Write-once technology will be important in archival applications. Maturation of the two technologies for read-write optical storage, that is, either phase change or magneto-optic recording, is a challenging task, but the driving force remains the very high resolution and freedom from close spacing tolerances of the laser beam technology.

The key challenge that I foresee in filing is the development of document base management systems. Tomorrow's document base management system will be in some ways analogous to the database management systems (DBMS) of today's data processing. The document base management system will be a storage, retrieval, and backup facility, integrated into a cohesive management framework. That framework will support the entire range of electronic publishing tasks and projects, from desktop and departmental publishing to corporate publishing. It will be the key element to support control and management of the publishing process.

**Traditional
Publishing Process**

Eventually, document base management system software technology will do for electronic publishing what DBMs have done to structure and speed the development of data processing applications. The figures (12-17) compare the traditional publishing process and the electronic publishing process. At the heart of the electronic process is the document management system. But the movement to an electric document management system will be evolutionary. The challenge here is two-fold.

Electronic Publishing Process

First, documents have much more complex structures that do data files. The document base will contain a great diversity of document size and types. There will be extensive interlinking of documents. Second is the distributed and more participative nature of the publishing process which requires a distributed document base and long complex transactions. A further challenge will be the management of active (i.e., computational) documents.

Tools can help in the distribution of documents to the people who need to see them. Tools can help make explicit some aspects of the content of documents for a document base. Quite sophisticated indexing will be based on adding linguistic technology to more pragmatic automatic indexing schemes. The possibilities in this direction are exciting and open up a wide range of uses. Today, statistical techniques (such as N-gram analysis) provide an impressive degree of functionality in retrieving documents by content. Pragmatic linguistic technology, based on morphological lemmatization and conceptual reduction by thesaurus lookup, can greatly improve our ability to recognize similar documents even when they are expressed quite differently in the surface language. When documents are semantically indexed, they can be easily retrieved from a document base.

Further, indexed documents can be automatically routed directly to people with matching interest profiles. Systems are being developed today that do this with electronic mail, but the concept can be easily extended to demand-printed documents. For example, Lens is an experimental system developed at MIT in cooperation with Xerox PARC; it is an expert system in that it can contain knowledge about the users on the network, the organizational structure, and the topics that people are interested in. By providing users with access to a rule-based filtering mechanism, it allows individual users to control the kind of information that gets sent to them (that is, control is in the hands of potential receivers, as well as senders). Senders do not have to worry about remembering who the right people are to send each document; the organizational knowledge base, which is built up by the individuals themselves, will determine who will be interested.

With indexing, demand printing can be carried a step further. If documents are constructed in modular pieces and the pieces are indexed, then specialized versions of documents can be constructed for particular people's needs. For example, a specialized instruction manual can be assembled to teach a worker how to do a new job, that particular manual being constructed to take account of the demands of the particular job, as well as what that worker knows from past experience. There are endless possibilities for such "micro-publishing" applications.

Output Technologies

Output technologies, especially those of raster printing, are the second of the two prime enablers of electronic publishing. (Fig. 18) The advent of electronic raster printers with a resolution of 300 dots per linear inch has permitted demand printing of documents containing multiple-font text, forms, and graphics. These printers permit near typeset quality material to be prepared rapidly and eliminate the need for forms storage. Raster printing is the bridge from the electronic master to the paper output.

Raster printing technology will make great advances over the next five years. Costs will drop steadily, leading to the proliferation and widespread availability of intermediate-quality printing. The output quality will be improved by the ready availability of printers capable of producing up to 600 dots per linear inch, although these will require a four times more powerful processor for the same output speed.

Color printing technology is being pressed to keep up with color display technology. But five years should see the introduction of printers with capabilities ranging from highlight color to full process color. The most demanding color tasks, especially pictorial, will continue to require special treatment. But the great majority of corporate color requirements for highlight color and color graphics will be fully integrated into corporate electronic publishing systems.

After the electronic master is converted to paper, the question arises of what production technology to use. Offset and xerography-based duplicators are the primary contenders. Two factors are accelerating the trend toward greater use of xerography, especially in corporate publishing. Xerographic technology is evolving faster than offset technology, and the trend is away from supply printing and toward demand printing with its shorter runs.

But will corporations really need all these printers, copiers, and duplicators? What about the paperless office that has received so much attention? Why can't electronic documents be produced, then sent them over tomorrow's broad bandwidth communications highways? In a flash, they could be displayed on workstations, the ones that by then are projected to be on every business desk.

In addressing this question, it is useful to distinguish between two major classes of documents. There are documents that convey significant information, not mere data, to humans. These are the documents that the focus for electronic publishing. There are documents that primarily support transactions, often for feedback to machines.

A canceled check, for instance, offers data confirming a transaction. But a bank statement conveys information needed to balance your checkbook. Much transaction support paper may disappear. Some banks have experimented with not returning canceled checks, for instance. So, as electronic-based, transaction-oriented systems become more pervasive, less of this kind of paper will be produced, especially between corporations.

Role of Paper in Electronic Publishing

But people like paper as the medium on which significant information is conveyed to them. They want to be able to read and study the information. They want to mark on it, carry it around, review it with others, hand it on, even crumple it, from time to time.

Paper has major advantages in tactile qualities, resolution, contrast, freedom from glare, transportability, and ease of scanning, to mention only a few. These advantages make it very unlikely that paper will be displaced from its position as the preferred output medium for electronic publishing. The proliferation of inexpensive raster printers only lends further support to this position.

So we believe that there will be more, not fewer, information-carrying documents. Experience bears out this prediction. As we have installed automated publishing systems, we have found that the amount of paper printed and reproduced increases significantly, while the amount of paper stored or mailed decreases. We regard this net phenomenon of more paper as evidence of improved communications, and not as a symptom of ineffective procedures. (Fig. 19)

Document Structure

A core and essential technology is that of document representation. A document has a complex structure. (Fig. 20) It has a logical structure, e.g., chapters and paragraphs, a layout structure including style, fonts, sizes, italicization, etc., and content. A document can be represented in a hierarchical architecture. (Fig. 21) The lowest level of the hierarchy is image form. In image form, as from an input scanner or for a printer master, a document could be imaged, but not edited or reformatted. Xerox' InterPress is an example of this form. In the processible form, the content could be edited, but the layout would be fixed. In the most general form, the content and layout structure could both be revised. (Fig. 22)

Definition of Document Forms

These three levels then give the user progressively more capability, although the user must, of course, have the right equipment and skills. In any large corporation, however, documents exist in many different electronic formats, usually incompatible or at best partially compatible. How can the transition to a more compatible situation be brought about?

Instead of changing or migrating to a common internal format, one approach is to establish an exchange encoding. (Fig. 23) The purpose is two-fold. First, to develop a method for different editors to communicate, and second, to bring a very complex conversion matrix down to a more manageable one based on the exchange encoding. Establishment of exchange encoding standards is essential to effective corporate publishing. The technology is available; the challenge will be the standards process.

Conclusion

This completes the overview of the component technologies that will be available to corporate electronic publishing five years from now. It is appropriate to address the challenge that users of this technology will face to see how to expedite its introduction.

One action for users is the prudent use of today's component technologies, especially those that are in the mainstream of technological development. Certainly, it would not be prudent to make a large investment in equipment to produce and scan OCR fonts. But an investment today in intelligent scanning can give a head start in tackling the long-term problem of capturing, for electronic manipulation, the existing paper document base in your organizations.

A second action for users is to keep an eye on the direction of rapidly evolving technologies. The integration of these technologies will create a new kind of environment for corporate publishing. That environment will differ for different kinds of organizations, but it is necessary today to envision what that environment could look like, and start today to build the architecture for that new environment

A user must start now to create the blueprints for the new systems architecture, blueprints that will enable preparation for tomorrow's integrated technologies, and the sizeable benefits and advantages that they will provide. That blueprint must address these, and other, fundamental issues: the degree to which the corporate publishing environment will be distributed, the communications requirements, from building cabling on up, what kind of document formats and standards have to be supported and how they will be evolved, how documents will be transmitted, and to whom they will be distributed.

As the information age advances, the strategic importance of information is becoming more widely realized. This importance implies a focus on information that supports strategic business decisions. These strategic decisions are those that can improve a company's competitive position, create new products or services, or give the company a head start in a new market.

The next realization is the strategic importance of documents, the vehicles for communicating strategic information to the people in and outside organizations. The information that we transmit to all levels of management must become more timely, more accurate, and more accessible. The quality of this information must be improved through the quality, the form and the content, of the documents carrying that information. These objectives can be achieved through better editing and composition, through better formatting, more creative use of graphics and color, and through the use of higher-quality displays and output devices.

To avoid drowning in the output of electronic publishing, doing a better job of communicating information is mandatory. The rate of transfer of information must be dramatically increased by making it easier for the users of that information to assimilate it. The information communicated must aid and abet insights and knowledge that support better decisions. Distributed demand publishing, publishing what corporate customers need, when they need it, where they need it, and how they can most effectively assimilate it, is the key to making electronic publishing of five years from now a powerful tool for the strategic exploitation of corporate information.

1. Electronic publishing functional processes

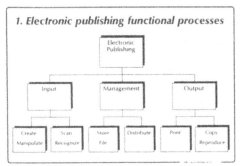

2. Technology groups for electronic publishing

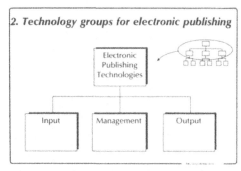

3. Input technologies

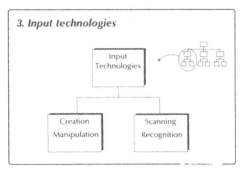

4. "3-M" workstation

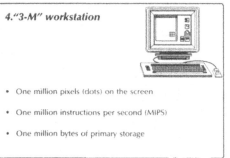

- One million pixels (dots) on the screen
- One million instructions per second (MIPS)
- One million bytes of primary storage

5. Publishing workstation in five years

- CRT technology
- One to four million pixels
- Five million instructions per second (MIPS)
- Eight million bytes of primary storage
- More powerful and effective software
  - Digital darkroom
  - Expert assistants
  - Ease of use
  - Management software
- Trend toward dynamic displays

6. Conversion bridges

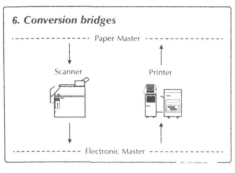

7. Typical effects of compression and recognition

Source	Size	
A4 sheet scanned @ 8 dots/mm	1	Mbyte
Compression of 10x typical using CCITT algorithm	100	Kbytes
Recognition, giving 300x total compression for text and data	3000	Bytes

8. Scan processing

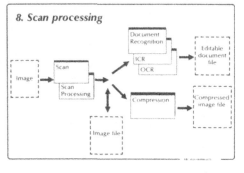

9. Management technologies

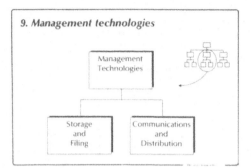

10. Communication technology trends

- Driving forces are fiber optics and deregulation

- Wider bandwidth local area networks (10 to 100 mbit/s)

- Wider bandwidth, shorter connection time, digital wide area connections (128 kbits/s, fractional second set-up time)

- Support trend toward decentralized and distributed publishing based on remote procedure calls

11. Storage/filing technology trends

- Continuing rapid evolution of magnetic read/write technology (quadruple in five years)

- Availability of CD ROM technology (read only)

- Advent of optical write once technology

- Emergence of optical read/write technology

- Introduction of document base management systems

12. Traditional document publishing process

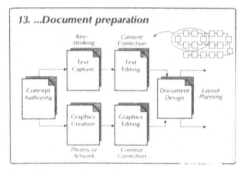

13. ...Document preparation

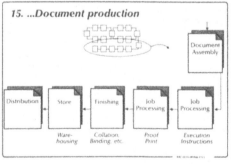

14. ...Document preparation

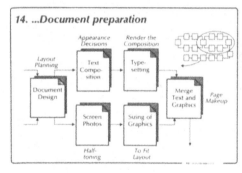

15. ...Document production

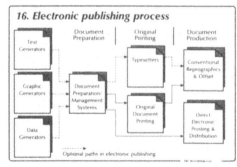

16. Electronic publishing process

17. Processes compared

Traditional publishing process

Electronic publishing process

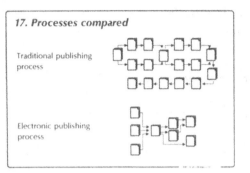

18. Output technologies

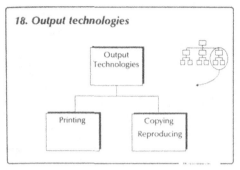

19. Role of paper in electronic publishing

- Advantages of paper as a presentation medium
  - Resolution, contrast, freedom from glare, tactile qualities, light weight, ease of annotation

- Disadvantages
  - Static, non-interactive

- Usage in storage and communications will decrease

- Usage in information presentations will increase

20. Document structure

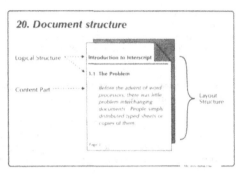

21. Document representation architecture

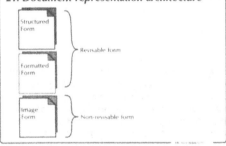

22. Definition of document forms

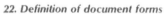

Form	User Capabilities		
	Image	Edit	Edit and Reformat
Structured	X	X	X
Formatted	X	X	
Image	X	X	

23. Document interchange

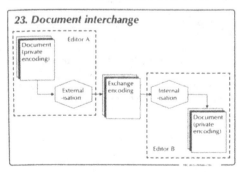

24. Fully featured electronic documents

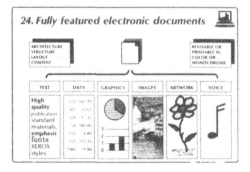

Page description languages

Concepts and implementations

Nenad Marovac
Department of mathematical Sciences
San Diego State University
San Diego, CA 92182.
and
CSS - Xerox, San Deigo.

Summary

A page description language is a programming language used to describe the structure and appearance of a document page, in a device (printer) independent way. A document description language is a language which not only specifies structure and appearance of a page, but also the structure of a document, the global document composing environment, and relationships between pages, combining pages of one document within another document, etc. The printing environment specification subset of a language, is used to specify printing options like one sided, and two sided printing, paper-shift during the printing of a page, tray used to feed in paper to print the entire document or on a page basis, etc.

There are two objectives in presenting this paper. First, to present the concepts of page and document description, as well as printing environment specification languages, and second to describe experience gained in two implementations related to Interpress, a XEROX developed document description language incorporating a printing environment specification subset.

Key words : Electronic Publishing, page description languages, printers and typeseters, raster imaging processors, and Interpress.

1. Introduction

A **page description language** is a programming language used to describe the structure and appearance of a document page in a device (printer) independent way. Using such a language we could program (encode) an entire page in a document and produce a form which we will refer to as a **page master**. Interpreting this master would produce a page in the appearance we envisaged. An encoded format of the entire document in a page description language is referred to as a **document master**. A page description language is used by an output generation program to encode a document, whether a book, or a computer listing, or a memo, into an output (printer or typesetter) format, to be interpreted by an output device (printer or typesetter or document display device) to produce a visual presentation of the document. A page description language is made device independent for two reasons.

First, we follow the idea that the language should be more document oriented rather than device oriented. In other words we formulate the language with the main objective to be optimal in describing the structure of document pages in terms of primitives, like paragraphs, text lines, rules (graphical lines), images, and similar. Further we incorporate in the language features specifying how these components will be rendered on paper, e.g. color and thickness of rules, typefaces to be used for different portions of text, and similar. In this we do not tailor the language to make it most suitable and optimal to any particular hardware printing device. However, it is a good design to make such language inherently optimal for hardware implementation. This means that the language should tend to incorporate features which can be implemented in imaging (printing or display) hardware in an efficient manner. This will be further dealt with in Section 6.1 of this paper.

Second, in this decade the computer community finally realized the need for standardization. This is apparent if one follows efforts in standardization of programming languages, interfaces to graphical software and graphical hardware devices, etc. In fact a page description language should be either a formal or industry standard for a printer interface, i.e. it should be a language which is directly interpreted by printing devices, regardless of manufacturer or model. The importance of this idea is readily apparent to an observer of the Electronic Publishing market. At the present we can identify three languages which fall into the category of page description languages. They are Interpress from Xerox, Postscript from Adobe Systems, and DDL from Imagen with the first two showing stronger presence on the market. Even after being in a public domain for a very short time, there is a large number of printing hardware and publishing software manufacturers who announced that they will implement either printers, typesetters, or software systems which will interpret or generate one or both of the languages.

Of the three languages mentioned I would classify Postscript and DDL as being page description languages, and Interpress as a document description and printing environment specifiction language. A document description language is a language which not only specifies structure and appearance of a page, but also the structure of a document, the global document composing environment, combining pages of one document within another document, combining two documents together, and similar. The printing environment specification language subset is used to specify printing options like on sided and two sided printing, which printer paper feed tray to use to feed paper to print the entire document or on a page basis, and similar. The printing environment specification, if present, is attached in front of a document master. This specification we will refer to as environment instructions. *

This paper is structured into six sections. The next section, Section Two, includes a functional overview of page description languages, and a more detailed discussion of the functional differences between the three types of languages. It also includes an overview of the Interpress language. Section Three presents the overall structure and functionality of Electronic Printing Systems in general and the Xerox XPS-700 system in particular. In Sections Four and Five Interpress generator and Interpress preview sub-systems for XPS-700 system are described respectively. Finally, in Section Six some observations made in generating Interpress masters are discussed.

2. Page, document and printing environment description languages

As stated previously a page description language is a programming language powerful enough to describe the structure of a printed page of any complexity and context, in a device independent manner. Printed pages, in general, are composed from three basic **publication primitives**. The primitives are **text, geometric figures** and **sections of photographs**. In other words a page comprises

---

* To simplify the discussion in the remainder of this paper, except in the next section, we will refer to all three types of languages as page description languages.

one or more columns of text, geometric figures, and sections of photographs in varied gray levels and colors. Such a language incorporates a number of data types and a number of operators as well as features to combine data types and operators into composite data types and operators. Basic and composite data types and operators in a page description language must allow for description of a page containing any composition of the basic graphics primitives needed to create a page of a desired complexity. Masters, e.g. programs in such languages, being descriptions of pages and documents, are typically generated and interpreted by machines. They are generated by (composition) programs running on computers for document creation and formating, and interpreted (executed) by programs running in printers, typesetters and display devices. Postscript is designed to allow for interactive master generation by users, and ready readability and understandability of documents masters in their encoded form by humans. It is believed that such property is more of a disadvantage rather than advantage, because masters in such form are inherently less efficient to interpret by machines. A master is generated automatically by a program as a user interactivelly places text, figures and visual representation of raster scan images on a WYSIWYG screen, or composes a page using a high level copymarking language. In the second case the user previews the page also on a screen. In either case the system can produce a document master, when the user indicates that he or she has accepted the context and appearance of the page. In such an environment it seems there is very little need for the user to program a page in a page description language directly, or to proof the master.

The functionality of a page description language typically provides for:
- setting a position anywhere within a page
- placing text, with or without justification within a desired measure
- creation, selection and modification of fonts
- creation of any graphics 2D figures from basic graphics primitives, like line segments, circular arcs, parts of 2nd degree curves, B-splines, closed filled outlines, etc.
- applying any combination of scaling, rotation and translation to graphics figures
- creation, scaling, and rotation of raster scan images

2.2 Document descriptiption languages

A document description language should provide all functionality as described above for page description languages as well as additional functionality enabling:

- specification of the structure of an entire document in terms of encoded formats of two or more pages.
- combining pages from two or more document masters into one document
- merging together a part of a page from one master in one or more instances with a page from another master. This is useful when a part of a page is an illustration generated at an illustrator's workstation and has to be pasted at different positions on a currently composed page.
- concatanation of two or more complete masters to be printed together as a unit.

2.3 Printing environment specification languages or Publishing environment integration languages.

Such a language should possess all functionality of document specification languages with some added system functionality. Since at this point only one such language exists, e.g. Interpress from Xerox , Interpress will be used to explain additional features of such languages [1].

Interpress allows for:
- Printing instructions for the entire document
  - -printing instructions on a page level
- Complete font encoding
  - Typefaces
  - Font metrics
  - Font distribution mechanism
  - User font definition
- Encoding of bit-map images
- File insert mechanism
  - In-line file insert
  - Local file insert
  - Remote file insert

Printing instructions. This feature allows a document creator to add to the document master additional information which will be either printed with the document, like document creator name, date of creation, etc. or will specify printing environment, like color of the paper to be printed on, one sided or two sided printing, stapling of documents, and similar. These printing environment instructions can be specified either on the document level, i.e. for the entire document as a whole, or on a page level, i.e. for each page prior to the section of the master for the page. Interpress allows for printing environment instructions on the document level to be overwritten when the document is actually sent to be printed.

Font encoding. Interpress is used to encode complete information about a font, including font metrics, font bit maps or contour structures for the font. For each font there is one Interpress master. This format of fonts is used for font distribution [2] to customers, either for their printing machines or for their document composition systems. Fonts are also to be stored in this format in font servers in office environments, and when a printer needs a font to render a document it will fetch it from the system font server. Furthermore, Interpress provides the means for a user to define fonts within document masters.

Encoding raster scan images. Scan images produced by scanners, or any other devices in the office environment are encoded into Interpress masters [3]. This allows for a general and generic merging mechanisms of documents and their parts into documents. Images produced by Xerox 150 scanners and the EPIC system are encoded into Interpress masters.

File insert mechanisms. Documents and images to be merged into another document can be merged in-line into a document during the creation and encoding of the document. Alternatively, the documents to be merged may already reside on the printer , or be stored in a filing server of the office environment. Interpress provides a mechanism for these documents to be recalled either from the printer disk storage, or from the office network filing server, during the printing of the document containing these documents or images.

Below are listed Interpress properties as perceived from a user's point of view.

Interpress properties

- Functional richness
- Multi-layer organization
- Page independent structure
- Device independence
- Priority important
- Compact encoding
- Performance
- Total environment

- Printing instructions
• Extensibility

The multi-layer organization or subsetting of Interpress has raised some controversy. Dividing a language into a hierarcy of functional subsets, forming a base for implementation alternatives, does present some problems. A master may incorporate some constructs which are not supported by a local printer. Images described by these constructs may not be rendered correctly at that printer. However, the printer should at least issue a warning message, and print the rest of the document correctly. This is not as difficult to ensure as it may seem. However, there is the other side of the coin also. Layer approach allows for both more efficient and cheaper implementations of subsets. A printer designed and implementing text and graphics figure primitives at black and white levels only, will be considerably cheaper and can be made faster than a printer implementing full Interpress supporting color. Experience with similar standards, e.g. GKS [4] seem to enforce this fact.

Interpress encoding is compact and designed for efficient decomposition of document masters. This is an important factor in designing and implementing printers with a high throughput and large volume publishing, like the Xerox 9700/8700 printer family.

Some additional observations and suggestions for the generation of efficient Interpress masters are included in Section Six of this paper.

3. Electronic publishing systems

An Electronic Publishing System (EPS) is an integrated publishing system for producing documents on demand, which incorporates computers, workstations, electronic printers, and digitizing scanners to input graphics. The use of such a system in producing documents encompasses four activities:

Text preparation
In this activity a writer prepares the text of the document, which is then typed into a word processor or a computer. He also identifies the drawings or artwork to be included in the document.

At this stage **style specifications** for the document are prepared. Style specifications define the layout of the document, i.e. they are composed of instructions to the composition and printing sections of the EPS instructing the latter how to process and print the document in accordance with the user's needs. The style specification includes indications for the kind of typefaces to be used for different sections of the document, settings for margins and column widths, the locations of chapter and section headings and the inclusion of previously generated and stored information such as forms, graphics and digital signatures. The style specifications are either prepared explicitly for the document or a previously generated one is identified and incorporated within the document. Usually, a company prepares a set of "standard" style specifications which are used over and over again for documents of desired similar visual characteristics.

Graphics input and preparation
There are two major sources of graphics images in electronic publishing: computer-generated images and images generated from hand-drawn art-work or photographs. Typically, in the past a user allocated spaces within the text to insert drawings and camera-ready artwork. More recently the user would generate digitized forms of artwork and photographs by using digitizing scanners like the Xerox 150 Graphics Input Station (GIS) to scan artwork, or computer programs to produce raster scan formats of drawings specified in mathematical forms. In either case the digital images are sent to the computing element of the EPS where they can be stored and directly used by the composition section of the EPS, like Xerox XICS [5], for merging and printing within the document.

Document composition
In this activity the document is formatted into elements that compose a page as we know it. During this formatting process the composing task deals with running heads; hyphenation and justification; change bars; selection and placement of tables, graphics, and captions, etc. This processing is done according to style specifications.

In the Xerox Publishing System XPS-700 [6], the composition process of a document is actually divided into two sub-tasks. The first sub-task is the *composer* or *composition task* proper, called COMPUSET, which processes the document and produces a so called "intermediate file" document format which is in a machine independent format. The second sub-task is composed of one or more *interpreters*. An interpreter produces output which is very machine dependent, and in fact is a translator from the intermediate file format of a document into an output format designated for a particular printer or typesetter. Therefore, it resembles a code generation section of a compiler. In an interpreter the final formatting of each page is made by determining such things as orientation of the final printed sheet, merging of graphics images and boiler plates with the text, etc. Xerox supports as many interpreters as there are different makes and models of printers and typesetters to be supported with the EPS.

One of these interpreters, called XIPINT, is for Interpress. It is also referred to as the Interpress Generator for XPS-700. It translates the output from COMPUSET for a document into the Interpress master for that document. The Interpress master being the output format for that document understood by Xerox printers. The Interpress master is all that is needed to print the document on any of those printers. Therefore, for our purpose COMPUSET and XIPINT together form a full composition section for Xerox XPS-700 system.

Printing
The printing section of an EPS may be comprised of a print machine like Xerox 9700/8700/4050 that will print the document including merging and collating of text and graphics, instantly and automatically at rates of up to 120 pages per minute.

The structure of an EPS and relationships between four activities in producing a document are shown in Figure 1.

More recent EPS, like the Xerox XPS-700, also include a **page design studio** activity. Through this activity using a WYSIWYG display, the user can design the structure and the appearance of a page. This activity makes use of two tasks: the composition tasks and the **screen preview** task. The preview task generates display dependent format for the page to be displayed. The structure and functionality of the preview task is very similar to the structure and functionality for previously discussed interpreters.

The structure of XPS-700, as shown in Figure 2, has three further additions. They are: the **library task**, the **receiving task**, and the **Interpress preview task**. The document library DCLIBs store documents in Interpress format. These documents are generated using the XPS-700, a document preparation workstation (like VIEWPOINT/STAR or similar), scanning devices (like Xerox 150 GIS), or artwork stations (like Xerox Publishing Illustrators Workstation). These documents can be later printed as individual documents, or merged (pasted) with other documents in preparation. When using an Interactive design studio, we might preview a document which contains one or more other merged documents and images in Interpress format, therefore the screen preview activity contains an Interpress preview subsection.

At this point we see clearly another use of Interpress language. It plays the role of an universal language functionally linking together all devices on the network. It allows for information exchange between different types of devices on a network in an office environment in an uniform format. It allows scanned images, which must be clearly encoded in a format different from text, to

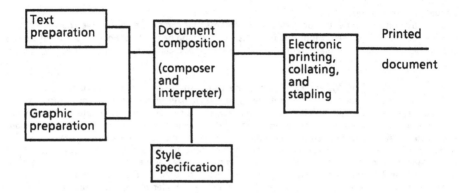

Figure 1. Structure of an Electronic Publishing System

be merged with text at document composition. It also allows documents, generated from any other source on the network, to be combined together, etc. Fonts and their metrics are distributed to printers and any other devices needing them, encapsulated in Interpress format. This feature of Interpress makes it unique when compared with other page definition languages. I referred to Interpress previously as document description language incorporating a printing environment specification. At this point it would be more precise to refer to it as language for the Office and Publishing Environment, or Publishing System Integration Language.

4. Interpress Generator for XPS-700 (XIPINT)

As stated earlier XIPINT is the code generation section for the composition activity in the Xerox XPS-700 publishing system. Composition calculations and decisions are made in the composition front-end called COMPUSET. The results from COMPUSET are a set of page specification directives, in the form of an intermediate language. XIPINT then sets the environment for each page and the entire document. It determines necessary transformations for each page as a whole, and for each individual item. It fetches documents and images to be merged (pasted) in the preparation of a document, and sets a document by generating Interpress code for a printer or a typesetter. Below is description of its functionality.

XIPINT functionality

- Generation of the Interpress representation of a document
- Incorporates printing instructions on request
- Supports head-to-head (in landscape printing), and head-to-toe (in portrait orientations) printing
- Supports all four printing orientations
- Supports saving of documents in Interpress format (output from XIPINT) into Document Libraries
- Supports pasting (merging) of scanned images within documents in all orientations

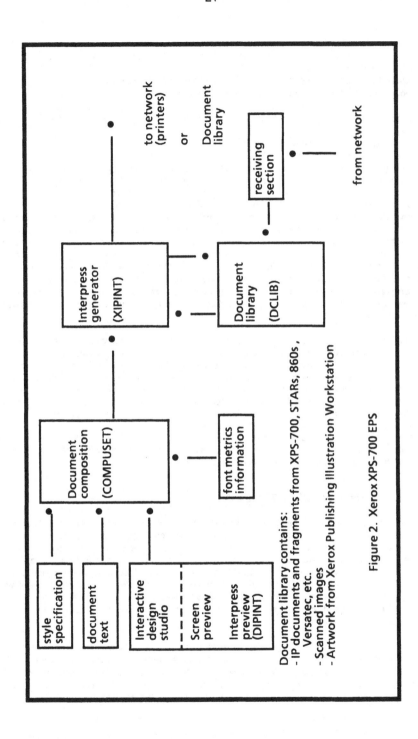

Figure 2. Xerox XPS-700 EPS

- Supports pasting (merging) documents (in Interpress formats) within a document currently being processed. Merged documents can be from any Interpress source (e.g. XPS-700, VIEWPOINT/STAR, 860, etc)
- Supports simplex and duplex (one sided and two sided) printing modes
- Support of paper feed from different trays for large printers

- It supports printing documents on all Xerox network Interpress printers, e.g. 9700, 8700, 4050, 8044, etc
- It will support multiple imposition printing.

In designing XIPINT one of the objectives was to use the smallest possible complete subset of Interpress which would incorporate the cheapest, i.e. the most time efficient, Interpress operators. At the time of initial design for XIPINT, Interpress was in its infancy and various Interpress printers available at that time supported different subsets of Interpress operators with varying efficiency. Since documents composed in XPS-700 had to be printed on every Interpress printer, research was conducted to determine what was a common set of operators supported at that time, and what was a likely subset that would be supported by every possible Interpress printer in a near future to offer guaranted printing within the XPS-700. Furthermore, printing speed and throughput of different printers differed considerably. Therefore, in order to guarantee a certain printing performance by a cross section of available Interpress printers, an additional study was conducted to identify which operators were inherently more efficient and tended to be optimized in most implementations of Interpress printers. The result of these two studies determined the subset of Interpress operators generated by XIPINT.

XIPINT architecture is illustrated in Figure 3. It has three levels of implementation. The first level, the composition and functionality level, is application dependent. It reflects constructs used in our composition activity. The second level, the Interpress functionality level, reflects the philosophy of Interpress. The third level, the basic Interpress operator level, implements each individual operator separately.   This division resulted from two objectives: easy maintenance of the system, and reusability of individual modules from different levels in other projects. XIPINT was implemented in FORTRAN IV. The reason behind this was to make it fast, and more important to make it transportable. Originally, XIPINT was part of the XICS system. XICS runs on a very large number of different machines under various operating systems. At that time (1984) only FORTRAN provided for a real portability accros main frames, mini computers and micro computers with different word sizes and different operating systems with different filling systems.

5. Interpress preview for XPS-700 (DIPINT)

This task is a software RIP (Raster Imaging Processor) for Interpress. An Interpress RIP accepts a document Interpress master. It decomposes the master and produces code to render the document on a typeseter or printer . DIPINT performs that function with the difference that it renders the document on a screen in order to preview a document which is already in Interpress format. Such a preview is done for two reasons. One reason is to examine the document before sending it to a printer. The second reason, more important in XPS-700, is to preview a document or image when merging it with the document being designed and composed interactively at a XYSIWYG terminal. Typically, these documents and images to be merged come from different sources, all of which have only Interpress format in common.

DIPINT organization is shown in Figure 4. It shows three levels. They are: the Interpress machine level, the Interpress operators level, and the graphics imaging level. The first level contains modules to parse the language, including the decomposition section, finite state machine implementing processing a master, and support for Interpress structures: stack, Interpress vectors, frame and imager data structures. The second level includes modules implementing each individual Interpress

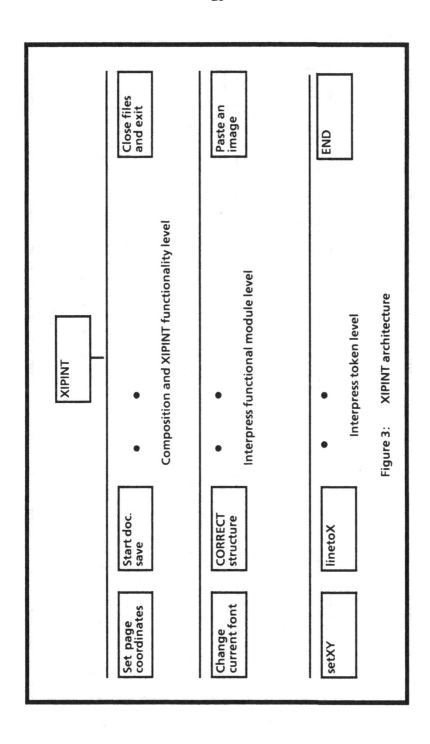

Figure 3: XIPINT architecture

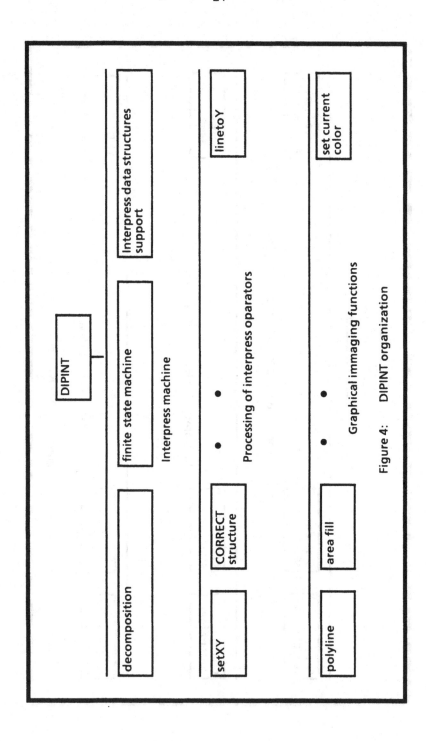

Figure 4: DIPINT organization

operator. The third level contains graphics modules to actually do all the imaging necessary to render a document. This architecture again resulted from the same two objectives as discussed in XIPINT, i.e. maintainability and reusability. Ideally, to use DIPINT to implement an Interpress machine of another type such as a printer, only the third level routines need to be redesigned and recoded. Also, to be compatible with graphics hardware of "tomorrow", the functionality and calling sequences of graphics modules were modeled as close as was feasible to CGI and GKS.

DIPINT is still in progress. Therefore no comments and observations related to this project will be put forward at this stage.

6. Experience with Interpress in EPS environment

Time spent in building and testing XIPINT was definitively exciting. It required involvement in many related activities. At that time high quality publishing fonts, like Mergenthaler's Optima, Helvetica and similar did not exist under Interpress. Therefore, one of the first task to undertake was to introduce these fonts into Interpress on 9700 series machines. However, these fonts did not exist on other Xerox Interpress machines like the 8044. The 8044 does an automatic font substitution, but the substituted font typically has different metrics. This could potentially degrade the quality of a printed page. To solve this problem use of the CORRECT Interpress operator, which is defined exactly for this purpose, was very valuable. However, the CORRECT operator is usually implemented on printers as a two pass operator, which makes it very expensive to use. In order to obtain the best compromise, an option was introduced into XIPINT allowing the user to decide whether to use CORRECT for justification (particularly in a font substitution environment) or to rely on the precision of the composer assuming no font substitution will be needed. In the second case the document will be printed much faster, an obvious advantage in large volume printing.

6.1 Optimization of Interpress masters

It was thought best to conclude this paper with some observations about Interpress master generators and optimization of Interpress masters. These observations result from involvement in both the XIPINT and the DIPINT projects.

In the generation of Interpress masters two optimization criterias can be followed:
- Size (encoding efficiency)
- Printing (decomposition and imaging) speed

The first criteria is generally important, when we wish to keep the entire master in main memory while decomposing it to reduce disc access time. This is relevant for smaller printers which are dedicated mainly for printing of smaller documents, and maybe for large printers for fast printing of large documents. Constantly decreasing price of memory combined with increasing addressing space of microprocessors makes this criteria less important than the second one, i.e. printing speed.

Printing speed is very much dependent on the content of Interpress masters. It is possible to formulate a number of rules, which if followed would result in more efficient Interpress masters. However, the most important optimization strategy for generating of Interpress masters is based on very basic common sense. A document is processed by a composer-printer pair. The real question is where does the composer end and where does the printer begin. Let's look at two very simple examples.

First, suppose that we need to plot a complex curve on a page of a document. Do we approximate this curve into line segments within the composer and request a printer to render the line segments, or do we construct a sequence of second degree curves and B-splines approximating the desired curve, and make the printer approximate these second degree curved and B-splines curves by line segments in order to render the desired curve.

Second, suppose again that we wish to produce a justified paragraph on the page. Do we do all required calculations within the composer and relatively position all words so that if the printer simply positions and paints the words, the paragraph will automatically be rendered justified? Or do we instruct the printer to put certain words into a certain measure to produce justified line of text which will again result into a justified paragraph?

It is believed that in both cases we come to the conclusion: let the Interpress generator do as much work as possible to reduce printer's work. This is correct for two reasons. First, a composer running on a main frame or a mini computer will have at its disposal a much better floating point arsenal than a printer in general. Sophisticated floating point hardware will make small and cheap printers too expensive. Second, a document may be composed once and printed many times in many copies on request.

This argument is similar to the implementation of compilers. An Interpress generator is no different really from a code generator in a compiler, and a printer being hardware for execution of a program. Do we wish more work to be done at compilation of a program, and less at its execution or vice versa.

These arguments do not lead to the conclusion that we should build less sophisticated printers. It just points to a more efficient division of labor in a composer-printer pair in an EPS. This is particularly relevant when we have a number of different printers with different degrees of processing speed connected to an EPS.

Conclusion

Concepts of page definition languages were presented. A closer look at Interpress in an Electronic Publishing Environment was made. Two projects related to Interpress were discussed, and finally some observations from experience in implementing an Interpress generator and a software Interpress RIP were given.

Acknowledgements

I wish to thank E.M. Palandri and D. Fregeau for valuable comments and help in preparing this document, and Brian R. Kavanagh for reading and proofing the text.

References

[1] INTERPRESS - Electronic Printing Standard, Xerox Corporation.
[2] Font Interchange Standard, Xerox Corporation.
[3] Raster Encoding Standard, Xerox Corporation.
[4] ISO/DIS 7942 - 1982 Information Processing: Graphical Kernel System (GKS).
[5] The Xerox Integrated Composition System (XICS). Reference Manual, Xerox Corporation.
[6] Xerox Publishing System. System Description Manual, Xerox Corporation.

SMSCRIPT:
AN INTERPRETOR FOR THE POSTSCRIPT[†] LANGUAGE UNDER UNIX[‡].

Stéphane QUEREL, Bruno BORGHI, Daniel de RAUGLAUDRE

GIPSI-SM90 [1]
c/o INRIA
BP 105
78153 LE CHESNAY CEDEX
FRANCE

---seismo!mcvax!inria!gipsy!stephane
---seismo!mcvax!inria!gipsy!borghi
---seismo!mcvax!inria!gipsy!daniel

Abstract: We present an interpretor for the PostScript page description language, running on the french workstation SM90 under Unix System V, designed to be the heart of a printing server. In the first part, we expose the choice of architecture that we made for the printing process and we explain the reasons that led us to implement PostScript. Then we expose some details of implementation. Finally we describe the new features offered to the graphic and document production programs, and the PostScript environnement that can be built around this interpretor.

Keywords: PostScript, Page description language, Unix.

[†] PostScript is a trademark of Adobe Systems Incorporated.

[‡] Unix is a trademark of Bell Laboratories.

[1] GIPSI-SM90 is sponsored by the French Ministry of Research and Technology under the contracts n° 83-B1032, 84-E0651 and 85-B0524.

1. A Printing Server for the SM90

1.1. The project.

The SM90 workstation uses a multimicroprocessor architecture[1], developed by CNET[2], based upon 680x0 CPUs and runs a version of Unix System V called SMX V.1. Modularity of the hardware allows to finely tune the workstation to the user requirements. The french national computer manufacturer BULL markets the SM90 workstation under the name: SPS7.

GIPSI-SM90 is a joint research and development group founded by CNET, BULL and INRIA[3] which sets up a scientific workstation environnement upon the SM90 architecture. To meet the requirements of the scientific community for which this workstation is designed, we are adding a full document production capability.

The usual Unix environment provides text editors such as *ed* or *emacs* to type documents in, and formators such as *troff* or *Tex* for typesetting. In the future, this production scheme should evolve to provide more interactivity, and the ability of easy including of illustrations.

The purpose of the printing server is to provide a way of imaging the final documents, whatever tool has been used to produce it. Its design implies the choice of a printer and the kind of hardware needed to connect it to the workstation, the choice of a software interface, the choice of a page description language, the choice of a printing protocol, etc...

The hardware has to be simple and cheap enough to be suitable for a workstation, and should be able to output illustrations.

The software interface has contraints among 3 domains:

- **Graphic Quality:** it must allow texts in any style and size, mixed with graphics and raster images; the location and orientation of every entity must be arbitrary and precise.

- **Communications:** the printing sytem can be operated on a single, possibly enhanced machine, and be shared as a remote server over a local area network.

- **Software Engineering:** to allow reusability of existing software, it must be compatible with some standard, and the gateways from the various and mostly incompatible current printable document formats should be feasible without excessive effort; to enable reusability of applications to come, it must be independant of the physical characteristics of the printer (resolution, imaging hardware).

---

[2] Centre National d'Etudes des Télécommunications

[3] Institut National de Recherche en Informatique et Automatique.

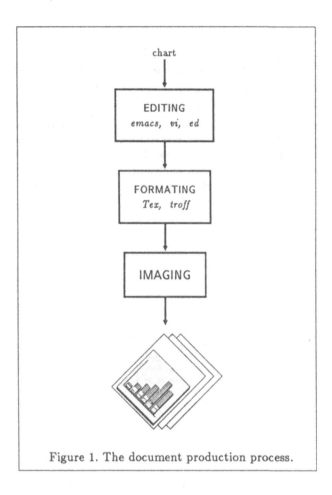

Figure 1. The document production process.

1.2. The architecture.

We choosed the well-known Canon LBP-CX as a marking engine. The characteristics of the printer (300 dots per inch, 8 pages per minute) allow good quality graphics and typography, at a reasonnable cost; and it is therefore usable as an individual printer. It is connected via a video cable to the workstation, inside which a special interface board, developed at GIPSI-SM90, converts the data into video signals.

We selected the PostScript page description language as the software interface through which the applications can drive the printer. The standard Unix spooling system performs the printing protocol functions.

The printing of a page is done as follow (See figure 2):

1) An application program running on the workstation has produced a PostScript file, or is currently feeding a pipe with a PostScript data flow.

2) A CPU runs our PostScript interpretor, so-called SmScript, to process the PostScript flow and builds a bitmap image of the page inside its own memory.

3) When a page is complete (i.e. when a *showpage* operator is encountered) the kernel, by means of a *write* system call, transfers the image from the memory to the printer through the hardware interface board, the role of which is first to serialize the bitmap image, then to convert it into a video signal and finally to regularly feed the marking engine during the 8 seconds needed for the laser beam to scan the page.

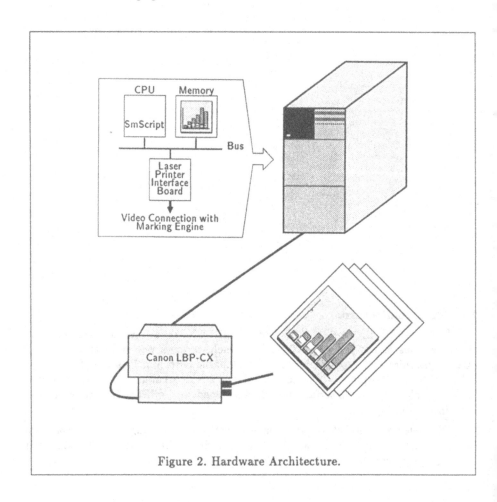

Figure 2. Hardware Architecture.

1.3. Why PostScript ?

At the time we started the study, two printer file formats were answering our software interface requirements: Adobe's PostScript[2] and Xerox's Interpress[3]. These two formats are in the same family, and we decided to implement PostScript for various reasons:

- every Interpress operator has its equivalent in PostScript or may be easily emulated, and graphic capabilities of PostScript were more powerful than those of Interpress[4].

- PostScript uses only US ASCII as input. This is important when developing applications, writing and debugging PostScript programs. In addition transmissions on any device such as magnetic tapes, asynchronous lines or networks are straightforward

- There was already one PostScript implementation available: the Apple LaserWriter. It gave us the assurance that PostScript would extend to a wide range of users and become rapidly a *de facto* standard. It was also useful to have a reference at hand to validate parts of our implementation.

The main objection that could be raised is that PostScript has no printing protocol functions. But this can be overheld by using document preprocessing with standard comments included in the document, according to Adobe's recommended conventions.

1.4. Features of the architecture.

All the PostScript interpretors commercially available today are embedded in a printer, and are accessible either via a RS-232 asynchronous line, or an Applenet connection, or a Centronics parallel interface.

In the opposite, our interpretor is a normal process running in the workstation. It does not reduce functionality, and it is convenient for some reasons:

- the dedicated hardware is reduced to the minimum, because there is no extra electronic component inside the printer. Almost every hardware element involved in the printing process is a standard resource of the workstation: CPU, memory, file system, disks, etc... The only exception, the interface board, is a quite simple piece of electronics. The interpretor can take advantage of the enhancements of most of these standard resources: for instance, if the usual 68010 CPU is replaced by a 68020, the printing process is immediately accelerated as a side-effect.

- like any other Unix process, PostScript can access an actual file system, which can be very convenient to modularize PostScript files and to reduce the space needed for standard prologues (using the *run* operator).

---

[4] At that time we were comparing PostScript and Interpress 2.0. With the third version of Interpress, both languages are now of the same graphical level.

- the same interpretor can drive multiple devices such as different printers, bitmap screens, windows of a window system, etc... Because 95% of the interpretor is generic and only a very small part is device specific, it is very simple to have a multi-device interpretor. We have a PostScript previewer by just writing the driver for a bitmap screen. We can also drive several physical printers with only one interpretor in-core instance, so that the program is not duplicated.

- PostScript can become a good candidate for a standard graphical data interchange format between Unix processes. An only-ASCII format enables data interchange between applications running on heterogeneous machines (such as SM90 and DEC Vax). Though restricted at present to pipes and files, communication between PostScript and other processes might use the various kinds of interprocess communication provided by Unix system V: shared memory, messages, sockets [5]. This is useful to build PostScript servers.

On the other hand, as SmScript uses common resources and consumes CPU time, at the printing time, the other processes may be slowed down. This effect is reduced when using a multi-processor configuration, and inexistant when using a remote server.

2. Implementation

2.1. Functionalities

When we started the implementation of SmScript, we first cut down to a coherent subset of the PostScript operators, such as the subset described in the Adobe's SubScript Specification[4]. We then got familiar with the objects and the concepts, and achieved an important work on basic algorithms. From this point, we are growing to reach a full PostScript functionality.

The current subset available through SmScript is (See figure 3):

- output printed on Canon laser printer, Numelec bitmap screen, and in a window of the SMX window system;

- most of the operators. Essentially, missing ones are related to raster images and complex clipping;

- use of bitmap and contour fonts;

We have almost achieved a complete PostScript interpretor although a lot of things have to be refined and cleaned up.

2.2. Implementation.

The software is structured in three levels (See figure 4):

---

[5] SMX V.1, which is System V based, offers some 4.2BSD facilities such as socket mechanism and TCP.IP network protocol.

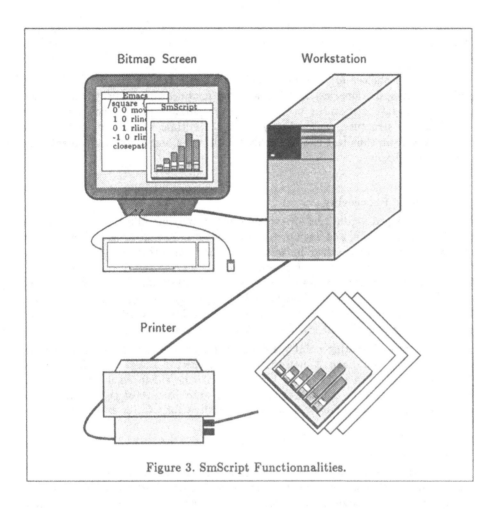

Figure 3. SmScript Functionnalities.

- *basic machines* which manipulate the data structures at the lowest level;
- *operators* which implement the native PostScript operators;
- *interpretor management modules* which perform an overall sequencing.

All modules are written in C language. The basic rasterops are taken from the standard SMX library: *libraster,* and are written in assembly language. The system-dependant functions are very few, and easy to isolate. This allows a good portability. The major non-portability is the use of the rasterop library, although this portability is provided for the machines with a 68000 familly based CPU.

The implementation itself is independent of the printer: whatever the printing device is, the task of the interpretor is to build a bitmap image, which the hardware is in charge of deposing on the final device. Thus it is an easy task to add new printing devices, as far as it can be considered some way or another as a memory[6].

The main choices for the implementation are related to the data structures (objects, stacks, dictionaries) and the way the modules communicate and handle errors. The data structures are always manipulated as abstract types. To modify a data structure, we need only, most of the time, update one of the basic machines: we can thus test it quite easily to select the best suited implementation to improve efficiency.

2.3. Graphic Processing

We developed algorithms for stroke drawing, polyline filling according to the non-zero winding rule, and region clipping. As we need a good precision, and for reasons of development schedule, we used floating point reals for the calculations related to the paths. The filling module uses an integer algorithm for efficiency. Our rasterop library is, in its current version, a little bit too coarse, and our algorithms have to do some low level job especially for region filling. We are working to provide a new library, with extended primitives, which will discharge the interpretor of inefficient low level raster manipulations.

The choice of floating point reals may not seem optimal for execution time, but the SM90 can have a powerfull array-processor board and 68020 cpus. Therefore the performances of the interpretor can be enhanced much more than with complex software optimisations. As the graphic part of the interpretor is almost complete, we are now refining the algorithms for a faster execution time.

3. Character Fonts

SmScript has to use various kinds of fonts (bitmap, vector, cubic spline). We started with bitmap fonts. Our font format was poor and not suited to manipulate and archive contour fonts. Thus, we have designed a new font format: GAFF[5] (General Application Font Format).

It is inspired by the PostScript font dictionaries architecture, the TEX font format, and our previous format. We built it versatile, self-descriptive and open. It is usable by various kind of software: typesetting, interactive graphic software, printing applications.

GAFF handles both high level informations on the characters, which are currently needed by a text formator (font name, point size, character widths, kerning, ligatures, etc...) and low level informations needed by the imaging process (bitmap descriptions, vectors and splines, etc...). The design of the format allows shortcuts for processes which only need a quick access to low level

---

[6] This is true for bitmap screens, with or without window systems and laser printers in raw mode such as the Canon LBP-CX printer.

35

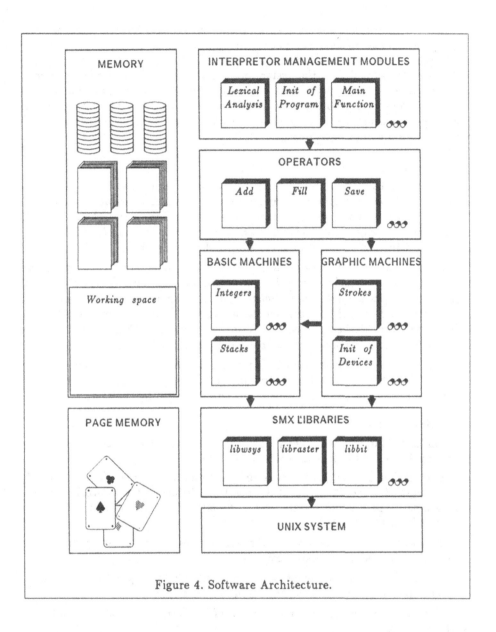

Figure 4. Software Architecture.

information. It is also designed to be modular in order to hide informations from processes which do not need or are not allowed to access them and permits data encryption for security.

We are developing a *character server* to handle this format, keep existing programs valid and to offer access to contour fonts to all programs without the heavy management of these fonts. This server will be in charge of managing the fonts currently available in the system or over the network, and offers a unique interface either to the various kinds of contour fonts or to the bitmap fonts. It is a nice solution to the problem of using contour fonts inside a program: a powerful PostScript-like character management, using caching mechanisms, accessible by any application without extra-cost.

4. SmScript server.

The generalisation of this server is a PostScript server. As the X[6] window system is intended to promote a standard way to communicate with windows, an SmScript server would promote a standard way to produce and exchange graphic datas between applications under a PostScript syntax. We can found the same idea in the SunDew[7] project of J. Gossling and D. Rosenthal.

Such a server can provide a full PostScript functionnality to programs without the need of including an interpretor inside their own code. The use of this server enables applications to image complex graphics while remaining small in code size, and to exchange graphic datas between them in a completely device independent way. Futhermore as PostScript contains only ASCII characters, the server may be on a remote machine connected through a network.

For example a program running on a machine A can open a window on the screen of a machine B, and draw its graphic in it. The communication between A and B is a PostScript ascii flow which is interpreted on B by the server.

5. Performances.

SmScript is in average slightly slower than a Laserwriter. We don't have any figures available, and in fact they wouldn't be very significant:

- PostScript on a LaserWriter is a unique process and the 68000 runs only PostScript. On the SM90 the CPU runs Unix, listens to the network, compiles programs, typesets documents, etc... Among all these processes SmScript doesn't have a special priority.

- If a floating-point array processor board is present in the workstation, the execution time is dramatically reduced.

- The current version of SmScript was not written to be efficient in terms of execution time but to be efficient in terms of developping time.

Actually, this is the weakest point of SmScript, and we are currently working to improve it.

6. Conclusions.

Even though SmScript has not yet reach the full PostScript functionnality, it is already in good working order and commonly used. The loss of general performance due to the CPU time consumed by the interpretor is widely

Carre   d'as

SmScript   -   1986

balanced by real advantages:

- capacity, ease to use and evolution of the interpretor are enhanced when it is a standard Unix process;
- the interpretor can be multi-screens and multi-printers;
- it takes advantage of all hardware enhancements of the workstation;
- finally the interpretor can be used as a server, and PostScript as a standard graphical data interchange format.

We presented our first version of the interpretor at the Journées SM90[8] in Versailles, in december 85. Our current version is far more powerful than the earlier ones and is still being developed. Among the major new features planed are the development of a driver for the Dataproducts LZR-2600 printer and a driver for a color bitmap screen.

7. References

[1]   U. Finger, G. Médigue, *"Multiprocessor Machines for Enhanced Availability : The SM90"*, L'Echo des Recherches, English issue, 1982.

[2]   Adobe Systems, *"PostScript Language Reference Manual"*, Addison-Wesley, 1985.

[3]   Xerox, *"Interpress Electronic Printing Standard"*, Xerox System Integration Standard, 1985.

[4]   Adobe Systems, *"SubScript Specification"*, 1984.

[5] B. Borghi, B. Chupin, *"GAFF: Un Format Pour les Fichiers de Polices de Caractères"*, internal document.

[6] J. Gettys, R. Newmann, T. Della Fera, *"Xlib – C Language X interface"*, MIT Project Athena, 1986.

[7] J. Gossling, D. Rosenthal, *"The SunDew Project"*, Usenix 86 Winter Conference Proceedings, 1986.

[8] B. Borghi, S. Quérel, *"Vers un serveur d'impression sur SM90"*, in *"Actes des journees SM90 1985"*, Eyrolles, pp 928-936, Dec 1985.

An Implementation of POSTSCRIPT

Crispin A. A. Goswell

Rutherford Appleton Laboratory
Chilton, Didcot,
OXON OX11 0QX.

ABSTRACT

This paper describes an implementation of POSTSCRIPT for previewing use on workstations with high resolution bitmapped displays.

It discusses implementation of storage management, area fill and line drawing, imaging, fonts and font caching. Treatment of bezier curves and dashing is explained.

Various hints are given on improving performance, including caching fonts on disk, treating thin lines specially and magnifying bitmaps.

Finally there is a brief discussion of porting experiences with the interpreter. It is written in the C language and runs on the UNIX† operating system.

1. INTRODUCTION

POSTSCRIPT has all the features required of a general purpose programming language[1] and, indeed, they can be separated from the graphics primitives to form a useful interpreted programming language.

POSTSCRIPT is simple to manipulate, as it is dynamically scoped and has a simple syntax.

It might be thought that a general purpose programming language would be overkill for such an application. It is observed, however, that the lack of a simple feature creates disproportionate problems for the user. For example, many graphics description languages have no general way of repeating a diagram in several guises. Also, some drawing algorithms need to know the device resolution in order to do rounding correctly. Without some kind of two-way communication, such algorithms could not be implemented portably. POSTSCRIPT solves this problem by putting the device dependent computation in the device.

The POSTSCRIPT language fits together neatly: all the features present are both necessary and sufficient. This approach of using the fewest number of concepts which provide the required functionality has proved successful on systems like UNIX. Our implementation was begun from the POSTSCRIPT Language Reference manual. We obtained an Apple LaserWriter which we have since used as a model implementation.

This paper assumes some programming knowledge of the POSTSCRIPT language.

2. THE POSTSCRIPT LANGUAGE

Figure 1 shows an architectural overview of our POSTSCRIPT interpreter and environment.

2.1. Postfix notation

POSTSCRIPT is a post-fix language, and while this is not the form that people prefer, it is by far the easiest for programs to generate. Almost all POSTSCRIPT source is machine generated, and the interpreter operates directly from source. This is so that there need be no worries about non-printing characters (most networks are not transparent to binary files).

---

† UNIX is a registered trademark of AT&T in the USA and other countries.

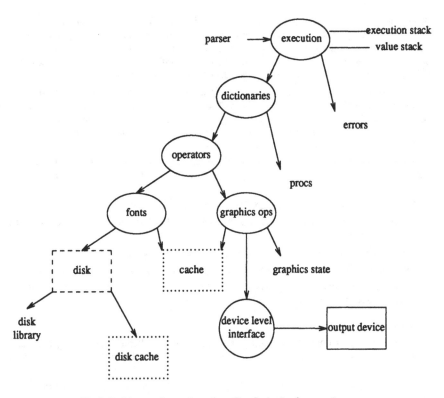

Fig 1. Architectural overview of our PostScript implementation.

2.2. Data types

POSTSCRIPT has a small fixed set of data types which describe objects in the system. Objects have a structure associated with them which contains type information, access control flags and a value.

Dictionaries, Names and *Operators* form the essential parts of the POSTSCRIPT execution environment. The interpreter looks up any names (symbols or tokens) which it encounters on the input stream in the dictionary stack. This stack can be dynamically added to by the user for creating local scopes. Dictionaries may take (almost) any data type as a key or value. It was observed that there are no operators for removing items from *dictionaries* (except save and **restore**), they were implemented by hash tables with linear chaining. This is the simplest scheme which fits the requirement. Most names in the system dictionary at the bottom of the stack are POSTSCRIPT operators, which do the real work. Because the naming is dynamic, extra names can be used to replace existing POSTSCRIPT functions with modified alternatives. This makes POSTSCRIPT very easy to alter.

Names in POSTSCRIPT can be compared quickly so that they can be used efficiently as dictionary keys. This requires a unique storage pointer. The *name* table was thus implemented by using a simple unbalanced tree structure with no garbage collection. When a *string* is converted to a *name*, it is looked up in the tree. This usually happens during parsing, though there is a separate POSTSCRIPT operator, token, for this purpose[1]. The resulting *name* object contains a unique reference to a tree node.

Operators were implemented by using function pointers with added argument type information. We arranged for arguments to be pulled off the stack and type-checked before being passed to the

---

[1] token is one of many key operators in POSTSCRIPT whose presence have a controlling influence on an implementation.

implementing function. This was an important feature, as it localised the type-checking for all but the most polymorphic operators. No escape mechanisms were added for operators with strange arguments, such operators simply declare themselves to have fewer arguments and then use extra ones off the stack. Result types are not checked, since they are tested as arguments by everything which uses them, but the number of results may be declared so that stack overflow and underflow checks can be localised.

Files, *Arrays*, and *Strings* are all usefully executable: an executable *Array* is a procedure body – there are special array literals for expressing these. This relies on the fact that parameters are passed on the stack and that binding is dynamic, so procedure bodies don't also have to be function closures. *Strings* are executed by parsing them like input. It is notable that the string quotes are parentheses, which are thus nestable.

There are a few subtleties with *files* - certain file names refer to pseudo-files which return complete syntactic units to the interpreter for processing. We implemented this by reading into a *string* and making that executable.

Integers, *Reals*, and *Booleans* are traditional.

Marks are used to mark unbounded lists on stacks, and have no interesting operations. *Nulls* are similar.

FontIDs are a means of internally referencing fonts (described later).

SaveObjs refer to saved contexts, which are described in the section on Storage Management.

There is no real notion of assignment in POSTSCRIPT but it is possible to replace key/value pairs in dictionaries or place values in *arrays* and *strings*.

2.3. Polymorphism

A large number of POSTSCRIPT operators take arguments of differing types. The get operator, for example, can get a value from an *array, string* or *dictionary*. It is a fairly simple extension of this idea to allow arbitrary polymorphism.

Our implementation has an extra dictionary for each data type which contains a simple operator implementing a version of a polymorphic operator for that data type. Many operators in the system dictionary point at a generic operator for the kind of polymorphism in question, and that generic operator calls a specific operator from a type dictionary. This is similar to the "discriminator functions" in COMMON-LOOPS[2] . This facility allows users to add or change the standard data types and operations. New operation/data type pairs can be added even in the POSTSCRIPT language itself.

It is not possible to construct new data types in POSTSCRIPT, as this involves changing data formats, but it is fairly easy to link new source modules into the interpreter with code for a new data type.

2.4. Error handling

POSTSCRIPT has an effective error handling mechanism, which is quite tidy and general when compared with many other systems.

When an error occurs, an error operator is called from a special dictionary. These operators are replaceable, like most other parts of the system. The change in control flow required by error handling is handled separately by two operators called stop and stopped. These implement "catch" and "throw", as found in some functional languages.

An executable array is passed to the stopped operator which calls it and normally returns false. If a stop is encountered, execution resumes immediately at the stopped operator, which then returns true. stop unwinds the "execution stack", which is directly accessible from POSTSCRIPT.

The above has a considerable influence on the design of the interpreter: Some operators need to take a POSTSCRIPT procedure as an argument, which they may call a number of times. The flow control operators work this way for example. When an operator needs to do this, it issues a "call-back". The obvious way to implement call-backs would be to call the interpreter recursively. To implement stop and stopped would then be difficult to do cleanly and portably (without manipulating the C runtime stack and compromising the reliability of the system). Instead of this, a virtual machine was built which executes

POSTSCRIPT objects, and allows POSTSCRIPT operators to explicitly alter the execution (return address) stack when necessary. This makes operators like **stopped** and **stop** fairly easy to implement, but makes call-backs into POSTSCRIPT code slightly more complicated. Call-backs are achieved by pushing a *continuation* operator on the execution stack, followed by the POSTSCRIPT object to be executed. When the operator finishes executing, the virtual machine will drop into the POSTSCRIPT code on the stack and when that finishes, the continuation function will be executed. In order to perform a loop, for example, the continuation would push the POSTSCRIPT object again, and another instance of the continuation function. Items such as the bounds of **for** loops and such are also placed on the execution stack, but they are removed by the continuation operators before the virtual machine attempts to execute them.

Implementing the **exit** operator in this context requires a little thought: how far should this operator unwind the execution stack? In our implementation the flow control operators place a marker on the execution stack. **exit** searches down the stack until it encounters one, and removes everything above it. Execution will then pick up just after the control operator. The **stop** and **stopped** operators work in a similar way, except that they use a different marker, so that some checking is possible.

Arrays and *Strings* are executed by placing their tail (sub array starting after the first element) back on the execution stack and placing the first element above it. If the array is of zero length, nothing happens.

Files manage their own file pointer. A custom lexical/syntax analyser was built to interpret *files* and *strings*, partly because POSTSCRIPT is very simple to interpret and partly for the control obtainable by doing this. The parser was parameterised on the character input function to avoid code duplication.

2.5. Storage Management

POSTSCRIPT has a simple model of storage management. Objects are created on request, and removed when the user loses his last pointer to them. This would seem to imply a requirement for garbage collection, but for the existence of **save** and **restore**. **save** means "save a snap-shot of everything" and **restore** means "restore a previous snap-shot". There are two aspects to **save** and **restore**: one is that the interpreter state is saved and restored, and the other is that garbage collection can be performed when the **restore** occurs. There are some curious exceptions which are relevant: the contents of the stacks are not disturbed, although if they would cause dangling references, a **restore** operation generates an error. Also the contents of a *string* is not defined after a **restore**. It is implicit that file pointers do not get moved back either, though it is not stated anywhere. The POSTSCRIPT Reference Manual also states that **save** and **restore** are efficient enough that they may reasonably be used to save context around a number of assignments and restore it afterwards.

One possible implementation of **save** and **restore** would be to copy the entire data space maintained by POSTSCRIPT, but the requirement of efficiency precludes this as a practical choice.

Another implementation would be as follows:

Note when an element of an array or dictionary is altered, and preserve the old value if it has not changed since the last **save**. This means that there would have to be a record of the save level at the last assignment for each element of an array or dictionary, and checking code on the **put** operator in its various disguises (e.g. **def**). A *SaveObj* would then have a pointer to a list of old values for items which have been assigned since its creation (initially null). **restore** would search this list, and put back all the old values and save levels. It would then deallocate all objects created since the save object was created. This could be done either by moving back an allocation pointer, if new objects are allocated in consecutive store, or by following through a list of allocated objects if they are not.

Although our implementation does not yet support **save** and **restore**, we will use the latter approach, as we allocate many data structures which are not bounded by scope constraints, e.g. bitmaps for windows, I/O buffers, cache table entries and so on. An implementation could use fixed size tables for these items in a dedicated environment such as a printer, but it is simpler in a virtual storage environment to allocate things dynamically.

One modification we might make, rather than stringing all new objects together, would be to batch allocation of objects, starting a new "bucket" at each save or when one fills up. This simple technique would vastly reduce the work done by the standard storage allocator and bring it in line with the efficiency of a contiguous allocation scheme.

Currently, our implementation does no garbage collection at all, and we rely on virtual memory to keep the interpreter running. Also, the only the thing our **save** and **restore** operators do is to save the graphics state. It turns out that this is sufficient for many purposes.

3. GRAPHICS

POSTSCRIPT distinguishes the generation of graphical shapes from their imaging. Shapes are called *paths*, and describe a set of possibly closed outlines. There is a variety of operators for adding lines, curves and arc segments to a path. Curiously a path is not a data type in POSTSCRIPT as such. The intention is that users should create procedures for generating paths and manipulate those instead.

A path is just one element of a fairly large *graphics state*, which can be altered prior to using an imaging operator. Much of it remains constant most of the time, so it forms an implicit parameter to these operators. In general very little of it needs to be changed frequently. The graphics state is also stacked so that changes made can be quickly undone with gsave and grestore.

There is also the notion of a current output page. This is the destination of the imaging operators and it accumulates the effects of them independently of gsave until a **showpage** or **erasepage** occurs.

3.1. Paths

POSTSCRIPT separates the generation of polygons from their imaging, so the same primitives produce shapes to draw and fill. This has the advantage that very complex shapes may be generated in a device independent manner and with no lack of generality.

Many operators in POSTSCRIPT do complicated things with paths, so a doubly linked list was used to implement them. This scheme proved very flexible and also simplified the storage management. A list of linked lists might have been better choice, since it would then have been easier to find "closepaths", however the use of a flat data structure kept the code simple. Most operations on paths require generating a new path from an old one, so very little juggling of path segments is necessary.

3.2. Painting model

An important feature of POSTSCRIPT is the graphical imaging model chosen. Because it was designed for printer devices, POSTSCRIPT uses a paint model for imaging (any output colour replaces any colour previously there). A path describes an outline which can be stroked with a pen or filled with colour. A path may also be used as a clipping region, which is like filling a region and then using it as a stencil.

3.3. Filling and Clipping

Filling regions needs a certain amount of thought. The intention is that filling should behave like paint, and cover anything previously painted. How then does one arrange to fill a self-intersecting polygon in such a way that it behaves like paint? Many systems use the so-called even/odd rule: starting at the outside of the region, count edges and paint when the count is odd and not when it is even. One problem with this is that if a region is self-intersecting, parts that are intersected do not always get filled.

POSTSCRIPT provides an alternative *non-zero winding number rule*, which counts the difference in the number of passes an edge makes across a line from any point to the outside. See figure 2. Clockwise passes count one way and anticlockwise passes count the other way. In this way, a self intersecting region gets completely filled where the difference is non-zero.

Implementing area fill in POSTSCRIPT is far from simple. Not only can one fill a possibly overlapping and self-intersecting path, but one can use it as a clip boundary to clip further output. Clipping is cumulative (i.e. each clip operation makes the clip area smaller). One of the most intriguing POSTSCRIPT operators is **clippath**, which gives you back a path description of the current clip boundary, taking multiple **clip** and **eoclip** operations into account.[2]

The first approach used to implement area fill was to scan the bounding box one raster scan line at a

---

[2] **clippath** is another example of a key POSTSCRIPT operator.

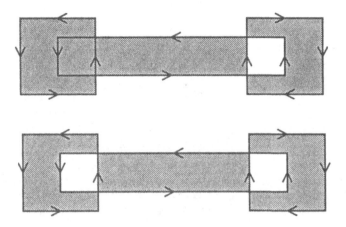

Fig 2. A comparison of the two rules for area fill.
Non-zero winding number above and Even/Odd below.

time. At each scan line, all line segments in the path which crossed the scan line were intersected with it (noting the direction of crossing) to establish a list of cross points. This was then sorted to produce raster line segments which could be filled according to the filling rule required (winding or even/odd). This algorithm is plainly inefficient, since it looks at every scanline, while most images drawn have interesting points which are widely spaced. Clipping could be achieved with this algorithm, but the clippaths produced would contain rectangular polygons describing raster line segments which would be unnecessarily large and slow to process.

A better way to implement fill and clip is to look only at scan lines (Y coordinates) where something interesting happens, such as a line starting or ending, or crossing another line. It is possible to scan in this fashion, generating trapezoid shapes at each interesting Y coordinate. This is described in a paper by Newell and Sequin[3] . See figure 3.

One reason why this algorithm has not yet been implemented is the problem of intersecting two sets of trapezoids to achieve clipping. It turns out that this is not the best way to think about the problem: clipping should be factored into the trapezoid generation so that the same code which does trapezoid decomposition also does clipping. From this, it is apparent that the clippath only needs to be reduced to trapezoids if it is intersected with another clip area, since the new clip area is getting clipped. This explains a feature of the Apple LaserWriter that puzzled us for sometime, which was that clip paths did not always seem to be reduced to trapezoids. This clue eventually hinted at the solution to the trapezoid intersection problem, above.

Some care is necessary in rendering trapezoids on an output device. With a scan line algorithm such as the one we are currently using, any deviations due to rounding are relatively minor, because they are localised. If two trapezoids share a vertical edge, the coordinates may be rounded so that the lines have slightly different gradients. If the trapezoids form the edge of a single line from the point of view of the user, he will be particularly disturbed if it doesn't look straight. One solution to this problem is to use floating point coordinates even at the output stage. A possible alternative is to define a trapezoid by the complete lines from which its vertical edges were formed, clipped by the interesting Y coordinates. If the vertical line segments are rounded, the minor differences in gradient are much less likely to be noticeable, especially since the line segments will be longer.

Fig 3. Trapezoid decomposition in action.

There are difficulties with clipping: how does one efficiently render text through a complex clipping boundary? One possible solution is to use a shadow mask bitmap containing a fill of the clip area. It may also be noted that bounding boxes on clip and fill areas may eliminate a large amount of work.

There are a number of techniques available here, but so far only simple area fill with no clipping has been implemented.

3.4. Strokes

Strokes (lines) in POSTSCRIPT are fairly complicated: most graphics systems provide line drawing, and some have facilities to allow thick lines to be drawn essentially by using a line drawing algorithm to drag a pen shape along a path and drawing it at every pixel. This generates poor results at corners and ends when the pen shape is large, as the Smalltalk book[4] demonstrates: it is fine for draft use, but not really good enough for printed copy.

POSTSCRIPT provides several options for finishing strokes at ends and corners to prevent ugly joins. Round, Mitered and Bevelled corners are filled in by describing the shapes which fill the gaps between the rectangles that form the line bodies.

POSTSCRIPT has a **strokepath** operator, which replaces the current path by a path which describes its outline, including the line ends and joins. The definition of this operator is that if the resulting path is filled, it will look the same as the original path if stroked, so **stroke** can be implemented by **strokepath fill**.[3] See figure 4. Working out exactly where to place the polygons which describe an arbitrary stroked path is simplified by transforming the coordinate system to make the stroke lie along an axis in a conventional direction. There are certain difficulties with closed paths, because the algorithm has to look to see if the path is closed before deciding whether to add end points.

We made one simple optimisation to the **stroke** operator to using native line-drawing for thin strokes. This made an enormous difference to performance, and also produced much better results for previewing output from programs such as *pic*(1). It is probably worthwhile treating two to five pixel lines specially also, but we haven't done this yet.

3.4.1. Curves

POSTSCRIPT paths can contain line and curve segments. In order to make the imaging and path transformation algorithms easier, an algorithm is used to convert curve segments into enough line segments to approximate the curve to the required accuracy.[4] POSTSCRIPT has a parameter in the graphics state which states by how many device pixels the flattened curve is allowed to deviate. A simple algorithm for Bezier curve flattening is recursive bisection[5]. The recursion is not to a fixed depth, since Bezier curves can have widely different curvatures along their length, but stops when the curve is sufficiently flat. See

---

[3] strokepath is another key POSTSCRIPT operator.
[4] There is another key POSTSCRIPT operator called **flattenpath** which does curve flattening explicitly.

Fig 4. This illuminating example demonstrates how miters are formed.

figure 5.

Circular arcs can be approximated be dividing them into Bezier curves of small enough curvature. The Apple LaserWriter uses 90 degree segments, so our implementation does the same.

The use of **flattenpath** inside the interpreter has the nice property that no other operator needs to know about curved lines.

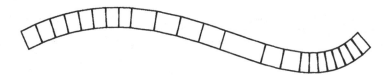

Fig 5. Curves can be flattened to line segments.

3.4.2. Dashing

PostScript supports dashing of lines in a very general way. Dashes are expected to follow around corners with the correct length, though no attempt is made to force them to appear at corners. The reason for this is so that curves may be flattened before the result is dashed. See figure 6.

In our implementation, a small amount of path juggling was necessary to get closed paths to connect up properly when they begin and end with the visible part of a dash. Since several connected line segments may form one curved dash segment immediately preceding the end of the path, a piece of the dash pattern may have to be chopped out and joined to the piece at the beginning of the path. This is one of the few cases where the new path has to be altered in situ as it is being generated.

strokepath calls **flattenpath**, then the dashing routine, and then it generates the path that would draw around the resulting path. This is so that the dashing routine doesn't need to know how to follow around curve segments. It is curious to note that there is no operator which returns a dash description in a manner similar to **flattenpath**.

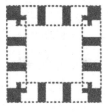 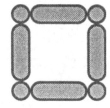 

Fig 6. Getting dashes to follow around corners is hard.

3.5. Images

POSTSCRIPT has support for bitmapped images, but in a device independent way. The model is that images are a short-hand for a grid of coloured squares. Two variations are supported: **imagemask** which allows a square to be either of the current colour, or absent; and **image** which allows a grayscale image of a range of pixel depths for the squares. The grid always occupies the unit square in user coordinates, so that the size of the definition does not affect the shape of resulting image. The unit square is transformed using the normal coordinate transformations to make the picture large enough to see.

Images can clearly be implemented by scanning the incoming data and generating small square paths, then filling them with colour. Our first implementation used this method, which is adequate for small images and large magnifications.

It is simple to detect when an image happens to correspond with the device resolution and orientation and use a display Raster Operation to render it quickly. An algorithm for simple magnification by integer amounts is described in Rob Pike's SIGGRAPH course notes on bitmapped graphics[6], and also in the Smalltalk book. See figure 7.

Fig 7. Integer magnification.

Magnification by non-integer amounts was not difficult to implement: essentially the difference is that there are two spacings between spread columns and rows, which together reach the correct width. The algorithm was adapted from the method of padding characters to a fixed width in text justification. The smear operation which follows the spread may in fact make some ''pixels'' too large by one pixel. A slower, but more accurate reverse sampling method would prevent this, but has not yet been done on our implementation.

Rotating an image by generalising reverse sampling should be fairly easy, but again this hasn't been done yet. Our code currently looks for fast simple cases and drops through into more general code when necessary.

Oddly, although there are facilities in the rest of POSTSCRIPT for supporting colour, there is no support for colour images. This is a curious and unfortunate omission.

3.6. Half-toning

POSTSCRIPT was specifically designed for use with bi-level raster devices, so half-toning is used to approximate gray shades. This is a familiar feature to users of bitmapped displays: typically a range of small speckle patterns is designed. They are replicated (tiled) over the area to be shaded, and clipped to its outline. An important feature of half-toning is that the tile shape should be aligned with the picture frame and not with the area being half-toned. If this is not done, seams will appear if two adjacent areas are tiled independently.

3.6.1. The half-tone screen

POSTSCRIPT adds a new twist to half-toning. Most bitmapped graphics systems do not actually provide a mapping between gray values and a suitable half-tone pattern. The user is expected to design each pattern himself, and that design is typically device dependent. POSTSCRIPT allows the user to specify a gray level intensity, and the interpreter maps this to an appropriate pattern. The user is permitted to specify a half-tone pattern by giving a solid spot function in POSTSCRIPT with a scaling size and rotation to an operator called setscreen. The spot function takes X and Y coordinates and returns a height (Z coordinate) at that point. The highest points are blackened first for the lightest grays and the lowest points last for the darkest grays. See figure 8.

Fig 8. Half-tone screens have a solid spot function.

Half-toning has been implemented partly in POSTSCRIPT and partly in the interpreter. Extra operators were added to allow POSTSCRIPT code to request a set of coordinate values at which to sample the spot function. This is then applied, and the resulting set of heights is passed back to the interpreter. The half-tone machinery then sorts the sample values by height and uses them to turn on bits in a half-tone pattern. Any gray value requested is scaled and used as an index into the array of sample coordinates. All coordinates above the scaled value have a bit turned on in the resulting half-tone. In practice, all the possible half-tone patterns are generated in advance in this way for efficiency.

Because we use bitmapped displays, half-toning is done by RasterOp code, so the tile patterns cannot be rotated; our implementation currently ignores the rotation parameter. It is possible to replicate rotated bitmaps, but a fast algorithm for replicating with $\log_2 n + \log_2 m$ RasterOps instead of $n \times m$ RasterOps (essentially by copying the area replicated so far at each stage) covers a large number of pixels more than once when used rotated. It is also harder because of the unusual clipping requirements, so we haven't implemented this yet.

If a half-toning (three-way) RasterOp function is not available, it is possible to simulate tiling by using the source bitmap as a clip mask and copying the tile through that with replication. Since memory is relatively cheap, we have used a shadow bitmap to retain the replicated tile and thus do half-toning in a constant number of RasterOps.

3.6.2. Brightness Transfer Function

One other complication is that POSTSCRIPT provides a mapping function between user gray levels and device gray levels. The user can set this *transfer* function (normally the identity function), to any piece of POSTSCRIPT source with **settransfer**. When the setting is done, it is sampled in a similar way to the above in POSTSCRIPT, then a table of values is passed to the half-toning machinery.

4. FONTS

4.1. Fonts as graphical shapes

POSTSCRIPT fonts are treated as graphical shapes, so they may be stretched, scaled and rotated as much as desired. POSTSCRIPT has been criticised because it does not scale fonts according to the typographical convention, which involve changing the shape of the characters at different sizes. One answer to this is that there is nothing to prevent headline fonts being added to a printer. POSTSCRIPT is flexible enough that it would be trivial to down-load a replacement **scalefont** operator which uses different fonts at different sizes. The ability to scale and rotate a font arbitrarily is useful in itself, if only for special effects.

4.2. Simple font rendering

The POSTSCRIPT model is that the show operator sets up the Current Transformation Matrix according to the current point and Font Matrix of the current font. It then scans a string calling **BuildChar** with the font and the character code as argument. Each font has its own definition of **BuildChar** which does the appropriate thing for that font.

BuildChar is expected to use the character code as an index into an Encoding vector where it finds a character name. The character name is then used to find some representation of the character to draw (often a POSTSCRIPT procedure to draw it). Since the transformation matrix has already been set up, the character drawing is independent of size.

It turned out to be much easier to implement the most general form of **show**, which is **awidthshow**. The other more restricted forms (**show**, **ashow**, and **widthshow**) can all be implemented with almost no loss of efficiency using **awidthshow**. Implementing them all separately is tedious. The reason that *strings* are the primitive type and not characters is for efficiency and convenience. With the operators provided, a complete line of text can be shown with a single operator. See figure 9.

kshow, which allows kerning between every character shown, is best implemented in POSTSCRIPT as there is little performance advantage in calling back to POSTSCRIPT for every character over showing one character at a time from POSTSCRIPT.

stringwidth is currently implemented in our interpreter by using **nulldevice** to prevent output and showing the characters using **show**. It is then simple to get the position of the current point to compute the width. It would be a simple optimisation to compute the widths by examining the metrics in a font dictionary.

show	here is some text which demonstrates the show operators
widthshow	here is some text which demonstrates the show operators
ashow	here is some text which demonstrates the show operators

Fig 9. The various forms of the show operator.

Adobe Systems evidently have some ingenious algorithms for making algorithmically generated fonts look reasonably good at low resolutions, though they have not revealed how this is achieved. The Apple LaserWriter output demonstrates that there is room for improvement, however: the tight curves at the bottom of small letters such as 'a' reveal small pimples. Naturally, our implementation cannot approach Adobe's rendering quality. It is also difficult to judge how good a job they do because of the resolution difference between laser printers and bitmapped displays.

4.3. Caching

Drawing every character algorithmically is too slow to be practical, so the POSTSCRIPT language provides elaborate mechanisms for caching character images into bitmaps. Unfortunately the mechanism is partly visible and partly hidden, but the effect is that **BuildChar** needs to know how to set up the cache, or prevent its use.

The model is that the contents of the cache is a mask, which is painted onto the page in the current colour. POSTSCRIPT does not support multi-coloured fonts with caching (though if the caching is not used, the rest of the machinery still works in colour). It is interesting to see how the **imagemask** operator fits into this scenario.

The mechanism for caching characters is somewhat involved: there is an operator called **setcachedevice** which alters the device in the graphics state so that further output goes into a saved bitmap. This operator only works in the context of a **show**. One curiosity of this operator is that it takes an implicit argument which is the character name to cache. This is magically passed from **show** in the graphics state. It cannot be global, as POSTSCRIPT is expected to be able to use other characters in the generation of compound characters such as ligatures, so in our implementation there is a small amount of extra graphics state associated with **show**.

The parameters to the **cachestatus** and **setcachelimit** operators give clues as to how the caching machinery might be organised. There is a doubly linked list of font caches which is kept ordered on a Least Recently Used basis, so that when too many characters have been cached, complete caches can be thrown away to make space.

There is a separate hash table of characters. When this fills up, the least recently used font cache and all associated characters are thrown away. There is also a maximum size beyond which characters are not cached at all (since characters of that size are used rarely enough to make caching them a waste of time and space). When a character is being drawn into the cache, the current colour is ignored.

All this accords with the description in the POSTSCRIPT Language Reference Manual, although some aspects of the Adobe implementation have recently changed.

4.3.1. Disk caching

In order to improve the start-up performance of our previewer, machinery was added for reading cached fonts from disk. These are keyed on the font name and final transformation matrix. It is not possible or even desirable to decide which cache to use until the actual **show** operator is executed, since this is dependent on the graphics state (i.e. current transformation matrix and font). At that point, the local cache is searched; if the font was present at the current transformation and scale, **show** will go on to render characters from the cache. If the cache was not found and the font bounding box is small enough, a new cache is generated. At this stage, the interpreter will attempt to add to the new cache from a disk copy. If it cannot find a disk cache, it simply continues. **show** will then attempt to render characters from the cache; if this fails at some point, it will drop out to perform a call-back into POSTSCRIPT code to execute **BuildChar** from the current font. When that returns, it will attempt to render from the cache again: if **BuildChar** added to the cache, this will succeed and show the character. If **BuildChar** defeated caching and drew the character itself, then **show** will fail to render from the cache and continue.

The nice feature of all this is that **show** is very fast as long as the characters it needs to show are cached. When they are not, it slows up briefly to add to the cache and then runs quickly for all subsequent renderings of that character. Apart from this, it never needs to return to interpreted code. Disk caches may be incomplete or even absent, but the interpreter always makes the best use of the information available.

Caches are not saved to disk automatically: if this were done, the disk would soon fill up with fonts in strange sizes and orientations. Instead, we have added a new operator, called **savecurrentfont** which writes the current font, as cached so far, to the appropriate disk cache directory.

4.3.2. Font library

Our font descriptions in POSTSCRIPT also do a certain amount of lazy evaluation: the **BuildChar** procedure which is initially loaded is in fact a stub which loads the complete font description when it is called. It then replaces itself by the real **BuildChar**, which does rendering. The advantage of this, is that as long as cached font sizes are used, the large font descriptions need never be loaded.

Even the font descriptions are loaded lazily by **findfont**. The internal **findfont** only knows how to search the *FontDirectory* within the interpreter, so a POSTSCRIPT version is wrapped around it which knows how to search a font library on disk. The first thing that does is to attempt to find the font in **FontDirectory**. If that fails, it goes to disk. An extra directory mapping font names to file names has been added so that fonts can be renamed. POSTSCRIPT documents tend to have names like "/Times-Roman" wired into them, so the ability to map these to the fonts available through a separate mechanism adds much flexibility.

When the interpreter was ported to a machine with a smaller display, an A4 page would not quite fit on the screen, so the default transformation matrix was adjusted to allow the page to be less than actual size. When this occurred, the interpreter automatically picked up slightly smaller cache entries for ordinary font sizes without any adjustment.

5. PORTING EXPERIENCES

Our implementation was designed for high performance, high resolution bitmapped graphical workstations. It was originally written on an ICL Perq 2 running PNX3 and later ported to PNX5 with virtual memory.

It was realised fairly early on that the interpreter would have to be portable, so some effort was expended to ensure that the graphics device dependencies were well isolated. To assist with this, a device interface was designed which could be re-implemented for each new display with minimal effort and size. The current system runs with device modules which each take less than 4% of the total code size. The first implementations used a locally written portable graphics library called ww: the interface for this is about 400 lines of C, the rest of the interpreter is about 10000 lines of C. The ww version runs unmodified on Perq 2s, Sun3s and Whitechapel MG1s. There is no conditional compilation, only an exchangeable object module.

A port was done to the High Level Hardware Orion workstation, which supports gray levels. This was done initially by porting enough of the ww library, and then by using the resident graphics system (when the latter was enhanced to support grayscale/colour graphics). All the half-toning work is done below the device independent interface, so half-toning algorithms were simply replaced by code set brightness levels. The first Orion port took a week.

A version has also been written for the X window manager, although X lacks certain essential features, such as the ability to half-tone a bitmap before drawing it, or perform off-screen RasterOps. X windows does not support general purpose RasterOp functions on or between off-screen bitmaps, so POSTSCRIPT has great difficulty caching fonts on X. There does not appear to be any reasonable way of getting drawn characters into an X font, even if the latter could support the requirements of POSTSCRIPT fonts.

5.1. Colour ports

Although the Orion and X windows both support colour, a full colour port has not been done yet, mostly because we cannot decide how best to deal with colour maps. POSTSCRIPT deals with colour in the abstract: it asks for a particular intensity of Red, Green and Blue or Hue, Saturation and Brightness, without regard to the abilities of the display. A reference to the colour model used is in the POSTSCRIPT language manual[7] . Most colour displays have a colour map which restricts the number of visible colours at any one time depending on the depth of the display. If a POSTSCRIPT program attempts to draw too many colours, the system would run out of colour map entries. This is not a problem on a grayscale implementation, because the colour space is one-dimensional, so it can be sampled reasonably. It would be possible to sample a colour space in three dimensions, but very sparsely.

An alternative is to half-tone the two closest colours in the colour map to the colour requested when the colour map is full. Unfortunately there may be times when there is nothing even remotely close in the colour map. It might be possible to prime the colour map with anchor points, but this would not work well without multicolour half-tones, for which a solid function is not sufficient. The problem deserves further research.

6. SUMMARY AND CONCLUSIONS

An implementation of POSTSCRIPT has been described, which is complete enough for most usage, and efficient enough to be a practical tool for previewing. The bottle-neck in execution time is in floating point arithmetic; this was amply demonstrated by compiling it on a Sun3 with and without hardware floating point support. We have considered the possibility of using fixed point arithmetic, but haven't tried this yet.

During the development, we encountered aliasing in various guises – thin lines vanishing as they fell between pixels and some fairly unpleasant examples of stair-casing along adjacent curves. This problem appears to be basically unsolvable.

We did a small amount work to make drawn characters look readable at small sizes, but this was not very successful. The only way to get reasonable characters is to buy properly designed raster fonts. We have not done this yet, so we haven't attempted to integrate bitmapped fonts with our caching machinery, though this should be automatic.

We have no clipping support yet, as our area fill is rather simplistic (though correct). Our implementation of the imaging operators is also somewhat simplistic.

Every POSTSCRIPT operator has some implementation, even if it doesn't provide complete functionality. This allows documents to print without failing, even if the output has bits missing when it is completed.

ACKNOWLEDGEMENTS

I would like to thank Tony Williams for his continual support and advice during the development of the interpreter, and also for his helpful comments on this paper.

I would also like to thank Mark Martin for writing the ww graphics package, which got me off the ground and saved me from battles with some bizarre window systems. Also for his comments on the paper.

REFERENCES

1. Adobe Systems Inc., *PostScript Language Reference Manual*, Addison Wesley, Reading, Mass.. ISBN 0-201-10174-2

2. D. G. Bobrow et al., "COMMONLOOPS: merging common lisp and Object-oriented programming.," *Intelligent Systems Laboratory Series*, Xerox, Palo Alto Research Center (1985).

3. Martin E Newell and Carlo H Sequin, "The Inside Story on Self-Intersecting Polygons," *Lambda* 1(2), pp. 20-24 (Second Quarter, 1980).

4. Adele Goldberg, *Smalltalk-80: The Interactive Programming Environment*, Addison-Wesley, Reading, Mass (1984).

5. B. A. Barsky and A. D. DeRose, "The Beta2-spline: A special Case of the Beta-spline Curve and Surface Representation," *IEEE Computer Graphics and Applications* (September 1985).

6. Rob Pike, Leo Guibas, and Dan Ingalls, "Bitmap Graphics," SIGGRAPH 84 Course Notes, AT&T Bell Laboratories (1984).

7. A. R. Smith, "Color Gamut Transform Pairs," *Computer Graphics* 12(3) (August 1978).

Integration of Graphics with Text in an Electronic Journal

N.S. Hall, S. Laflin, W.P. Dodd

Department of Computing and Computer Science
University of Birmingham

Abstract

The overall aim of this paper is to describe a diagram classification that has been carried out with a view to suggesting the most convenient methods of storage and reproduction.

This work has been conducted in support of the British Library (BLEND) project designed to integrate text and graphics within an electronic journal.

The preliminary goal is to identify problems associated with the inclusion of graphics in an environment that uses low bandwidth communications channels. This means that the efficiency of compression and image-representation techniques is of vital importance. The particular method chosen will be dictated by the type and complexity of the diagram.

Key words: BLEND, typology of diagrams, GKS.

1. Introduction

The main purpose of this paper is to describe the particular classification scheme that has been set up to describe diagrams according to their complexity, and suggest efficient methods of representing them.

This work forms part of a preliminary study being carried out at Birmingham to investigate various problems associated with the design of a graphics system for an electronic journal, such as BLEND, (Birmingham and Loughborough Electronic Network Development), and compare different techniques for their compression and transmission.

The discussion is divided into three sections. In order to place the current study in context, the first section will provide a brief description of the BLEND project and proposals for the graphics study within it. Here it is intended to give a brief overview of how a prospective user might interact with an "electronic browsing" facility in a computer based journal and the likely requirements of its graphics subsystem.

The constraints imposed on graphics management software within such a system include, minimizing storage requirements, minimizing image reproduction times, while, at the same time giving as high quality reproduction as possible. It is obvious that these requirements conflict. The current study will address such problems and some of the necessary compromises.

The second part of this paper contains a detailed description of the classification scheme. A number of "images" will be used to illustrate the type of graphics found within the different groupings. It is also very important to consider those borderline cases that lie midway between categories. When this happens it may not be obvious which representation methods are most appropriate and additional criteria have to be considered.

The third section very briefly outlines some current work within the project. In particular, there is an interest in methods that allow images to be requested at low resolution and subsequently upgraded. This corresponds nicely with the envisaged operation of an electronic browsing facility, but it also achieves an effective data compression.

2. An Overview of the BLEND Project

BLEND (6), (7), was a four-year program jointly organized by two universities. The aims were to assess the cost, efficiency and subjective impact of an electronic communication system, and to explore and evaluate alternative forms of user communication through an electronic journal and information network.

Using a host computer at the University of Birmingham, a community of about 50 scientists (Loughborough Information Network Community - LINC) was connected through the public telephone network to explore various types of communication including journals, annotated abstracts, workshop conferences, cooperative authorship, etc. Following this start in 1981, five other communities have been using the system for these various types of communication.

The BLEND project made use of a computer conferencing suite called NOTEPAD, supplied by the InfoMedia Corporation based in San Bruno, California. This suite was selected on the basis of its well-researched human interface, but also, there were very few alternatives available and the timescale of the project would not have permitted the development of in house software. In any event, it would have proved difficult to produce a detailed specification for an electronic journal system without prior experimentation. NOTEPAD and the BLEND system were exclusively text orientated and therefore one feature of hard-copy journals that had not been replicated in the BLEND experiment, except in a very rudimentary manner, was the provision of a graphics facility. The only graphics that have been provided were obtained by direct mapping onto the standard ASCII character set. This is a very severe limitation on the development of an electronic journal. There has been some work on the use of extended character sets, including enhanced facilities for graphics. Such work has been carried out by various bodies including PIRA and ECMA.

Alternative approaches will be made possible with the Teletex terminals and distribution systems. However, when the project was in its embryo stages, neither of these systems were available. It was also thought that the Teletex system was likely to be expensive or of limited market penetration initially. In addition, the extended code solution might still not have a sufficiently versatile code set for the reproduction of all diagrams.

As a consequence, it was proposed (4) to investigate solutions based on equipment currently available or shortly to become available to the user, i.e. the microcomputer with communications hardware and software. In fact many of the participants involved in the BLEND/LINC experiment used these devices to communicate with the DEC-2060 host located at Birmingham. However, the local processing power these micros provide has been very much underutilized except for certain automatic logging procedures and off line file/document preparation.

The solutions mentioned, Teletex and extended character sets, rely primarily on transmitting "screen fulls" of data which are then simply displayed on the user's device. In this case the level of sophistication is entirely within the data transmitted and local decoding. These methods do not make very much use of the processing power usually available at the user's terminal. Many micros that provide hardware graphics facilities also include a comprehensive software library to manipulate these.

The proposals therefore suggested a comparative study of alternative methods of utilizing this local processing power and accompanying software in order to reconstruct source diagrams on a variety of microcomputers. The information transmitted from the host would be further processed by local software to produce a given screen of information. It was suggested the comparative study should consider the following three methods for representing graphics:

(a) Bit map techniques
(b) Picture description language to be interpreted by some locally running process
(c) Representation in terms of a high level language code, the same code as the local process, so that it is able to use the local graphics subroutine library

Finally, in order to direct the project towards a tangible goal, the suggested subject area for use in the pilot study was, "Computer Applications in Archaeology". Several reasons for this are that there is interest within the department on the subject and archaeology was considered likely to provide a very wide variety of material with a minimum bias toward computer techniques. The graphics content in journals is expected to be subject dependent and it is necessary to consider and be able to represent the widest possible range of diagrams. The chosen subject area would appear to give this range.

The main purpose of the current graphics research is to investigate methods for the representation and reproduction of pictorial information within an electronic journal. The methods will be subject to constraints imposed by the electronic journal environment. Such constraints as slow communications channels, fast reproduction speeds (at the user's terminal), and image fidelity will require methods to be tailored to the diagram type and even the output devices.

3. Necessity for a Diagram Classification

As was mentioned previously, the content of pictorial material will be subject dependent. For example, the images in a certain journal on electronics are almost exclusively circuit diagrams, whereas astrophysics texts contain many black and white photographs. These are fundamentally very different and require different amounts of information to be fully specified.

There would be no need for a diagram classification if either (a) one catch-all method could be used with impunity in all cases, or (b) the subject matter were to be restricted so much that only one specific, well defined type of diagram need ever be represented. Unfortunately, the constraints imposed by the electronic journal environment make the first strategy (a) impractical, and it is obvious that the second option (b) would be so restrictive that it may become difficult to find a subject or journal which could be represented using the system. This would in turn reduce the type and number of users or user communities and hence the amount of "hands-on" practical experience to a level which jeopardizes the usefulness of the project.

With these considerations, it seems that the most realistic approach is one which could accommodate the whole spectrum of pictorial information likely to be found in learned texts. However, as no single method of representation is efficient for all pictures, this must be subject to the proviso that representation methods be tailored to the "type" and complexity of the image. It is necessary to have some objective strategy for choosing the most efficient method of storing any given image from the journal and the diagram classification scheme is designed to provide a mechanism for doing this and also for identifying those instances where a diagram could be equally well represented by more than one method. The latter point may be important if, for example, the particular local hardware and software configuration provides more support for one method.

There was a second related reason for performing the diagram survey. In an attempt to impose order on the work and provide some experimental material, it was decided to choose a set of sample diagrams from different archaeological texts. The diagrams could then be used as control material by which various methods of representation and storage may be compared. To ensure a complete coverage, diagrams representing the different types were selected for use as a set of test data for the different methods.

4. Diagram Classification (A Description)

Throughout the following discussion, reference will be made to GKS (Graphical Kernel System) (1), an ISO standard for device independent representation and manipulation of computer graphics.

5. Use of the Term "Complexity"

Illustrations have been placed in groups according to their typology. In this context, the term "complexity" is related to the quantity of data needed to represent the diagram using GKS output functions. Thus, a "complex diagram" is anything that is inconvenient, difficult or inefficient (i.e., that can be achieved more quickly or in less space by other means) to represent using standard GKS constructs. In this sense complexity is almost directly related to the information content of the image in GKS format. This is not the case if an uncompressed memory map technique is used to represent the image, when it is immaterial whether the image happens to contain one single straight line or a photograph.

6. Basis for the Classification

Why base the definition of complexity (and hence, the classification) on GKS? The classification was carried out for purely practical reasons, with certain hardware and software configurations in mind. It was decided at an early stage that wherever possible, use would be made of graphics libraries to implement most of the non-machine dependent vector type functions. GKS provides a convenient set of utilities for just this purpose but, more importantly, it is an international standard already available on many systems and likely to become even more widely available in the future.

7. Description of Diagram Classification

Having stated that the classification will be based loosely on a "GKS description" of images, the following "assumptions" clarify the concept of image complexity as used here:

(a) An "image is composed of a collection of lines and uniformly shaded areas. (At a microscopic level everything is uniformly shaded, i.e. if the particular diagram has areas of variable density shading it is still possible to define small strips or areas that can be uniformly shaded. In terms of the display, these areas may be one or a cluster of pixels illuminated to the same intensity.)

(b) A "line" is an ordered set of two or more vertices between which straight line segments are drawn. Each vertex in the set, except the first and the last, is a point where two straight line segments touch.

(c) A "shaded area" is an enclosed region whose interior has a specified colour, usually different from its surroundings.

(d) A "colour" is anything from black to white (i.e. dark gray and light gray will be regarded as different colours as will light red and dark red). Colour is an attribute of lines and shaded areas within an image.

It is important to keep the above definitions in mind when making comparisons. For example, according to these definitions, a diagram which is constructed from n "curved" lines will be more complex, i.e. require more information, than another constructed from n straight lines. It is for this reason that the classification scheme described below makes a distinction between pictures with and without curves.

In order to simplify matters, item (d) defines what is meant by "colour" in this context. With definition (a) it is intended to imply that a black and white photograph containing say 16 shades of gray will be regarded as having 16 different colours. Thus, as far as the classification is concerned, different shades and different colours are treated on the same footing. This is a useful concept when it is possible to swap one colour set for another.

The actual classes or groups have been based on diagram complexity measured rather loosely in terms of parameters such as whether the diagram is a photograph or line drawing, is composed entirely of straight lines or contains generalized curves, has non-uniform shading, etc. These groups were originally conceived in terms of a binary tree of attributes (Figure 1). Many other classifications are possible, but it was mainly intended to identify different diagram types and provide some guide to help determine an appropriate method of representation.

The following tree diagram describes the basic structure of the classification scheme. It is only intended to illustrate the combination of factors used to catagorize diagrams found in printed journals.

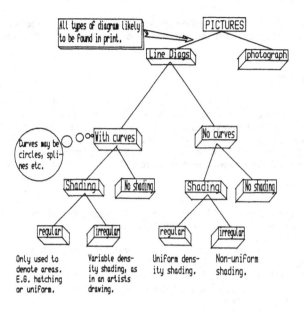

Traversing this diagram from the root produces a list of attributes that have been used to define seven separate groups or classes of diagrams as follows:

Type (1)   Line diagrams without curves
                        without shading.

Type (2)   Line diagrams without curves,
                        with regular shading.

Type (3)   Line diagrams without curves
                        with irregular shading.

Type (4)   Line diagrams with curves,
                        without shading.

Type (5)   Line diagrams with curves,
                        with regular shading.

Type (6)   Line diagrams with curves,
                        with irregular shading.

Type (7)   Photographs

Note that no mention has been made of colour in the above classification. This is because although information has to be included as to what colour a line or region is (in the sense defined by item (d) above) it does not directly dictate the choice of representation. However, the rate at which colour varies with displacement across the image does. This has been accommodated by reference to the type of shading.

8. Example Images to Illustrate the Various Groups

This section contains a selection of diagrams/images taken from archaeological texts. These illustrate two main points:

(1) The wide range of material likely to be encountered even within a single discipline.

(2) Which group, within the above classification these diagrams fall into, and as a result, how they could be represented.

The diagrams in Figure 2 fall into type (1). They are constructed entirely of straight lines and contain no shaded areas. One of the diagrams is fairly simple. The other uses very many short, linear segments for the outline of a distribution group.

Figure 3, on the other hand, falls into type (2) since it contains no curved lines but does have uniform shading. Ignoring attribute setting functions, both figures could conveniently be described in GKS terms, using only "polyline" and "polymarker" constructs in the case of Figure 2, plus the "fill_area" construct for Figure 3. These diagrams could therefore be coded symbolically as collections of "polyline", "polymarker", and "fill_area" constructs. Reproduction software could decode the symbols into the appropriate GKS functions and reproduce the image. This should be qualified by noting that if the original diagram happens to contain a high degree of stylization (e.g. if it is contructed solely say of square boxes) a more convenient representation may be afforded by describing the positions of the boxes rather than the co-ordinates of every vertex. There are many examples of this in both types (1) and (2) diagrams. It is a consequence of the kind of information they usually represent.

Type (3) is not represented. No examples have been found and it is probably a redundant type. Figure 4 illustrates the type (4), which is more complex than type (1) because it includes curved lines. Diagrams in this group could be represented by collections of GKS polyline primitives as for type (1). In this case however the number of points along a curve would have to be large in order for the curves to appear smooth. It would make more sense in terms of storage requirements to represent such shapes using spline techniques (2), (3).

Type (5) is illustrated by Figure 5 which in addition to curved lines contains uniformly shaded areas. In this case the same considerations as for type (4) apply, but with the addition of uniform shading.

The remaining two groups types (6) and (7) contain images that may be far more complex (in the sense defined above). These are illustrated by Figures 6 and 7, respectively. It is difficult to see how such images could reasonably be represented using the GKS polyline and fill_area functions because it is not easy to locate a polygon that defines the boundary of any area to be shaded. In these examples, most of the important detail is implicit within the shading alone. In the case of Figure 7, there is only an intensity distribution across the surface of the picture. Under these circumstances, one has little choice but to resort to the catch-all method by using some form of compressed intensity map.

Here it is worth mentioning the relationship between types (6) and (7). Category (6) will contain images which are obviously drawings, such as pencil sketches (these may contain intricately shaded areas). On the other hand, category (7) are photographs. However, in terms of intensity distribution across the page, the images in category (6) may be almost as complex as the photographs of category (7). The distinction between these two groups may become fuzzy depending on the resolution at which they are to be displayed. It is easy to find diagrams which contain so much detail that they become as economical, in terms of storage, to represent by intensity maps as by the GKS based vector form. In addition, since many PC hardware configurations use memory map displays, the processing overhead of having to decode the individual GKS commands would be avoided. This particularly important trade off must be considered by the current study.

The more intricate diagram in Figure 2 could be placed in either type (1) or type (4). It is a borderline case. If it is taken to be type (1), then it will be represented solely by polyline constructs

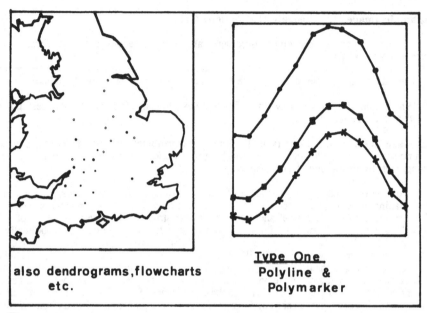

also dendrograms, flowcharts
etc.

Type One
Polyline &
Polymarker

Figure 2

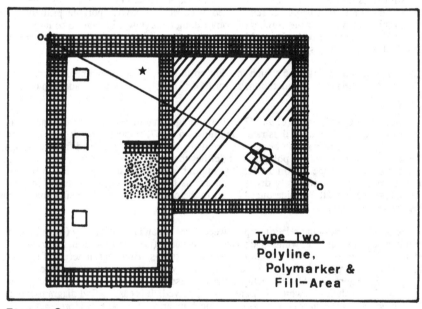

Type Two
Polyline,
Polymarker &
Fill-Area

Figure 3

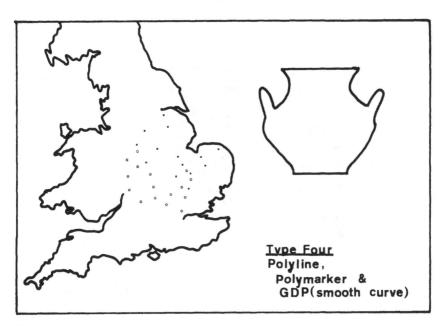

Figure 4

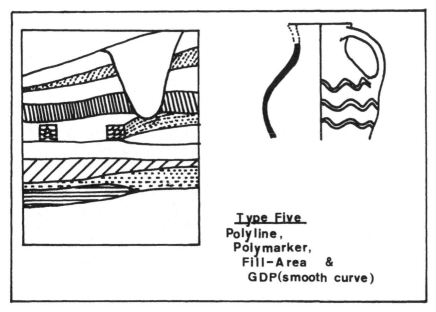

Figure 5

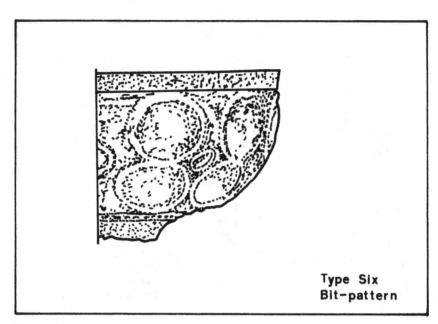

Type Six
Bit-pattern

Figure 6

Type Seven
Bit-pattern

Figure 7

within GKS. Each polyline will consist of many points. If it is placed in type (4), a mathematical spline description of each "curve" will be used. This will avoid the necessity to describe every incremental position but obviously carries a much greater processing overhead. The latter may or may not be important. For the electronic journal, where the picture data is held remotely, the communications channel is slow (say 1200 baud) and the local computer is used mainly for display processing it may be faster overall to use the spline techniques of type (4).

9. Current Work Within the Project (Concluding Remarks)

The diagram classification scheme will be used to guide the choice of an image representation method when archiving graphical data for the computer based journal. In addition, it has been used to select a set of sample images so that graphics work in this domain may proceed in a controlled environment. It is therefore appropriate to conclude this article with a very brief description of some graphics research being carried out at Birmingham in support of the electronic journal study.

The important constraints that an electronic journal environment would impose on its graphics subsystem have already been outlined. Often, a user of the journal may want to browse through "pages" of an article (or group of articles) for a particular diagram. He will want to skip quickly through those images/illustrations that are irrelevant in order to find the material which is of interest. Images should appear quickly mainly because many of them will be discarded and it is frustrating to wait 15 minutes while an image is received only to find it is not the one you wanted. Part of the current work at Birmingham focuses on methods to support browsing when the images are hosted remotely and communication is via relatively slow channels. The overall strategy of such methods is to receive images at the remote sites in degraded but recognizable form. It is then up to the user either to discard the current image and request another, or to request more detail of the current image.

There are a number of techniques which allow images to be transmitted from the picture archive to a workstation in degraded form. Some of them send composite values constructed by averaging groups of image pixels. These methods provide a low resolution preview of the image, but when higher resolution is desired it may become difficult locally to infer the values of constituent pixels without roundoff errors. In other methods (5), the whole image is encoded (prior to archiving) in such a manner that it is easy to increase the resolution of the image currently on display. Such methods transmit information about how to split the logical composite pixels on display. This has the advantage that all subsequent data from the archive is used in a non-redundant fashion to improve the current picture rather than just redraw it at higher resolution. Since many of the images will be recognized by the user as being irrelevant at a very early stage in the transmission, an effective data compression is achieved. Experiments have indicated (5) that with careful encoding, a user is often able to recognize whether an image is going to be of interest after having received only 2% of the data.

Future work will continue in this area with a view to producing a number of usable demonstration systems based on several different techniques. Feedback gained by "hands-on" user experience with such systems should provide valuable information about how best to integrate graphics into the electronic journal environment. It will also lead to greater appreciation of what users actually require from a graphics facility in an electronic journal.

References

1. Introduction to the Graphical Kernel System, F.R.A. Hopgood, D.A. Duce, J.R. Gallop and D.C. Sutcliffe. (Aric Studios in Data Processing, No 1), Academic Press.

2. Applied Numerical Analysis, p 90., C.F. Gerald, Addison Wesley series in Mathematics.

3. Mathematical Elements for Computer Graphics, D.F. Rogers and J.A. Adams, McGraw-Hill.

4. A proposal for the investigation of "The Provision Of A Graphics Facility For Computer-based Electronic Journals", W.P. Dodd and Mrs. S. LaflinBarker, Centre for Computing and Computer Science, University of Birmingham.

5. Interactive Image Query System using Progressing Transmission, F.S. Hill, Jr., S. Walker, Jr., and F. Gao, p 323, Computer Graphics, Vol 17, No 3, July 83.

6. The BLEND system: Program for the Study of some Electronic Journals´, B. Shackel, Department of Human Sciences, University of Technology, Loughborough, The Computer Journal, Vol 25, No 2, p 161.

7. The BLEND/LINC Project on `Electronic Journals´ After Two Years, B.Shackel and D.J. Pullinger, Department of Human Sciences, University of Technology, Loughborough, T.I. Maude and W.P. Dobb, The Centre for Computing and Computer Science, University of Birmingham.

Publication Systems at TODAY

John Honeywell

TODAY Newspaper   London, England   UK

TODAY is a totally computerised national daily newspaper, the first in Britain, and one of only a few in the world. While other national newspapers in this country move over to computer typesetting and direct input on screen by journalists, most are still relying on cut-and-paste for page make-up, outputting stories, headlines and pictures to bromide and pasting them up onto a full page, **TODAY** has full on-screen make-up, mostly done by the journalists themselves, and a small team of page layout terminal operators.

We use a Hastech front-end system, with more than 100 terminals. Of these, 20 are 'non-intelligent' Edit VIIIs, used by reporters and copytakers simply for inputting text. The majority are 'intelligent' Hastech Magician terminals, of which we have 90, with more complex editing facilities, and on which we can copyfit stories onto the pages created by our eight PagePro terminals.

The main system is broken down into five sub-systems, each with its own CPU, with full networking between each system. The total capacity is in the region of 2500Mbytes, and there are six off-line disc drives with 300 Mbyte hard discs.

As well as being Britain's first fully-computerised national daily, **TODAY** is also the first with full on-the-run colour pictures and graphics. We have two Crosfield Magnascan full-colour scanners. Colour pages are planned on two Crosfield 860 make-up tables.

We originally planned to use ImagiTex equipment to handle monochrome artwork and pictures. This would have allowed a low resolution display on the page layout terminal screen, with the ability to rotate and crop the image on the front-end system. However, the operating slowness of the ImagiTex created a serious bottleneck, and one week before launch this unit was replaced by two Autocon cameras, each linked to a Monotype graphics sub-system and to the Monotype Lasercomps. Although they do not offer as many facilities as the ImagiTex, they are a workable, reliable, and speedy alternative.

Pages are output to film through three Monotype Lasercomps. At this stage the pages are almost complete and ready for transmission, except for advertisements, which in most cases are shot from camera-ready art work, and pasted onto the film, which is then copied, or duped, and passed to the Datrax for transmission to the print sites. We have two Datrax readers at our Vauxhall Bridge Road offices, and two receivers at each of the three satellite printing plants at Poyle, near Heathrow airport; Birmingham, and Manchester.

Each page is scanned by red laser and the image is sent to the sites down Mercury lines. The data is received on film in negative form, and is then shot photographically onto the printing plate.

We can also send pages direct from the Hastech system, via Monotype raster image processor, to the Datrax writers at the print sites. This achieves better quality by cutting out the process of going to film and the subsequent Datrax scanning of that film.

A further computer process is brought in on the actual printing presses. The on-run colour registration and ink flow is fully computerised, and minute changes to maintain colour quality can be made while the presses are running at their full speed of 40,000 copies per hour.

So much for a brief description of the computer systems in use at **TODAY**. How do we use them to produce a 32-page, 36-page, or 40-page national daily newspaper, seven days a week, 52 weeks of the year?

Stories come into a newspaper from its own staff reporters, from freelance reporters, news agencies here and abroad, and from specialist writers. Pictures too are provided by staff photographers freelances and agencies. The reporters are controlled by the news editor and the newsdesk staff, and the photographers by the picture editor and the picture desk. Reporters on **TODAY** write their stories in the office on Edit VIII terminals, or file them from out of the office using portable computers connected to the office by modem and telephone line. Stories can be dictated to copytakers over the telephone, or can be wired direct into the system by Telex. Copy from the Press Association, Britain's national news agency, and from foreign news agencies Reuter and Associated Press is also input to the system by direct wire.

Staff photographers would normally bring their pictures, black and white or colour, to be processed in the office, though we have facilities for mobile colour developing, so the pictures can be processed in the back of a car or van on the way back from an assignment. Pictures can also be wired into the electronic picture desk from agencies and transmitters around the world. These are stored on disc, can be called up on screen for selection, and then printed out as required.

Ignoring for now the copy for features and sports pages, which are dealt with in their own departments, all news items are fed through the copytaster. His job is to weed out the insignificant and the insubstantial, and pass on only the best stories of the day for inclusion in the paper. He sits at a terminal, reading stories coming in from all sources, and routeing them to the 'back bench,' the executives who make the ultimate decisions on which stories to use and where.

They decide which story will be the front page lead, or 'splash,' which to lead inside pages with, which are going to be used as smaller stories, and which are the fillers, or nibs. The back bench also assesses the pictures supplied by the picture desk, and will arrange for the graphics department to create explanatory maps, diagrams and other graphics where necessary.

The night editor, or his assistant, having weighed the value and importance of each story and picture, draws a rough lay-out scheme for each page. This is then redrawn, accurately, with the sizes of headlines and pictures carefully marked, by a design artist.

On an 'old-tech' newspaper, one copy of this layout would then go to the chief sub-editor, whose subs would edit the stories to fit and write the headlines. The copy would then be sent for typesetting, and the other copy of the layout would be passed to the compositors who would follow it when making up the page, using either cut-and-paste, or, now much more rarely, hot metal.

At **TODAY**, however, the layout goes first to the Page Layout Terminal, where an operator creates the page on the system, accurately following the instructions from the plan.

The PagePro terminal has two screens, one displaying text and commands being input; the other the actual page being created. The keyboard contains a large number of function keys as well as the alphanumeric QWERTY keys, and there is a built-in joystick for placing the graphics screen cursor. Four of the PagePro terminals are also equipped with an AdPro tablet and a mouse, which can replicate most keyboard commands, and are also used for more accurate cursor control, and for drawing, cutting, and carving rules.

At its simplest, the creation of a page is just a matter of assigning space for advertisements, graphics, headlines, and text. The space for ads and pictures is reserved by inputting parameters for width and depth, and for the position on the page. Headlines are input by creating a filename and giving commands for the typeface, the width of the head, and the number of lines required. The head is then placed on the page in the required position. The remaining space on the page is then assigned for the stories, each of which has its own filename. Grids can be called up or created to ensure accurate splitting of column widths.

As the items on the page build up, they are shown on the graphics screen, and once the page is complete, it is output through a Printronix printer for a hard copy to be passed to the chief sub-editor.

Once completed, the page is available to the subs for copyfitting, a simple enough term, but a process which can be complex and time-consuming. Occasionally, a story will be written in exactly the way the editor wants it to appear in tomorrow's paper. It may even be the exact length required to fit the space allotted. That, however, is very rare, and even then the sub will have to insert typesetting instructions.

More often than not, the story will need re-writing to some extent. Freelance copy may have been written by an inexperienced correspondent. The Press Association supplies the same copy to each subscriber, and we will not want our version of the story to be the same as everyone else's. The point of the story that the editor wishes to emphasise may be buried half-way down, and need bringing up. A story may have to be cut to half its length, or less, and the sub will have to boil it down to the most salient points. The original story may need up-dating with later information, or points of fact will need correcting. Very often a sub will have to combine two or more versions of the same story, selecting facts and quotes from each.

For initial rough subbing, the sub can split his Magician display screen into up to four windows. Three of these would display original versions of the story, and the fourth would be the version he is creating. Sentences or paragraphs can be moved from each window to be combined in the final version, and by hitting the 'estimate' key, the sub can find out the length of his story.

When it comes to actual copyfitting, the sub calls up the page on his terminal. Several subs can work on one page simultaneously, each dealing with a separate item on the page. Each sub works on a copy of the page, assigning completed stories to the master copy, but only one person can work on a story at a time.

On calling up the page on his terminal, the sub is presented with a split screen display. On the left is a low resolution graphic representation of the screen, and on the right a catalogue of file names. Scrolling through the file names highlights the associated space in the page alongside. When the appropriate item is selected, the left-hand display changes to a representation of the space into which the story is to be fitted. The story's filename is called up and a copy of the story is burst into the space. Hitting the copyfit key sets off the composition process; the story is hyphenated and justified, a representation of the typeset lines appears in the box, and the display informs the sub whether it is over (too long) or loose (too short). Further cuts or additions can be made to the story until it fits accurately, and when the sub is satisfied, he assigns it to the page.

Then the sub turns his attention to the headline, for which another window in the page has been assigned. On some stories, particularly page leads, the head will already have been conceived by the back bench, drawn on the layout, and input on the Page Layout Terminal. More often, the sub has to write his own. The typeface will already have been decided, and the sub has to write words to fit the lines. Obviously, whereas in the text of the story hyphenation is inevitable, this is not acceptable in headlines. Therefore the system will not break words when in headline mode, and will tell the sub the head is over if the words are too wide for the available space.

With the low-resolution available on the Magician's graphic display, we do not see the actual letters of the headlines, or the words of each story displayed, merely bars of tone, or lines which depict how deep and how wide the heads are in a graphic representation of the space they take up.

Once the stories, headlines, captions, etc are complete, the chief sub-editor will re-read each item, checking for consistency of style, avoiding clashes of words in headlines, making sure different headlines on the same or facing pages do not contain the same words, and double-checking spelling, etc. While the system contains a hyphenation dictionary, we do not have an automatic spelling checker. Such things are still best left to human operators, particularly in a newspaper which contains so many different personal names and place names each day.

When the chief sub is satisfied with the page, it is 'returned' to the PLT department. There it is opened up on screen once more for a visual check on positioning of headlines and graphics, and the column rules separating individual items. The PagePro gives a much higher resolution display, and while it does not, at the moment, display the graphics, in full-page mode it displays the page smaller than actual size, with readable representations of the headlines. The display can be blown up to full-size, and the operator can scroll round the page, at which point it is possible to read even the smallest typeface, and place rules and graphics very accurately.

The page is then sent to the Monotype Lasercomp for output through a Laserprinter for proofing. This is the first time we see the page on paper, and it is given a final 'quality control' check, before being sent to the Lasercomp again for output to film.

At this stage of our development, advertisements are not usually included on the pages. These, prepared on film from camera-ready artwork usually produced outside the office, are pasted onto the film. Pairs of pages (eg front and back) are then stuck onto clear plastic foil, shot once more photographically, and then transferred to the Datrax for transmission to the print sites.

For a colour page, as well as the film carrying the black text, there are three further foils for the colour separations. These are output from the Crosfield colour tables, each is carefully punched to ensure perfect registration, and they are Datraxed separately. It takes approximately four minutes to scan and transmit each pair of pages, so transmitting a colour page is much more time-consuming, as four films have to be scanned to create four separate printing plates.

All this work has to be carried out within very strict deadlines. In order to print enough copies to reach the whole of the country, even with three print sites in different parts of England, printing of the first edition has to commence at 10.30pm. In an ideal world, the decisions about which stories and pictures to be used in the paper, and which are to be given the greatest prominence, would be made at about 8.30pm, when it would be possible to assess the events of the day as a whole. It would, however, be impossible, or at least impractical, to have an army of staff working flat-out to produce 32, 36, or 40 pages within a hour. Even then, because we do not print from the same site as we produce the paper, those pages have to be Datraxed, and that takes further time.

Instead, production has to phased throughout the day, in a fairly constant stream. Many features pages, such as television, fashion, horoscopes, etc, are created 'overnight' or two days ahead of the date of issue. The on-the-day news, sport, features and city pages have to be fed through the system in a regular, ordered manner to avoid log-jams in critical areas which would create delays and jeopardise production.

The news pages, which are the pages I am most concerned with, go through at roughly half-hour intervals. From conception of the original idea, it can take about 15 to 20 minutes for the design artist to complete the layout. A further half-hour is allowed for creation of the page on the Page Layout Terminal. Subbing and revising can take $2\frac{1}{2}$ to 3 hours for an average page, and another half-hour is allotted for checking on the PLTs, outputting to proof, and reading and correcting the proof.

That, in outline, is how we use the system to create **TODAY**. I can now explain in a little more detail how each individual uses the system.

Each user has his own personal queue, or electronic in-tray, to which he signs on at the start of a shift. News reporters working on System 2 write stories which are created in their own queues then assigned to a newsdesk queue, and thence to the copytaster. Agency copy is automatically assigned to queues for news, parliamentary stories, law reports, City, etc. Agency sports copy is automatically routed to different queues for racecards, soccer results, league tables, etc. The news copytaster reads through the stories in each news queue and assigns them to the back bench queue on System 0, and from there they are sent on to the chief sub-editor. All news pages are created on System 0. Sport and features use System 1. System crashes, which are still, unfortunately, a regular, though not a daily, occurrence, usually affect only one system, so only one department is incapacitated at a time.

Queues are not only assigned to users, but also to each input/output device connected to the system. A file is sent to another user, or to an output device such as a printer or typesetter, by assigning the file to the proper queue. A directory, or list of files in a queue can be displayed by the user at any time.

Any queue on the system can be designated as an auto-purge queue. It is given a maximum file capacity, and when the number of files matches the limit specified, each new file entering the queue (at the bottom) causes the file at the top of the queue to be deleted. These auto-purge queues help to prevent the system from becoming overloaded, especially with continuous input devices such as newswires. Auto-purge queues also provide automatic maintenance of the 'done' queues, into which files are assigned once an output process, such as printing or typesetting, is complete.

The system automatically ensures that no two filenames residing in it can carry the same name. If it did not, two reporters could conceivably be writing separate stories simultaneously about different subjects, but carrying the same catchline, or filename, and confusion and disaster could ensue. When copying files, so that a reporter can retain his own copy of the story once it has been sent to the newsdesk, or in order to make sure a spare copy of a story still resides in a holding queue should the working copy be lost, mutilated or corrupted, the system adds a digit or a character to the filename each time. Thus the filename remains identifiable, but is nevertheless unique.

Similarly, each page has its own unique filename, and that filename automatically generates the folio and dateline which appears at the top of each page of the newspaper.

What are the advantages of computerised newspaper production as employed at **TODAY**, and what are the disadvantages, compared with more traditional methods of newspaper production?

Obviously,there is a tremendous cost saving by combining the roles of journalists and compositors. Reporters writing their stories, or more particularly sub-editors copyfitting the stories into the pages, are actually setting the type, thus getting rid of the whole composing room set-up still in use in almost all other national newspapers. The PLT department, the nearest thing we have to a composing room, consists of just a dozen people, most of them very young, and with little or no previous experience of newspaper production. They have been able to acquire their new skills very quickly.

The journalists, who joined **TODAY** from national and provincial newspapers and magazines, were not, on the whole, familiar with VDTs when they arrived, but they too picked up their new skills in a very short time.

However, two weeks before launch at the beginning of March, serious electrical problems were discovered at the Vauxhall Bridge Road offices, necessitating a complete rewire at an extremely critical time when the staff should have been producing dummy issues every night to iron out problems before the paper hit the streets. Immediately after launch, it was realised that we were understaffed in certain key production areas, and new staff was taken on.

Reproduction of colour pictures and advertisements, one of the paper's biggest selling points, was initially rather disappointing, largely due to technical and manual problems on the presses. The content of the paper was criticised, often unfairly by our Fleet Street rivals, as being rather bland. Distribution problems in the early days often left large areas of the country without supplies of the paper.

These problems are now all being overcome, more finance has been injected by Lonrho, and the paper 'relaunched' last month with a new advertising campaign.

The lead established by **TODAY** and the technology it exploits, in bringing down the cost of launching a new newspaper, has been followed by others, such as The Independent, and Sunday Sport, and the threat posed by **TODAY** was one of the major factors behind the move of Rupert Murdoch's News International group to Wapping, and the changes brought in at Mirror Group Newspapers by Robert Maxwell.

TODAY, having changed the face of national newspapers, is here to stay, and ready to use further advances in newspaper technology to keep it at the forefront of the industry.

PLEIADE,
a system for interactive manipulation of structured documents

J. Nanard[1], M. Nanard[1], G. Cottin[2]

[1] *Centre de Recherche en Informatique de Montpellier
CNIAM, 860 Rue de Saint Priest
34100 MONTPELLIER, FRANCE*

[2] *Société AXEL IRIS
Avenue de Coppenhague
91946 Les ULLIS, FRANCE*

ABSTRACT

Pleiade is a professional document manipulation system designed to manipulate interactively structured documents including texts, graphics, formulaes, tables and any kind of structured objects defined by the user. It is an integrated editor formattor providing a nearly exact representation of the document on the screen. It is based on a structured description of the document. User defined logical types are used to specify the formatting rules. Though it uses a declarative approach, it has no written language neither for the commands nor the specifications. An iconic language and an object oriented approach are used to operate directly through the visual representation of the entities on the screen.

KEYWORDS

structure, nearly wysiwyg, declarative approach, document manipulation, iconic language

1. INTRODUCTION

Interactive manipulation of structured documents based on a direct pointing mechanism on the screen is a trend in recent works in the document preparation area.

First systems were batch processing ones and more tailored to produce the final document than to offer an environment for its manipulation. So is T_EX, which provides a powerfull tool to describe the geometrical aspect of documents. SCRIBE, for its own, has shown how to abstract the presentation concepts and to separate the presentation rules from the content of the document. Graphical devices such as high resolution bit map screens and mouses, now available at low cost, allow interactive manipulation of the document at its representation level. Some recent research prototypes [Furuta 86, Coray 86, Quint 86, Nanard 83] take into account the document structure to guide its manipulation. At the professional level, INTERLEAF is an example of an efficient and user friendly tool able to deal with slightly structured documents with objects of different types.

PLEIADE[*], the professional tool derived from our research prototype GTX [Nanard 83], is a system designed to interactively manipulate structured documents including text, graphics, formulaes, tables and any kind of structured objects defined by the user. PLEIADE is available on higher level micro computers such as the HP Veçtra[**], or the IBM AT or BULL BM60 with an added on high resolution bit map and laser printer or phototypesetter. PLEIADE allows as well the interactive editing of the document, as the interactive manipulation of the document layout and its final printing.

This system is characterized by a user friendly man-machine interface and a very high level of interactivity. It keeps updated on the screen, a nearly exact visual representation of the document even for the page breaks. All the entities are interactively manipulated by direct object selection on the screen. Pleiade does not require any written language to describe the document model or the presentation rules : the structures of the document are operated on directly through their visual representation with a mouse.

Three aspects of structuration are taken into account by PLEIADE :

1) the logical structure of the document expresses how the author wishes to organize the semantics of the document.
2) the page structure describes the macroscopic geometrical organization of the page areas in which the logical content is poured.
3) the geometrical structure characterizes the aspect of the final document. The formatting rules are expressed as logical type attributes.

As a consequence, with PLEIADE, a document is not statically described but can be considered as a dynamical entity compound of a logical content (logical structure and actual content) and a 'presentation environment' (attributes of the types and page structure). Any change in either the content or the environment updates the document representation. So, it is possible to obtain different views of the same document by specifying different environments, or to produce many documents with an homogeneous presentation style by using the same environment.

PLEIADE is a professional tool taking advantage of many concepts arised among research prototypes (boxes, logical structure, page structure, separation between presentation rules and document content, use of logically typed objects, multiviews of a document). The environment mechanism helps the user to create easily homogeneous documents, by providing him a document model and all associated types. But, as the user may update and create new types by his own without complex syntactic description, he may also take advantage of freedom to create his own structures and presentation rules.

This paper does not intend to present all the features available in Pleiade, but focuss on some original points : the structures, the man machine dialogue, the declarative aspect, and so on...

---

[*] PLEIADE is a registred trademark of AXEL.

[**] The development of Pleiade has been sponsorized by Hewlett Packard France

2. THE STRUCTURES

The Knuth's box model [Knuth 79] is adapted to express the geometrical structure of documents. It does not take account of their logical structure such as, for example in a book, chapters, sections, subsections, and so on... Systems based on a syntax directed mechanism such as Mentor [Donzeau 83], Grif [QUINT 86] take account of the document logical structure and use it to induce the geometrical aspect of the document, but do not consider the page breaking rules and the page structure as a part of the document description, but only as a printing specification. Interscript [Ayers 84] suggests a pouring mechanism to formalize the general page layout filling. These three points must be taken into account to describe completely a document.

A Pleiade document is defined through three concurrent structures :

- the logical structure expresses how the document components are hierarchically ordered and is used as a framework on which the formatting rules are described.

- the page structure expresses the macroscopic geometrical aspect of the page. Areas are used as containers into which the document components are poured. Permanent areas such page headers, logos... are distinguished from flowing areas into which the document body is spread out and from specific areas which exist only on some pages.

- the geometrical structure is induced by the positionning rules associated to the logical components. It uses the Knuth's box model.

As an example, in a 'page body' (element of the page structure) of some document , one can find a 'lemma proof' (element of the logical structure) in which stands a 'centered mathematical formula' (both logical and geometrical structure). At its numerator (geometrical structure, implicit logical structure) is a square root... With the Pleiade system, the user is allowed to select as a whole the 'lemma proof' entity that he has defined in the logical structure even if this entity is spread over several pages. This entity is purely logical and has no associated formatting rules. The centered mathematical formula is both an element of the logical structure and of the geometrical structure, since the user may specify the positionning rules for the box containing this formula. Within the formula, implicit formatting rules are used depending on the usual mathematical syntax : if the user creates a fraction, he implicitely creates a numerator and a denominator with implicit formatting rules.

2.1. The page structure

Pleiade can deal with several different macroscopic page layout within the same document. One of them is called the standard layout. The user can introduce an explicit break at any point in its document to specify the use of special page layout. Any non explicit page break brings back to the standard layout. As an example, a letter has a first page with a special layout, next pages are automatically formatted with the standard layout. As another example, the page layout of a technical data sheet may be very complex with a specific page layout for each page.

A page layout is described as a set of page areas. A set of attributes specifies the formatting rules of each area (position, size, number of columns, graphical enhancements such as frames and grey or patterned background, default font...). The informational content of the document is associated to these areas, each area being the root of one of the trees of the logical structure of the document. If an area has the attribute 'permanent', the same data is replicated on each page where this area is present. If an area has the attribute 'document body', the associated data can be spread out on several pages in this area. (Fig 1)

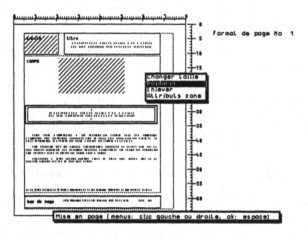

Fig 1 : The screen of Pleiade when operating on a page structure

2.2. The logical and the geometrical structures

The document logical structure is a set of independant trees, one per page area. Logical types decorate the nodes of the trees. The leaves of the trees are the elementary components (tokens) of the document (a paragraph, a picture, a formula...). The logical structure is used as the framework for the geometrical structure organized according to the box model. The formatting rules are described at the logical structure level as attributes associated to the logical types. Each logical type is referenced by a name given by the user. The manipulator of the content of a node and most of the attributes depend on the 'nature' of the node : pure logic, box, textual, image, formula, table,...synchro.

The non terminal nodes of the logical structure which have geometrical attributes are called 'boxes' in the Pleiade terminology. They comply with the Knuth's box model.

The types of nature 'Pure logic' have no associated formatting rules. The layout of the objects of these types results from the layout of their subcomponents and such nodes are only used to describe the logical structure . So, they can be directly selected or manipulated as a whole in the logical structure. This is the case, for example, of a 'chapter' which cannot be seen as a single geometrical box.

The terminal nodes can be of nature 'textual', 'image', 'formula' or 'table'. Specific manipulators are used to deal with them. As example, the attributes of a textual component are shown on figure 1. These attributes concern as well the positionning rules of the component (size and margins in relation to the mother box, stretchability or shrinkability of the margins, footnote flag, new page flag...) as the rules about the ornemental aspect of the content (fonts, color, frames, backgrounds, word hyphenation threshold...).

For some strongly structured objects such as mathematical formulas or tables, the user does not need to express explicitly their logical structure. Their specific manipulators are able to automatically synthesize their logical structure and the associated geometrical structure directly from their constructs. The mathematical manipulator of Pleiade is based on similar principles as those of Edimath [Quint 83].

The components of type 'synchro' are virtual nodes used to express constraints between the page structure and the logical structure such as explicit page breaks.

The three different structures presented here are necessary to describe completely the document and to manipulate it efficiently. In this section, we have delt with the document model. Now, we explain how the documents are manipulated with the Pleiade system.

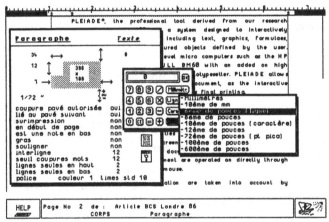

Fig 2 : The screen of Pleiade : Updating the attributes of a logical type

3. A NEARLY EXACT REPRESENTATION ON THE SCREEN

As seen earlier, the internal representation of a document consists of data describing the structures of the document with their associated types and attributes. Pleiade processes the document by mapping this internal representation into several external representations called views [Reiss 84]. One of these views, the 'main view', is a nearly exact representation of the printed document, including line and page breaks, and differs only by the elementary font representation on the screen. This view is updated on the screen at any key stroke. The abstractions such as the logical structure and the formatting rules associated to the types can be observed and accessed on the different views.

3.1. The main view

On the main view (Fig 3), the lines breaks, the page breaks and the page structure are exact. The position of the characters on the screen are computed from the effective spacing on the printer. The shape of the characters on the screen is an approximation of their printed shape according to the used font. So, for eight points fonts, no distinction is done between the particular fonts, but from ten points fonts, normal, bold and italic can be distinguished on the screen. A font editor provided with Pleiade allows the user to create new symbols or new fonts for the HP laserjet printer and to build their screen representation. Only grey and patterned backgrounds are not simulated on the screen to improve the legibility. As bitmap images, drawings and any graphical items of the document may have large size, they are kept into databases on the disk and their description are loaded only on request. So, graphics included into the document are symbolized only with a shade of their exact size to improve the response time. The user can observe their exact view when he selects and opens the corresponding area.

Pleiade had be designed to be used on a full page bit map screen 780*1024 but it can also be run with a not full page high resolution graphical screen (such as the IBM EGA or the internal graphical screen of the HP Vectra). In such a case, a scrolling allows to watch the full page, and a zooming (Fig 1) is used to provide full page facilities when page structure manipulation is required.

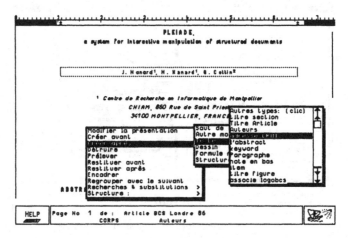

Fig 3 : Aspect of the Pleiade main view

3.2. Formatting quality versus response time

The choice of implementing a nearly WYSIWYG giving the exact page breaks comes from the wished class of users who prefer to operate directly on the document rather than to write an abstract description of it. But a WYSIWYG implementation enjoins speed constraints for the formatting algorithms which had to maintain at real time the view of the document without restraints for the user. Since the display must be exact at any time during the typing in of the document, the formatting algorithms used by Pleiade to break lines into paragraphs and paragraphs into pages have to conciliate a high quality for formatting and a correct response time. It is nevertherless very important, when a choice is necessary, to give advantage to the formatting quality on the response time in order the user could always trust the system and obtain an exact layout when important changes are to be done in the document layout.

The complexity of these algorithms has led, on one hand, to choose powerfull microcomputers (IBM AT compatible) to run Pleiade, and on the other hand, to use concurrent programming for formatting and typing in. The mean response time for display updating is slightly a few hundredth of a second but can rise up to a few tenth of a second when a full page change is to be done. But in any case, the user may go on typing while the screen is updated.

The formatting algorithms used in Pleiade cover a large range : hyphenation, possibility of use of tabulations even in justified lines, multifonts capability, simultaneous subscript and superscript notations allowed on the same symbol, mathematical formulae 'in the line', generalized independant formulae, page breaking avoiding widows or orphans, possibility of page balancing with stretching or shrinking of the spacing between paragraphs... On any of these problems, more complete algorithms than those used in Pleiade can be obviously found, mainly in high quality batch formattors, since the Pleiade implementation has to take account of the response time. However, owing to its interactivity and the easiness of its use, one can locally express the wished formatting. As an example, the Pleiade French hyphenation algorithm uses the Grevisse rules [Grévisse 82] in an implementation close to the one proposed in [André 84]. This algorithm finds 98% of valid hyphenations. They are less complete but faster than those used in TEX. The use of an exception dictionnary had not been choosen, it would have greatly penalised the response time in Pleiade. To avoid the disadvantage of this choice, the user can express by his own exceptions when necessary either by inhibiting hyphenation on a word or by suggesting an hyphenation point.

In general terms, on every system, the response time grows exponentially when the subjective quality of the result improves. So, it is very important to find a just balance. Pleiade has choosen to maintain its average response time under a tenth of a second to avoid disturbing the user while he is typing.

The display on a WYSIWYG system is considered as being unsteady while typing : justifying or centering causes the current line to be reorganized at each key stroke. This cannot be considered as a disadvantage because most of the users do not look at their screen while typing and the screen is at a steady state whenever they stop typing and they rise up their eyes. The only surprising behaviour of the system might be sometimes a delayed page changing due to the shrinking of the page to avoid a widow line at the next page when starting the typing of this line in a new paragraph at the bottom of the page, because the layout has to conform to the formatting rules in every case.

The advantage of the WYSIWYG approach is its naturaliness : at any time the user can see exactly what he has done and may correct his document at once.

3.3. The multiview mechanism of Pleiade

The main view displayed provides a nearly exact representation of the printed document but other views are also available.

The view of the logical structure of the document looks like a table of contents as shown on figure 4. Each terminal component of the document is described on one line, starting with the name of the element type followed, if it had a textual content, by the beginning of it. Images are referenced to by their pathname. These lines are indented according to the logical structure and each non terminal node of type xxx of this structure is displayed as two lines ('begin xxx' and 'end xxx'). Page changing and numbering is indicated in the margin. This view makes it possible for the user to catch a global sight of the logical structure of the document and to point directly and quickly anywhere in the document. Operations on the logical structure such as moving or deleting large parts of it can be expressed on this view.

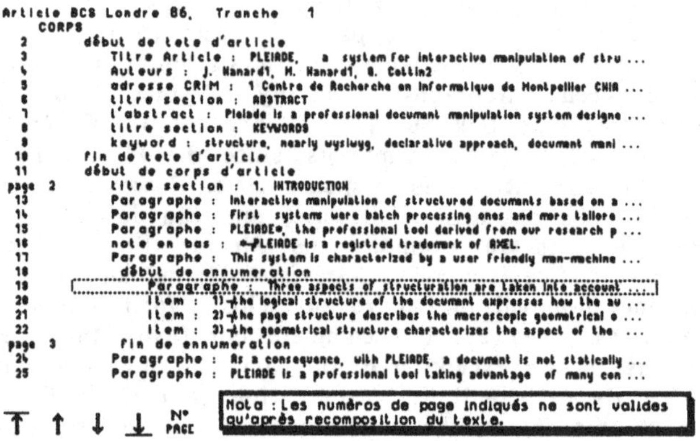

Fig 4 : The screen of Pleiade : A view of the logical structure.

The concept of 'environment' allows to obtain easily some variants of the main view without changing the logical structure. A Pleiade environment is a set of formatting rules adapted to format documents according to some specifications (letters, reports, scientific papers, technical manuals...). The layout of a document can be globally modified only by specifying a new environment. Some special effects can also be obtained using this mechanism : as an example, when the dummy flag, which is one of the attributes of a type is true, all the components of this type are voided at the formatting level. So, views containing only the tokens of some given types (e.g. : images and their captions or only titles, ...) may be obtained by observing the document in an environment voiding all types except the wished ones. A similar, but automatic, mechanism allows any object or any part of an object to be formatted but not painted. This can be used to obtain multicolor documents since colour printing can be done on a laser jet printer by changing the toner and printing the different coloured views of the document. Pleiade provides an 'environment manager' to create and update specific environments.

4. THE MAN-MACHINE DIALOGUE

The man-machine dialogue is based on an iconic language. There is no written expression neither for the editing commands nor for the formatting specifications. An object oriented approach underlies this dialogue. Any transaction between the user and the machine is done by pointing an entity on the screen and selecting the message to be sent in a menu or a control board. The basic communication device is here a two buttons mouse. Nevertherless, for keyboard lovers, they may define dynamically shortened commands by associating key strokes to the most usual Pleiade menu selections. In the Pleiade system a uniform mouse model makes it easy to learn how to use it. The right button is used for selection and the left one to bring up generalized menus or control boards depending upon the context.

4.1. The object selection

The object selection mechanism is drawn from the GTX one : pointing a textual area both selects the pointed character on which character level operations may be applied and the surrounding token in the logical structure of the document, on which component level operations can be applied. The pathname of this component in the logical structure is displayed in a window at the bottom of the screen. Pointing in this pathname selects the wished node in the structure. This mechanism allows to select with only two mouse button strokes any subtree of the part of the structure displayed on the screen.

This being so, the cursor of Pleiade is compound of two elements (figure 3) :

- an arrow for geometrical pointing
- a dashed box frame around the terminal component.

Since a non terminal logical node does not necessary correspond to a box representation in the document (it can be spread on columns or pages), the dashed box used in GTX cannot be applied to the logical structure of Pleiade. So, two markers 'from here' and 'to here' are overplaced at the limits of the selected logical subtree.

4.2. The message sending

The message is elaborated using menus. The Pleiade menu system is the same one as in the Biostation [Nanard 86] : the menus appear near where they are to be used, minimizing the mouse travel. Menus are structured as trees. Pressing the left button of the mouse makes the root of the menu to pop up. The lines with an arrow on their right side are the nodes of the menu structure. Moving out the mouse rightwards causes the opening of the associated submenus on the right of the current menu, and so on. Moving out the mouse leftwards closes the current submenu. The selection is validated when the user clics in a terminal node. This tree mechanism allows for the user a reversible exploration of all the available choices and a structured presentation of the commands allowing the user to build messages which look like sentences (fig 5) without any key stroke ('create here, a picture, copied from the base of images' : the names of the images in the base are then presented on the screen to the user who will select one of them with the mouse).

Fig 5 : Building a sentence with the tree menu mechanism.

This mechanism is not restrictive to strict menus. It has been generalized to access panel boards or scrolling windows as leaves of menus. A panel board allows the user to observe the state of some system variables without modifying them (as examples the typographical attributes of a character). Thereby, a panel board makes it possible to continue the browsing of the tree menu by closing the panel board rolling the mouse leftwards and then exploring again the menu.

A control board is a variant of a panel board but which allows to modify the variables. It is displayed when a function selected into the menu is not monadic, and makes it possible to have a global view of the actual values of the parameters and to modify them. So, an effective choice in a control board is considered as a menu validation. Icons are often used to represent these parameters as shown on fig 1. As an example, the formatting rules associated to the type of a given component are displayed on such a board. Operating on this panel is done according to the standard convention. One attribute is selected by pointing to its icon. An associated menu or control board then pops up allowing to specify the new value. All numerical value may be given either from the keyboard or via a calculator displayed on the screen and providing automatic unit conversion between millimeters, inches fractions and pica points.

4.3. The error handling

The man machine dialogue of Pleiade provides a syntax-directed mechanism to build the messages. This is due both to the object oriented approach and to the non written language which allows the user to build only valid messages. The language is iconic and could be defined by an action grammar [Payne 85]. Even user defined identifiers cannot cause errors : the user cannot invokate a non existing type since he has never to spell it but only to choose it in a menu dynamically built with the name defined at creation time. He can no more enter invalid values for the attributes because only the correct values to be choosen are presented on the screen. Similarly, when manipulating, actions invalid in the current context are avoided since only the valid messages appliable to each object can be selected.

Nevertheless, at the context sensitive level, some correct action may induce, as side effect, that a layout satisfying all the constraints could not be found. In this case, Pleiade temporarily overrides some of the attributes to obtain a valid layout. As an example, let us suppose that the first paragraph of an area is specified as non breakable and grows up until it overflows this area. If this area is the document body, it could neither be on this page nor on the following ones. So, Pleiade has to break temporarily the paragraph, overriding the non breakable attribute specified by the user. Such events are not considered as errors but generates warnings. The warnings are flagged by blinking the warning icon in the corner of the screen but the user can go on working without being worried by any message. The list of active warnings is available in a panel board on user call. It is the user responsibility to choose the best way in the context and the opportunity to suppress the causes of the warnings. The classical 'message on error' strategy would be very worrying since the same error would be caught at every formatting cycle!

5. THE DECLARATIVE ASPECT

Compared with the procedural mechanism, the declarative ones such as those used to express the formatting in Scribe [Reid 81] have proven their efficiency, allowing a very good homogeneity of the formatting : to each abstraction are associated the corresponding formatting rules, so that any change in the formatting rules is automatically propagated in the document everywhere the abstraction is invoked. This allows to distinguish between the structural description, the content description and the formatting rules. Such an approach become common in most of the new systems either directly at the system organization level (Grif [Quint 86], [Furuta 86]) or as an additionnal layer in a system which was not declarative at first (LATEX [Lamport 85]) .

The design of Pleiade is based on an interesting declarative mechanism which does not use any written language either for the abstraction declaration or for their invokation. All the informations about the formatting specifications are carried by means of attributes associated to the types. A document is mainly compound on one hand of a part describing the logical structure and its content, on the other hand of a table of the types used in the document with their associated attributes. The structure trees are described as linear lists with brackets. Each element of this list is a pair of pointers, one in the table of types and one in the table containing the textual material. A non terminal node is represented as a pair of two associated elements used as brackets to parenthesize the subtree associated to this node. In the same way, the page organization is a list of pointers to the table describing the page area with attributes, and where each area points to a tree of the logical structure. It will be shown now with examples how the dialogue method described earlier allows a declarative approach without any written language allowing to give values to attributes.

The first example concerns the object creation. If the user wishes to create, after a figure, a new object for example of the already existing type 'figure caption', then, after selectionning the figure with the mouse, he needs only to choose in the tree menu 'create after / a textual entity / of type "figure caption"'. Immediately, the structural cursor delimits on the screen a new area in which the mouse position indicates where the text of the figure caption will be typed with the adequate font. In this way, the user does not need to specify any of the formatting rules details again and again, they are given by the type.

The second example is about the declaration of a new type. So, it is now supposed that the type 'figure caption' does not exist. Since there is no explicit type declaration command, the user must operate in the same manner as earlier. He creates a component regardless to its type. In practice, he chooses a type the attributes of which are the most similar to those of the futur type. So, an object is created with the attributes of the old selectionned type. The user then chooses in the tree menu 'modify formatting'. All the attributes of the old type are then displayed on a control board (figure 2) on which the formatting rules will be modified according to the standard dialog to obtain the new specific attributes of figure caption. When the control board is left by rolling out leftward the mouse, the user is asked if the modifications concern all the objects with the old type (this case simply corresponds to the modification of the formatting rules associated to the old type) or if the modifications only concern the new object. If so, this is considered as a new type declaration and the user must chose a name for this new type, here 'figure caption'. The new type is now available in the list of local types in the tree menu.

As seen on the examples, with Pleiade as it was with GTX, the user does not need to create objects or types 'ex nihilo'. He always operate from existing entities. So, the declaration method choosen in Pleiade minimizes the quantity of informations that the user has to give since only a few atributes need to be changed. As the same, the document creation does not exist as so. To build a new document, the user receives a copy of a document model with a list of predefined types and he has only to fill up this copy or to modify it to obtain his document. Furthermore, the list of the predefined types provided with the document model from the 'environment' makes it possible for most of the users to type a document without new type declarations. Several environments may be available allowing the user to manipulate all kinds of documents and types (i.e. layout rules).

Another aspect to be pointed out is the fact that dialogue method allows to declare the types at the moment when they are needed. The user does not have to leave the document as it will be the case with a written approach where the declaration part is separated from the document description. The same dialogue method is used everywhere. This implicit declaration method is simpler for the user who operates on the new created component as if he used a procedural system, so he has not to abstract by his own the different entities which he manipulates but only to express how the new ones differ from the preexisting ones.

As a conclusion, the declarative approach of Pleiade provides power and flexibility and allows document homogeneity without the frequent disadvantages of this type of approach because of the friendly and direct non written dialogue method.

7. THE GRAPHICS

This well known logo has been digitized and processed by Pleiade. One of the purpose of Pleiade is to produce technical documents. To do so, it provides large graphical capabilities. An integrated graphical editor allows to create or update drawings without quitting Pleiade. Pictures, drawings or images produced by foreign programs as bitmaps can be processed. As an example, the scanner Agfa S200 and the CAD program Picador has been interfaced with Pleiade. All graphical items can be independently stored in an external base and referenced from the document. This allows different documents to share images. The graphical editor provides classical tools for dealing with standard geometrical shapes and hand drawing. Its main originality is the use of libraries of user defined symbols usefull for chemical, electrical, technical drawing. The association of the scanner, the font editor and the graphical editor makes the graphical features of Pleiade very efficient.

6. CONCLUSION

Pleiade results form an efficient cooperation between a research team of the Montpellier University, and the french computer manufacturer AXEL. It has taken advantage both of our GTX prototype and of all the improvments we have studied since, and of professional means leading to a commercial package. Obviously, the Pleiade implementation has required an arbitration between the natural trend of the university towards more abstraction and the nessecity of creating in a fixed delay an efficient and attractive system running on a small machine.

We take up the wager that abstractions such as structuration, logical types and declarative approach can be accepted and used efficiently by common users, as far as they will be presented in a user friendly way. The declarative mechanism of Pleiade based on the modification of existing entities relies on the common knowledge idea that it is far more easier and natural for common people, to express how two objects differ than to fully describe them. Perhaps, the most interesting point of the cooperation takes place at a pedagogical level. We have tried to make attractive and user friendly to non specialists most of the concepts which are the up to date topics for specialists in document manipulation. The frequency of the word 'user' in this paper is surely significant of the important place given to the design of the user interface in Pleiade.

The fourth structured aspect of Pleiade that we have not yet presented, (and has not been studied at the university!) is its 'marketting structuration'. Different versions have been designed to fit with several classes of users, and to make them progressively familiar to all these concepts.

For example, in the present versions of Pleiade, as in the GTX prototype, the structure of the document is the consequence of its existence and not a constraint imposed by a grammar. So, Pleiade document model is not really a model of document as in Grif. A syntax directed approach as not been choosen yet, to guide the creation of documents since it is based on abstractions such as grammars and description languages which are difficult to be learned by common users. Nevertheless, Pleiade have been designed to support this mechanism which will be implemented in the future versions.

BIBLIOGRAPHY

[André 85] J. André, J. Menu, J.P. Mueller, *Un exemple pédagogique pour Prolog*, TSI vol 3 no 5.

[Ayers 84] R.M. Ayers, J.T. Horning, B.W. Lampson, *Interscript : A proposal for a standard for the interchange of editable documents,* Xerox Palo Alto Research center. 3333 Coyote Hill Road, Palo Alto, California

[Coray 86] R. Coray, R. Ingold, C. Vanoirbeek, *Formatting structure documents : batch versus interactive*, International conference on text processing and document manipulation, EP86, Nottingham, April 86.

[Donzeau 83] V. Donzeau, G. Kahn, B. Lang, B. Mélèze, *Outline of a tool for document manipulation*, 9ième congrès mondial d'informatique, Paris 1983.

[Furuta 86] R. Furuta, *A non exact representation integrated editor formattor*, International conference on text processing and document manipulation, EP86, Nottingham, April 86.

[Grévisse 82] Grévisse, *Le bon usage*, Duculot, Bruxelles 1982.

[Knuth 79] D. E. Knuth, *TEX and METAFONT, a new direction in typsetting*, Digital Press, 1979.

[Morris 85] R. A. Morris, *Is what you see enough to get? A description of the INTERLEAF publishing system*, Protext II, Dublin Oct 85.

[Nanard 83] M. Nanard, J. Nanard, *GTX, un système interactif de manipulation directe de la structure de documents illustrés*, Journées Manipulation de documents, Rennes, Mai 83.

[Nanard 86] M. Nanard, J. Nanard, *Semantic guided editing : a case study on genetic manipulation*, International conference on text processing and document manipulation, EP86, Nottingham, april 86.

[Payne 85] S. J. Payne, *Task-actions grammars*, INTERACT'84, B. Shackel (ed), Northolland.

[Quint 83] V. Quint, *Un système interactif pour la production de documents mathématiques*, TSI vol 2 no 3, 1983.

[Quint 86] V. Quint, I. Vatton, *Grif : an interactive system for structured document manipulation*, International conference on text processing and document manipulation, EP86, Nottingham, April 86.

[Reid 81] B. K. Reid, *The Scribe document specification language and its compiler*, International conference on research and trends in document preparation systems, Lausanne, Feb 81.

[Reiss 84] S. P. Reiss, *Graphical program development with Pecan program development system*, ACM Sigplan notices 19,5.

This paper has been prepared and printed with the PLEIADE SYSTEM. The printing device was a HEWLETT PACKARD LASERJET[+]. The logo has been scanned with an AGFA S200 scanner at 400 dots per inch. The followings symbols have been created with the PLEIADE Font Editor.

Embedding Graphics into Documents by using a Graphics Editor

Ulrike Harke, Manfred Burger, and Dr. Gall
Siemens AG
Otto-Hahn-Ring 6
D-8000 Munich 83

Abstract

This paper is concerned with the description of an editor for creation and manipulation of graphics and their integration into documents. It informs about functionality and specific forms of a graphics editor and experiences in implementation. The graphics editor is part of a document editor containing an user interface based on a window management system.

Keywords: graphics, documents, editor, portability, user interface, CGI, CGM, ODA, ODIF

1. Introduction

Documents usually contain both text and graphics in an arbitrary arrangement. They represent letters, scientific reports, articles in newspapers, etc . Beyond this it may be desirable to print the output of a CAD-program which is represented graphically on the screen within a scientific report. Including graphics produced on different machines into one single document is required, too. Editing of documents, development and execution of programs should be enabled on the same machine, e.g. a personal workstation.

To fulfill these requirements a powerful document editor is being developed. The document editor is based on subeditors. The subeditors work in an object oriented way. Each of them is dedicated to handle a special data type of the document. Examples of data types are text, graphics, facsimiles, etc.

This paper is concerned with the description of the subeditor associated with graphics. It discusses the functionality, the forms of the subeditor and the experience gained during implementation.

To associate the task of the graphics editor within its embedding environment the construction of a document is also introduced.

2. Document

Usually a document consists of a mixture of different data types (see Fig. 2.1.). Data types may be text, graphics, facsimiles, etc. [SIEM]. Each data type is manipulated by a subeditor.The whole document is administered by the

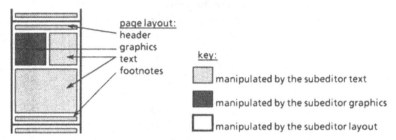

Fig. 2.1.   General Construction of a Document

document editor. Each editor is associated with a window which represents a virtual terminal of the type ANSI X3.64 or CGI [CGI]. Windows are handled by a window management system. The following sections describe some significant aspects of the graphics editor's design. A graphics editor is assigned to the window-type CGI.

3. Design of the Graphics Editor

3.1. Functionality

The functionality of the subeditor **GRAPHICS** includes the manipulation of graphical objects. Graphical objects are divided into two classes: basic graphical objects (line, circle, graphical text, ...) (see Fig. 3.1.) and composed graphical objects (see Fig. 3.3.).

To represent a graphical object, the graphics editor needs all information about its external appearance. This includes both coordinates for exactly placing objects and object specific attributes. For example: the graphical object circle is described by its centre coordinates, its radius, the properties of its border (structure, colour, width) and the properties of its interior style (shade, pattern, pattern-colour, shading-colour, ...).

If the graphics editor manipulates a composed graphical object it needs knowledge about its hierarchical structure (see Fig. 3.3.).

Each graphical object receives an identifier when it is created. This identifier is valid during the lifetime of the graphical object.

The graphics editor keeps all information about all graphical objects in its display

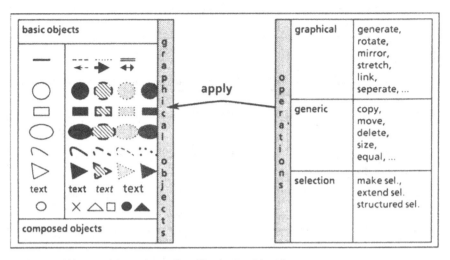

Fig. 3.1.   Objects and Operations offered by the Graphics Editor

file which is based on ODA [ODA] and CGM [CGM]. ODA determines the structure of a document represented by two different trees: the logical tree and the layout tree (see Fig. 3.2.). These two tree structures are connected by common leaves. The contents of the leaves are CGM-like. They contain relevant information for the representation of the graphical objects.

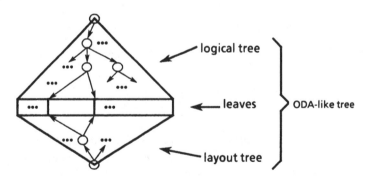

Fig. 3.2.   Overview of the Display File

The manipulation of graphical objects is achieved by carrying out operations. Operations are - like objects - divided into different classes: graphical operations (rotate, mirror, change attributes, etc.), generic operations (copy, move, delete, etc.), and selection (make selection, extend selection, structured selection). All operations manipulate the display file. Typical primitive operations defined on the ODA-like tree structure are insertion and removal of individual elements or subtrees, tree traversal and comparison tests.

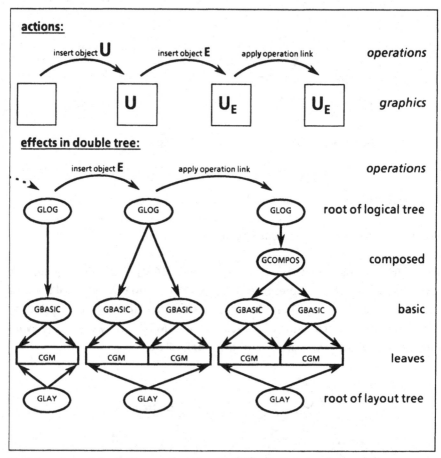

Fig. 3.3.   Example for Linking two Basic Graphical Objects

If for instance several graphical objects are linked together they represent a new graphical object, a composed graphical object. Then a new node in the double tree is inserted (see Fig. 3.3.).

The functionality of the graphics editor can be changed dynamically during its lifetime. The decision about the range of its functionality is made by the current application of the graphics editor (see section 3.4.).

3.2. Forms

The graphics editor presented in this paper is able to manipulate graphical output of an application (for example CAD graphics) as well as graphics produced interactively by the user. It can consequently be used purely as **CAD front-end** or as **general purpose** graphics editor. A **combination** of both forms is offered, too. The differences between the forms mentioned above are explained in section (3.4.).

3.3. Header and Body

The graphics editor consists of a header and a body. The header contains information about the maximum available and current display region. The header contains information about the background colour of the display region and units of measurement, too. The header can be modified either by the application of the graphics editor (see section 3.4.) or by the user at any time.
The body is represented by the display file. It can be modified by manipulation of graphical objects.

3.4. Application

The graphics editor is reentrant, i.e. it can be instantiated more than once. Each of these instances is subordinated to an application whereby an application can use more than one of these instances. The application determines the editor's functionality. It is also responsible for the editor's form and header. Form, header, and functionality of the graphics editor can be changed at any time during its lifetime by its application.

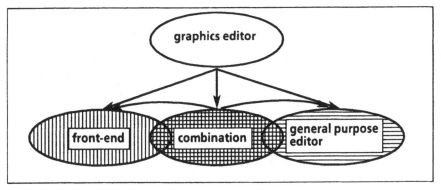

Fig. 3.4.   Different Forms of the Graphics Editor

a) front-end

If the editor is used purely as a front-end, there is no interaction with the user at all (see Fig. 3.5.). The editor is completely controlled by its own application (for example: the editor is used for presenting CAD graphics on the screen). If the application wants to manipulate a specific graphical object it can address this graphical object by its identifier.

To manipulate graphical objects the graphics editor offers functions with predefined parameters to its application.

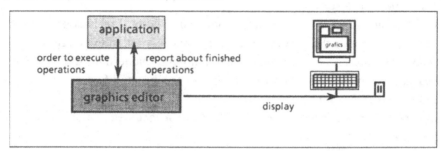

Fig. 3.5.   Graphics Editor used as Front-End

b) general purpose graphics editor

If the editor is used as a general purpose graphics editor, the application only starts its own editor. The application does not have any knowledge of the user's interactions on the screen. If the user wants to terminate the graphics editor the application is informed and has the chance to save the actual graphics produced interactively by the user (see Fig. 3.6.). The user interface is described in section 4.

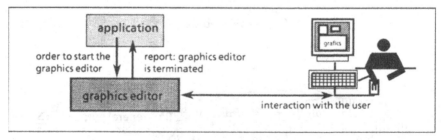

Fig. 3.6.   Graphics Editor used as General-Purpose-Editor

c) combination

If the editor is used as a combination of the forms mentioned above, its application can specify which functions should be under its control, which functions should inform the application of their end, and which functions should

completely be excluded from its control. Function control can be extended to object specific control, too:
- An application can request control about the execution of a specific operation, if this operation is applied to a specific graphical object.
- The editor should inform its application after the execution of a specific operation, if it is applied to a specific graphical object.
- An application forbids the execution of a specific operation applied to a specific graphical object.

Example:
   (1) The application generally does not want to have any knowledge, if the operation *rotate* is executed, but
   (2) The application wants to be informed, if the user creates any graphical object of type line.
   (3) The application forbids rotation of the line *a*
   (4) The application wants to be informed, if the line *b* should be rotated.

Meaning:
   (1) If the user wants to *rotate* any graphical object except line *a* and line *b*, the application does not have any knowledge about the execution of the *rotate*-operation.
   (2) When creating graphical objects of type line the application will be informed about their identifiers, resp.
   (3) The operation *rotate* cannot be applied to the line *a*.
   (4) The application can decide whether line *b* may be rotated or eventually manipulated by other functions.

The different forms, header information, and the dynamic functionality of the editor allow its use within a wide range of editing purposes. One specific application is exempted from keeping the attributes of all graphical objects it uses and can assign its own semantics to any graphical object.

4. User-Interface

Good design of the user interface should insure that the resulting application supports, not distracts from, a user's task [XEROX]. It should support both experienced and novice user as well as the occasional and frequent user of the graphics editor.

The design for this graphics editor prefers "seeing and pointing" to "remembering and typing".

To interact with the user the graphics editor offers menus. There is e.g. a menu showing the basic graphical objects which can be created as well as a menu showing graphical operations offered. The contents of the menus depend on the functionality with which the graphics editor is equipped.

The general procedure of interacting with the editor looks as follows:

<select operand 1> <select operator> <[select operand 2]...[select operand n]>

whereby the operand 2 ... operand n are optional.

Example: The user wants to create a line.

User-actions:
(1) select coordinates of the starting point within the current display-area
(2) select *line* in the menue offering the basic graphical objects which can be created
(3) select coordinates of the end point

If the user has chosen any function which must be completed by some further user action he will be prompted how to finish this function correctly. Wrong user actions cause messages prompted on the screen. Ghost figures are drawn if it is helpful for further inputs. Interruption of a chosen function is allowed at any time and will be executed when selecting another function.

Scrolling the current display area within the maximum display region is established by the graphics editor by offering two scroll bars.

Figure 3.7. shows one possible screen layout of the graphics editor.

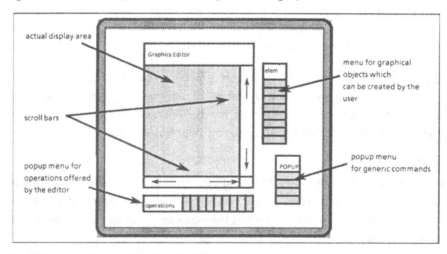

Fig. 3.7.   Screen Layout of the Graphics Editor

Modern computer workstations with bitmap displays allow the user to work on a number of different tasks at the same time. The screen is divided into a set of distinct areas called windows. By selecting different windows, the user can interact with several tasks concurrently.

As already mentioned the graphics editor is assigned to a window within its embedding environment. The window management system supports working in an object oriented way. To this it offers a popup menu with universal commands like copy, move, delete, etc. These commands are applied to the current selection whereby the type of the current selected object (window, graphical object, text, etc.) is irrelevant. The window management system guarantees that there is only one selection at any time. A command's execution is controlled by the administrator of a selected object. In case of the graphics editor all created graphical objects (interactively or by the application) are administered by the graphics editor itself.

The generic operations as printed out in Figure 3.1. are equivalent to these universal commands.

The window management system also supports the exchange of graphical information between different instances of the graphics editor. Exchange can be caused by selecting (interactively or by the application) graphical objects administered by an instance of the graphics editor, choosing the generic operation *move* or *copy* and selecting the destination in the current display region of another instance of the editor.

5. Portability

Portability of software is a topic of increasing importance. The architecture and structure of the graphics editor is designed to meet these requirements:

It is based on the draft standard CGI (Computer Graphics Interface) which makes software independent from hardware. The portability of the graphics editor is additionally guaranteed by the structure of its display file.

If graphics should be exchanged via electronic mail it should not only be possible to display, print/plot, and manipulate its own graphics but also to handle graphics procuded on any machine. To support this kind of working a model for document architecture will be introduced. It is called ODA (Office Document Architecture) [KRON]. To transmit ODA-like documents within a LAN (Local Area Network) the document interchange format ODIF (Office Document Interchange Format) is derived from ODA. ODIF describes the conversion of ODA-objects to a sequential data stream and reverse.

The approved contents of a document are described in so called "content architectures". Today content architectures can only be of type character or facsimile, but not yet graphics. Graphics will however be soon integrated in ODIF. CGM (Computer Graphical Metafile) will be used for the description of the relevant content architecture.

The display file used by the graphics editor is based on the draft standards ODA and CGM. These facts enable the graphics editor to operate independently of its working environment.

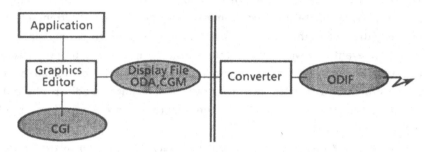

Fig. 5.1.   Draft Standards used by the Graphics Editor

The portability of created graphics is achieved by transforming the display file into ODIF by a converter and vice versa.

6. Example for Applications

Assumptions:

An user wishes to construct a switching diagram interactively and embed the created diagram into a design document. To this the user starts a CAD-application and a document editor. When the user starts running the CAD-application the CAD-menus showing the CAD-symbol U_E and the possible connection rules are presented on the screen. He also is presented with the graphics window, where he can create his diagram. The command menus containing *copy / global selection* can be popped up if needed. The window assigned to the document was created by starting the document editor. Information for the user is prompted on top of the screen.

The CAD-symbol U_E will be copied interactively but under control of the CAD-application. Copying of this CAD-symbol causes a new name of the copied symbol e.g. U_{E1} or U_{E2} (see Fig. 6.1.). Copied CAD-symbols can be composed in a specified way by so called connection rules. The composition is controlled by the CAD-application. It offers the user a menu from which he can select a desired connection rule. The CAD-application itself will then cause the graphics editor to draw the switching diagram.

If the user wishes to *connect* two CAD-symbols he has to select the first symbol, select the desired connection rule within the application specific menu, and then select the second symbol if necessary. To copy the created CAD-graphics into a document the user has to select it, select *copy* within the popup menu, and select the destination within the current display area of the document. A possible screen layout is shown in Fig. 6.1..

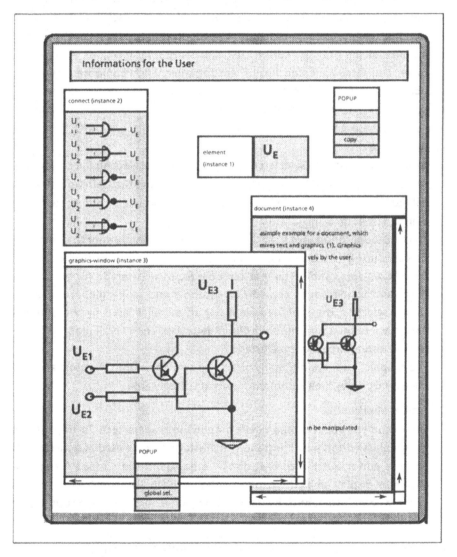

Fig. 6.1   Example for Embedding CAD-Graphics into a Document

Realization:

CAD-application:

The CAD-application uses the graphics editor to create the CAD-symbol U_E out of two basic graphical objects of type text. Furthermore the CAD-application informs the graphics editor that this composed graphical object may be selected and copied interactively only but under its control. No other operation is allowed. The CAD-application offers the user a menu showing the different symbols of allowed connection rules. For this it uses a second instance of the graphics editor, creates basic graphical objects of type *line*, *circle*, and *closed arc* and links them together. Each composed graphical object may only be selected interactively under the control of the CAD-application. No other operation is allowed. The CAD-application itself assigns each of these connection rules their own semantics e.g. AND, OR, NOT, NAND, NOR.

Assuming the user has selected a CAD-symbol and is selecting the connection rule corresponding NOR, the selected CAD-symbol and the CAD-symbol which will be selected next will be connected by drawing the according switching diagram (see Fig. 6.1.).

The CAD-application uses a third instance of the graphics editor to enable the user producing CAD-graphics interactively. Its creation happens under control of the CAD-application. The user can only copy the offered CAD-symbol U_E, select and connect the copied CAD-symbols and make global selection. Global selection is established via a popup menu offered by the graphics editor where the user can select *global selection*. The overall graphics in the current display area is then selected.

The graphics editor additionally offers two scroll bars, thus the user can scroll the actual display area within the maximum display area.

Document application:

The document application embeds graphics into some text. To this it starts the graphics editor, the 4th instance. This instance can be used as pure general purpose editor but the current display area cannot be scrolled within the maximum display area (The scroll bars shown in Fig. 6.1. enable the contents of the whole document to be scrolled.). The units of measurement of the 3rd and 4th instance are different.

Example of user interactions to create the diagram and embed it into the document as shown in Fig. 6.1.: (see Fig. 6.2.)

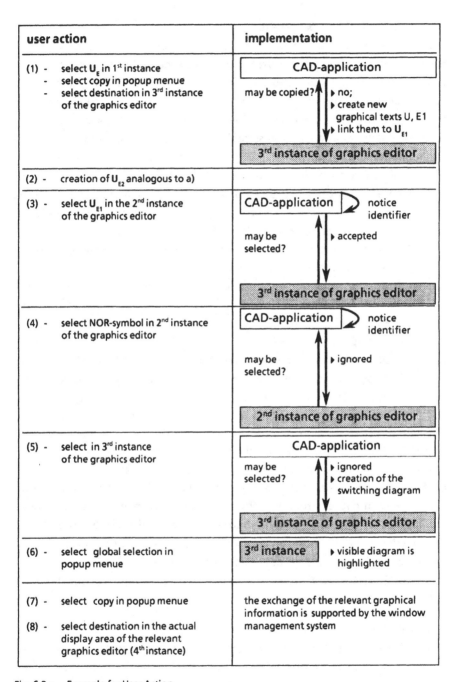

user action	implementation
(1) - select U_E in 1st instance - select copy in popup menue - select destination in 3rd instance of the graphics editor	**CAD-application** may be copied? ▶ no; ▶ create new graphical texts U, E1 ▶ link them to U_{E1} **3rd instance of graphics editor**
(2) - creation of U_{E2} analogous to a)	
(3) - select U_{E1} in the 2nd instance of the graphics editor	**CAD-application** notice identifier may be selected? ▶ accepted **3rd instance of graphics editor**
(4) - select NOR-symbol in 2nd instance of the graphics editor	**CAD-application** notice identifier may be selected? ▶ ignored **2nd instance of graphics editor**
(5) - select in 3rd instance of the graphics editor	**CAD-application** may be selected? ▶ ignored ▶ creation of the switching diagram **3rd instance of graphics editor**
(6) - select global selection in popup menue	**3rd instance** ▶ visible diagram is highlighted
(7) - select copy in popup menue (8) - select destination in the actual display area of the relevant graphics editor (4th instance)	the exchange of the relevant graphical information is supported by the window management system

Fig. 6.2.: Example for User Action

7. Implementation Experience

The graphics editor described in this paper has been implemented in a 1st product version. It runs under UNIX and is implemented in C-language. Much experience was gained in using the draft standards CGI, CGM are noted in. As mentioned above the graphics editor has its own display file and does not use the segment storage concept of CGI. There are several reasons for this fact:

- Segment storage is not a suitable device for dynamic modification of images.
- CGI output elements can be gathered within a segment but a specific element cannot be adressed afterwards. CGI only allows the whole segment to be addressed. The single solution for this problem would be: one segment per CGI output element.
- Graphical output elements cannot be stored hierarchically by CGI. This fact makes it impossible to create graphical symbols.
- CGI does not provide the inclusion of special attributes to CGI output elements, which can be interpreted by the application of CGI. It only allows the segment attributes (selectable, detectable, visible, etc.) or purely graphical attributes.

Further experiences were made in using the input concept of CGI as well as embedding the graphics editor within its environment. The basic idea of a modern user interface is that the user should be the chairman, e.g. he should make decisions about the actions to be executed. He should have the chance to interrupt any started action. The editor must guarantee the correct execution.

Using CGI input the editor must put the CGI input devices (locator, choice, string) into the EVENT-mode, i.e. the input events are saved in an event queue. This enables the graphics editor to guarantee correct execution. If the graphics editor is embedded into its environment, the window management system receives all user inputs first and then passes them to the editor e.g. the inputs passed by the window management system must be interpreted as inputs of CGI input devices. If not the graphics editor does not meet the portability requirements.

Using CGI/CGM, ODA/ODIF today is difficult because they are not yet standards but drafts.

8. Conclusions

Today many graphical representations originally generated on computer terminals, personal computers etc. have to be regenerated once or even several times by hand. This is caused by different coding of the relevant information. This underlines the need for standards. However a lot of work remains to be done to establish and refine a standardized ODA and ODIF, CGI and CGM. The use of standards has been mandatory for the implementation of the graphics editor. Its full functionality could not be described however this paper represents a short overview about the power of this graphics editor. The possible applications are wide-spread.

References

ODA	1986	ISO/TC97/SC18/WG3 N469: ISO/DIS 8613/2, Information Processing - Text and Office Systems - Office Document Architecture (ODA) and Interchange Format - Part 2: Document Structures, First Draft International Standard, June 1986
ODIF	1986	ISO/TC97/SC18/WG3 N561: ISO/DP 8613/5, Information Processing - Text and Office Systems - Document Structures - Part 5: Office Document Interchange Format, Second Draft Proposal, Oct. 1985
CGI	1985	ISO/TC97/SC21/WG2 N356: Information Processing Systems - Computer Graphics - Interfacing techniques for dialogues with graphical devices (CGI), Second Initial Draft, Nov. 1985
CGM	1985	ISO/TC97/SC21/WG2 N191: ISO/DIS 8613/1-3, Information Processing Systems - Computer Graphics - Metafile for the Transfer and Storage of Picture Description Information (CGM), Nov. 1985
PCTE	1986	ESPRIT-Projekt: A Basis for a Portable Common Tool Environment, Functional Specification, July 1986
SEIGIS	1985	A. Seigis: Interactive Structure Oriented Editing of Text and Graphics Based on Modern Workstations, Proceedings of CAMP 85
SEIGIS	1986	A. Seigis: Architektur eines Dokumenten-Editors in einer objektorientierten Benutzerumgebung, Informatik Fachberichte 119, GI-Fachgespräch Bremen, Springer-Verlag, März 1986
SIEM	1986	Burgstaller, Gall, Hess, Kneißl, Seigis: Ein interaktiver, objektorientierter Dokumenteneditor für graphikfähige Arbeitsplatzrechner, H. Schwärtzel (Ed.): Angewandte Informatik- Ein Fachbericht der Siemens AG, Informatik Fachbericht, Springer Verlag, 1986 (soon published)
KRÖN	1985	G. Krönert: Anforderungen an ein Textverarbeitungssystem auf der Basis des Standard-Dokumentenarchitekturmodels Proceedings of IG/OCG/ÖGI-Jahrestagung 1985
HORAK	1983	W. Horak: Interchanging mixed text-image documents in the office environment, Computer & Graphics, no. 7.1, pp. 13-29, 1983
SCHELL	1985	A. Scheller: Dezentrale Verarbeitung von Dokumenten im Rahmen des Deutschen Forschungsnetzes (DFN) auf der Basis internationaler Standards, Proceedings of IG/OCG/ÖGI-Jahrestagung 1985
FEINER	1981	S. Feiner et al.: An Integrated System for Creating and Presenting Complex Computer-Based Documents, ACM Computer Graphics, no. 15.3, pp. 181-189, 1981
XEROX	1985	Sara A. Bly: User Interface Design for Graphics Applications, Proceedings of CAMP 85

A GRAMMAR FORMALISM AS A BASIS FOR THE SYNTAX-DIRECTED EDITING OF GRAPHICAL NOTATIONS

M. Woodman, D. Ince, J. Preece and G. Davies.

Computer Science Department, Faculty of Mathematics
Open University, Walton Hall, Milton Keynes, MK7AA.

Abstract

Software Engineering graphical notations exhibit a regular structure. This holds out the possibility that they can be described as grammars. If so then all the power of compilers and syntax directed editors can be employed in the production of software tools for such notations. This paper examines the possibility that picture grammars can be used to describe software engineering notations. Current picture grammars are found wanting and a new formalism: the relational/attribute grammar proposed.

1. Introduction

This paper describes a picture grammar formalism which has been developed to drive a syntax-directed editor for graphical notations. In particular, the editor will process notations from the field of software engineering. The editor is a component of a documentation and tools environment currently under development in the Open University Syntactic Graphics Project[*]. Rather than supporting only the programmer, this environment will support other types of user who are involved in the software development process. These users include: project managers, requirements analysts and designers.

The requirement that our environment caters for a wide range of users means that it must be possible to create and change documents expressed in a wide variety of notations and to rapidly create ad-hoc tools to process such documents [1]. Furthermore, documents may contain a number of graphical notations which must be recognized and correctly dealt with [2].

---

[*]The work is supported as project SE/066 by the Alvey Directorate

The view that we have taken is that, in order to facilitate such processing, documents must be created and maintained in a syntactically correct form, and that this is preferable to syntax checking after input. While syntax-directed editors for programming languages (and their grammar formalisms) are common, editors for graphical notations are not. Previous work has demonstrated that grammar systems intended for configuring syntax-driven program editors [3] may be applied to documents and that syntax-based editing of pictures is feasible [4].
However, the novel requirement that graphical notations be similarly handled has necessitated the development of a suitable grammar formalism describing such notations.

The formalism presented in this paper is inspired by work carried out by workers in the field of pattern recognition. Here graphics are described by means of picture grammars. These are notations similar to programming grammars [5,6,7]. Recognition of such pictures being carried out by means of syntax directed compiler technology. Although our work has been influenced by developments in pattern recognition we have found that in order to process complex graphics a new approach to syntactically defining pictures is required.

First, the paper will review existing picture grammars. Second, the grammar formalism itself is described and the deviation from existing picture grammars justified, and a metasyntax given. By way of example, a grammar for the graphical notation of Data Flow Diagrams [8] is developed; first, the notation is described informally in order to explain its syntax; second, a grammar is described with reference to the informal description; third, the paper describes the uses of the support environment, in particular the syntax-directed editor—its applicability to a range of document types and notations through the picture grammar formalism.

The paper concludes with a description of work in progress, and an evaluation of the grammar system for describing picture data. The main work to be carried on the grammar formalism is to extend it to include rules for generating semantic information which can be used by the ad-hoc tools [9]. We believe that the grammar formalism described here is generally applicable and is superior to most in its ability to specify non-graphical relationships between graphical elements (such as the decomposition of hierarchical diagrams).

2. Grammar, Pictures and Software Engineering Notations

2.1 Software tools and picture grammars

A major application where graphics and formal grammars come into contact is that of pattern recognition. Here pictures are described by sets of production rules and specific instances of pictures are encoded in a form that enables a syntax directed parser to pass judgement on whether a particular picture conforms to the rules [10,11,12].

This is a simple explanation of syntax directed pattern recognition. There is never a clear cut decision whether a pattern matches a grammar. What usually happens in practice is that each production is given a finite probability and the parser, instead of giving a simple yes/no judgement about the pattern produces a figure of likelihood based on conditional probabilities. The grammars used in pattern recognition can be employed as recognisers for software engineering notations.

There is a need to produce software tools to process graphical software engineering graphical notations. Typical examples of such notations are: data flow diagrams, structure charts [8] and Nassi-Shneiderman charts [13]. There is a set of requirements for tools which process such notations.

- The tools should process and syntactically check the notations for correctness. For example, in a data flow diagram a source should not be directly connected to a sink.

- The tools should process and semantically check the notations. For example, in a data flow diagram a data flow diagram should not contain more than seven bubbles.

- The tools should generate information structures which enable the user to extract data from the notations being constructed. For example, the user of a structure chart tool should be able to ask what program units are subsidiary to a given program unit.

- The tools should be able to display instances of a particular notation in an acceptable form or at least warn the user that the notation instance created is not acceptable. For example, if the user of a structure chart tool creates a chart that has a large number of intercrossing lines then, at the very least, the tool should warn the user about this.

- The tools should provide a limited amount of knowledge processing. For example, there is no reason why production rules should not guide the layout of notation instances on a display screen.

The way in which we see such tools being used is in processing documents which are known to be syntactically correct. The processing itself will depend on the function which the tool is to perform and is driven by a different set of rules. Correct syntax can be guaranteed by a successful edit/compile loop; however, since editing must take place and the manipulation of graphical notations benefits from computer assistance, we have adopted a syntax-driven approach.

2.2 Picture grammars and software engineering notations

Two software engineering notations were chosen as a medium for examining the feasibility of representing them using picture grammars. The grammars used were tree grammars, plex grammars and web grammars [6]. The notations used were structure charts and data flow diagrams Each grammar was examined using a number of criteria. These were: expressability of the grammar formalism, i.e. how easy it was to represent the software engineering notation, the ease with which the formalism can be modified to accommodate the description of the notations and the ease with which the grammars could be compiled.

The results were relatively straightforward. Tree grammars were dismissed as their basic lexical element was the line and even for relatively simple notations this lead to too many productions. Web grammars are more general than tree grammars but often lead to context sensitive rules. Unfortunately, this would result in major parsing problems. The only grammar that remained was the plex grammar. A more detailed discussion of this grammar is reproduced in the following section.

3. Plex Grammar

From the foregoing it can be seen that grammar which has the greatest potential for describing software engineering graphics is a *plex grammar* . It describes structures which have an arbitrary number n of attaching points for joining to other symbols. A structure of this sort is called an n attaching-point entity (NAPE). Structures formed by interconnecting such entities are called plex structures. These structures are quite general in nature and include strings, trees and webs as sub-cases. A plex grammar is a six tuple:

$$G_p = (N, T, P, S, I, i_0)$$

N is a finite non-empty set of NAPE's called the *non-terminal vocabulary*.
T is a finite non-empty set of NAPE's called the *terminal vocabulary*.
P is a finite set of *productions* or *replacement rules*.
S in N is a special NAPE called the *initial NAPE*.

I is a finite set of symbols called *identifiers*.

i_0 in I is a special identifier called the *null identifier*.

The restrictions on this grammar are that

$$T \cap N = \{\}$$

$$I \cap (T \cup N) = \{\}$$

The symbols of I are used to identify the attaching points of NAPE's. Every attaching point of a NAPE has an identifier in I, and no two attaching points of the same NAPE have the same identifier. The null identifier i_0 serves as a place marker and is not associated with any attaching points. Interconnections of NAPEs can only be made at the specified attaching points; "imaginary" connections using the null identifiers are not allowed. A set of NAPEs is said to be connected if a path exists between any two NAPE's in the set.

An *unrestricted plex grammar* has productions of the form

$$LT_L D_L \rightarrow WT_W D_W$$

where L is called the *left-side component list*; W the *right-side component list*, T_L the *left-side joint list*; and T_W the *right-side joint list*; D_L the *left-side tie-point list*; and D_W the *right-side tie-point list*.

The component lists are strings of the form

$$L = a_1 a_2 \ldots \ldots a_i \ldots \ldots a_m$$

and

$$W = b_1 b_2 \ldots \ldots b_j \ldots \ldots b_n$$

where a_i and b_j are single NAPEs called *components*; L and W list and provide an ordering for the groups of connected NAPEs that comprise the respective component lists. The connection of attaching points of two or more NAPE's form a joint, and T_L and T_W specify the way in which the NAPEs of their respective component lists connect. The joint lists, which are unordered, are divided into *fields* that specify which attaching points of which NAPE's connect at each joint. The lengths of the field for the left and right hand side of each production are given by l(L) and l(W) respectively, where l denotes the length of its string argument. An entry i_k in the jth position of a field indicates that attaching point i_k of the jth element (i.e. NAPE) of the component list preceding T connects at the joint associated with that field. If the jth. NAPE is not involved in that particular joint, the null identifier appears in the jth. position of the field.

The component and joint lists LT_L and WT_W when taken as pairs, define the structures involved in a rewriting rule. These structures attach to the remainder of the plex at a finite number of points called *tie points*. The tie-point lists D_L and D_W give the correspondence between these external connections for the left and right hand sides of a production. The tie-point lists are also divided into fields, with exactly one field specifying each tie point. Since the number of tie points for the left and right hand sides of a production must be the same, the number of fields in each tie point list is the same. Moreover, the tie-point lists are ordered, with the kth field on the left corresponding to the kth field on the right.

4. Plex Grammar and Software Engineering Notations

There are a number of drawbacks to the use of a plex formalism with software engineering notations. Firstly, there are potentially an infinite number of attaching points. At least there will be a large number of attaching points. This would lead to a grammar which is unwieldy. Secondly, a number of lines can be attached to the same attaching point this is very difficult to handle in a plex grammar.

Thirdly, there is the problem of text. Almost all software engineering notations have text attachments associated with the graphics. The pure plex grammar approach described above has no facilities for coping with this problem.

Fourthly, the simple line approach would not work for software engineering notations. The reason for this is that many graphical software engineering notations have lines with arrows attached to them to indicate data flow or flow of control.

Plex grammars are a good way of describing structures which have a degree of regularity. What is required is a formalism which, although it is based on the concept of a plex grammar is able to express fairly general notations. Such a grammar should express connectivity, position and, possibly text, associated with the entities described by the grammar. This is valid because the connection point is not important in defining the syntax of notations such as data flow diagrams and structure charts.

One possible new grammar formalism is shown below. This paper gives a formal definition of the syntax of data flow diagrams using this formalism. Some discussion of what constitutes a valid data flow diagram and an informal syntax precedes the definition.

5. Data Flow Diagrams and Formal Syntaxes

5.1 Data flow diagrams

A *Data Flow Specification* consists of a set of *Data Flow Diagrams*. The first of these is the top-level or *overview* of the system being described. The basic vocabulary of DFDs is as follows:

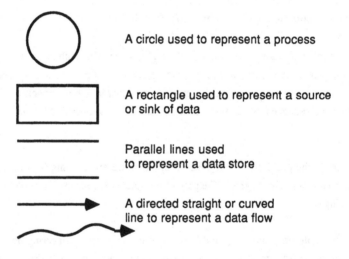

A circle used to represent a process

A rectangle used to represent a source or sink of data

Parallel lines used to represent a data store

A directed straight or curved line to represent a data flow

Each data flow diagram is a decomposition of some process in a higher level diagram (or the overview). Conceptually, therefore, the data flow specification consists of sets of planes containing a number of diagrams; and an editor should be able to move from one plane to another with ease.

Now consider some diagrams:

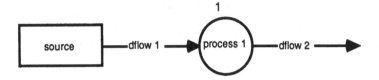

This is not a valid data flow diagram: it cannot be a system overview (a figure zero) because there is no sink (or data store) for the output from the process; it cannot be the decomposition of a process because there is no data flow coming from "nowhere" (i.e. from some source, data store or process at a higher level).

The following is correct in one context, but not another:

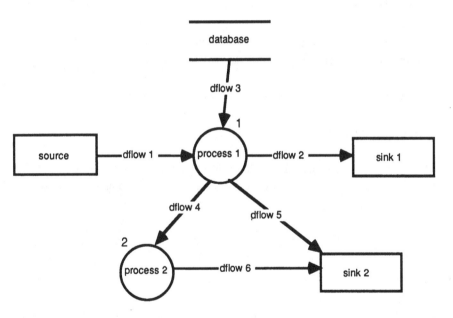

It is a valid (though arguably over-complicated) overview, but not a syntactically valid decomposition. Removing *source* and *sink1* would make it a valid decomposition, but not a valid overview.

5.2 Informal Syntax

The syntax of a data flow specification is now given informally:

1. A data flow specification is an overview diagram which may be decomposed into a number of data flow diagrams. Only the processes of a diagram may be decomposed.

2. As a minimum the overview must contain a source with a data flow emanating from it to a process; from that process a data flow must go to a data store or sink. The rules of juxtaposition apply (cf. 4 below).

3. A data flow diagram must consist of at least one process with at least one data flow as input to it and at least one output from it. These minimal data flows must come from ,and go to, "nowhere", representing sources, sinks, data stores and processes from the previous (higher) level.

4. Only certain objects may be juxtaposed. Sources only with data flows; data flows with sinks, processes or data stores. Processes may only be juxtaposed with data flows.

5. All objects must have text "centered" on them (see examples above).

6. Processes must be numbered.

7. All diagrams must have captions (not shown above). A convention for these might be "Figure" followed by number of process which was decomposed followed by a colon and some descriptive text.

5.3 Formal syntax

The formalism we have designed combines a number of rule sets which will be needed to define the structured, graphical documents produced in the software development process. It consists of a number of "declarations" which specify the metasymbols and three sets of production rules.

The grammar is a 9-tuple of the form:

> (Non terminals, Start, Terminals, Objects, Relations, Attributes,
> Production rules, Relation Rules, Object definitions)

Non terminals is the set of meta-identifiers denoting the non-terminals of the language.

Start is the start-symbol of the language (which must be a member of *non terminals*).

Terminals is the set of terminal symbols of the language. The graphical shapes and text used in a notation will be enumerated in this set.

Objects defines a set of meta-identifiers which denote terminal symbols that have *attributes* associated with them (in the *object definitions*). They are special non-terminals, of limited derivation, which, in some sense, define composite objects that are more abstract than the terminals. Thus, for example, a process object is made up of a circle terminal, with some text centred within it, and must be labeled.

Relations is a subset of the set of all common positional and directional relationships between elements of two-dimensional diagrams. The *relation rules* define which objects (or non-terminals) may be related.

Attributes define typed variables associated with objects. These variables may either have some range of values or be fixed. For example, a circle will have a centre position (variable) and diameter (fixed).

Production rules are a set of rewriting rules which define the language using *non terminals, objects,* and *relations*. The metasyntax for this rule set is based on EBNF but rather than overload the use of braces (used for denoting sets) the $^{+}$ superscript is used to denote one or more repetitions of a syntactic element, while the superscript * is used to denote zero or more repetitions. Square brackets are used to group zero or one occurrences of a syntactic element. By convention, objects are underlined, while attributes are shown in italics; relations are shown in bold.

Relation rules are a set of axioms which declare the allowable relationships between objects or non-terminals. Thus, in a data flow specification, <u>text</u> may be **co-centred** with any object, but only a <u>process</u> may be **decomposed**.

Object definitions specify how objects and terminal symbols are combined to make abstract objects. For example, a caption will be made up of <u>text</u> a <u>process-number</u> (a hierarchical number) and more <u>text</u>.

The grammar for data flow diagrams is given below

Non terminals ≡
{data-flow-specification, overview, process-seq, database-seq, data-flow-diagram, diagram}.

Start ≡
data-flow-specification.

Objects ≡
{<u>process, database, data-flow, source, sink, text, process-number, caption</u>}.

Relations ≡
{**juxtapose, decompose, co-centred, labeled**}.

Attributes ≡
{start-pos, mid-pos, end-pos, centre-pos: **(real, real)**; diameter, diagonal: **real**}.

Terminals ≡
{"   ", "   ","   ", "   ", "   ","A".."Z", "a".."z", "0".."9", "_", "-", "(", ")"}.

Production rules ≡
data-flow-specification =
    overview (**decompose** data-flow-diagram)*.
overview =
    (<u>source</u> **juxtapose** <u>data-flow</u> **juxtapose** process-seq **juxtapose** <u>data-flow</u> **juxtapose** (<u>sink</u> | database-seq))$^+$ <u>caption</u>.
process-seq =
    <u>process</u> (**juxtapose** <u>data-flow</u> **juxtapose** (<u>sink</u> | process-seq | database-seq))$^+$.
database-seq =
    <u>database</u> (**juxtapose** <u>data-flow</u> **juxtapose** process-seq)*.
data-flow-diagram =

diagram (**decompose** diagram)*.

diagram =

    ([source] dataflow **juxtapose** process-seq **juxtapose** data-flow [sink])$^+$ caption.

Relation rules ≡

  co-centred:

    text **co-centred** (source | data-flow | sink | source | process).

  juxtapose:

    source **juxtapose** data-flow | data-flow **juxtapose** (sink | process | database) |

    process **juxtapose** data-flow | database **juxtapose** data-flow.

  decompose:

    process **decompose** data-flow-diagram.

  labeled:

    process labeled process-number.

Object Definitions ≡

process ::=

    (("   " *centre-pos diameter=5*) **co-centred** text) **labeled** process-number.

process-number ::= ("0".."9")$^+$ ("." ("0".."9")$^+$)*.

caption ::= text process-number text.

database ::= ("   " *centre-pos length=12*) **co-centred** text.

data-flow ::=

    ("   " *start-pos end-pos* | "   " *start-pos mid-pos$^+$ end-pos*) **co-centred** text.

source ::= ("   " *centre-pos diagonal=10*) **co-centred** text.

sink ::= ("   " *centre-pos diagonal=10*) **co-centred** text.

text ::= ("A".."Z" | "a".."z" | "(" | ")" | "-")$^+$ *centre-pos*.

6. Conclusions and Discussion

We have developed a formalism which can be used to describe graphical notations in software engineering. The formalism can be used for defining notations regardless of any need to drive an editor. This is itself a major advance: too many of the notations used in software engineering are defined by example, let alone informal text. To be able to rigorously fix a notation is significant.

Another useful facet of our work is that the existence of a formal definition of a notation allows decisions about the user interface to be considered at an early stage. For example, a directed line in a data flow diagram is a terminal symbol but not an object of the notation; it requires annotating with text to make it such. Thus, the design issue arises as to whether one menu icon in the editor for data flow diagrams should be a directed line on which text should be placed, or should be a line with a "text place holder" which must be filled.

The formalism is itself not fixed; it will not become so until we have more experience in constructing notations and in building associated parsers. We have already defined Jackson structure diagrams [14] and JSD networks [15] and are beginning to recognize the system-wide *relations* and *attribute types* which we need. For example, Nassi-Shneiderman charts [13] consist of nested rectangles and triangles with most rectangles coincident at the bottom right hand corner of the outermost one; the triangles are juxtaposed as two identical right angle triangles between an isosceles triangle on its apex (text omitted):

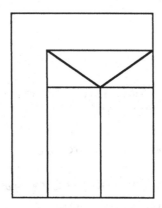

Which is an appropriate relation to use here—**coincident-at-bottom-left**?

The main parsing problem arises from the unpredictability of how the user will wish to type a notation. For example, a data flow diagram in construction is unlikely to conform to its grammar—a user might choose to place process bubble at appropriate points on the screen *before* connecting them with dataflows. Also, a simple approach to adding the required text to objects in a data flow diagram would be to permit its addition after the object (minus text) had been placed in the document, but no object in a DFD is valid without text. Hence the DFD, except when completed, would not adhere to the grammar. This problem is akin to those encountered by the designers of syntax-directed program editors [16]: their aim is to allow the construction of valid computer programs, but at any stage the user may have input an illegal program. Incremental parsing techniques have been used to overcome these problems, and we will need to follow a similar approach.

Related to the need to tolerate partially correct documents, is the need to be able to store and read them. While this makes sense to allow a number of editing sessions on a document, any tools which assume correct syntax must be prevented from processing the ill-formed documents.

The grammar formalism should settle within a year as we define more grammars and experiment with parsing techniques, while prototyping of the editor continues in parallel.

References

[1] Ince D.C. and Woodman M., The Rapid Generation of a Class of Software Tools, *The Computer Journal*, **29**, 2, 1986.

[2] Woodman M., Formatting Syntactically Nested Documents, *Proc. PROTEXT 1 International Conference on Text Processing*, Dublin, 1984.

[3] Rose G and Roper T., Generation of Program Preparation Systems for Formatted Languages, *Proc. IFIP '83*, 1983.

[4] Ince D.C. and Woodman M., A Software Tool for Structured Analysis, *Software Practice and Experience*, **11**, 11, 1985.

[5] Clowes M.B., Transformational Grammars and the Organization of Pictures, in *Automatic Interpretation and Classification of Images*, A Grasselli (Ed.), New York, N.Y.: Academic Press. 1969.

[6] Fu K.S., *Syntactic Methods in Pattern Recognition*, New York, N.Y.:Academic Press, 1977.

[7] Velasco F.R.D. and Souza C.R., An Application of Formal Linguistics to Scene Recognition, *International Journal of Computers and Information Science*, **6**, 4, 1977.

[8] Yourdon E. and Constantine L.L., *Structured Design*, New York, N.Y.: Yourdon Press, 1978.

[9] Woodman M. and Ince D.C., Towards a Unified Representation of Life-Cycle Notations for the Rapid Synthesis of Software Tools, *Proc. 6th. International Workshop on Software Design and Specification*, London, 1985.

[10] Gonzales R.C. and Thomason M.G., On the Inference of Tree Grammars for Syntactic Pattern Recognition, *Proc. International Conference on Systems, Man and Cybernetics*, Texas, 1974.

[11] Lee E.T., Shape Orientated Chromosome Classification, *IEEE Transactions Systems, Man and Cybernetics*, **5**, 7, 1975.

[12] Fu K.S., *Syntactic Pattern Recognition, Applications*, New York, N.Y.:Springer Verlag, 1977.

[13] Yoder C.M. and Schrag M.L., Nassi-Shneiderman Charts: An Alternative to Flowcharts for Design, *Proc.ACM SIGSOFT/SIGMETRICS Software Quality Assurance Workshop*, 1978.

[14] Jackson M.A., *Principles of Program Design*, London: Academic Press 1975.

[15] Cameron J.R., An Overview of JSD, *IEEE Transactions on Software Engineering*, **12**, 2, 1986.

[16] Allison L., Syntax Directed Program Editing, *Software—Practice and Experience*, **13**, pp453–465, 1983.

Electronic Publishing System Based Upon Dec Vax Minicomputers at the BP Research Centre, Sunbury

B. Spicer

BP Research Centre
Sunbury, UK

Abstract

This paper briefly describes the activities of the British Petroleum Group Research Centre, the type of technical documentation produced by research staff, and how a VAX based technical document publishing system is increasing the efficiency and effectiveness of the research effort. The system includes compatible PC and VAX based technical Word Processing software, typesetting software, local and central laser printers and image scanners. Future developments include links to telex and facsimile and to Information Retrieval Systems.

1. Background

British Petroleum Group is an energy resources organisation consisting of 1900 subsidiary and related companies with 12,000 personnel working in over 70 countries on six continents. Group turnover in 1985 was £41.7 Bn, with profits after taxation of £1.8 Bn. The group has a major stake in the US through its 55% interest in the Standard Oil Company.

The BP Research Centre, at Sunbury-on-Thames, England, is the Group´s primary research and development facility with more than 2000 staff on a ca. 75 acre site - one of the best equipped multi-disciplinary research centres in Western Europe. The work of the Research Centre is funded in two ways: 60% of funds are provided by individual Group companies/businesses "buying" specific R & D and 40% of the funds are corporate, provided for fundamental research.

The Research Centre uses a range of on- and off-site computing facilities. On-site facilities will, by the end of 1986, provide a central total of 26+ MIPS (millions of instructions per second) computing power based on a cluster of Digital Equipment Corporation (DEC) VAX 8000 and 11/7XX minicomputers. Some 700 terminals are (or will be) attached to this cluster. Distributed processing facilities consist of more than 300 desktop/personal computers, including powerful workstations, and a number of highly specialised minicomputers connected to laboratory systems.

2. Scope of the Problem

The Research Centre is organised into technical divisions which in turn are sub-divided into specialist branches and research project teams. There are ca. 90 project teams operating simultaneously on ca. 800 projects on-site. Of the 2000 plus staff at Sunbury, close to 1200 are qualified scientists/technologists, with the remainder being administrative and technical support personnel.

Much of the work of the site results in the production of technical documentation - both to record the results of research work and to present findings and proposals to sponsors.

The technical documentation and report work produced at Sunbury is, because of the nature of research work, complex with large numeric and textual tables, scientific equations and chemical compounds embedded in text along with both graphical and imaginal data. Documents which mix text, equations, graphics and image on a page are known as Compound Documents. An example is shown in Figure 1.

A COMPOUND DOCUMENT

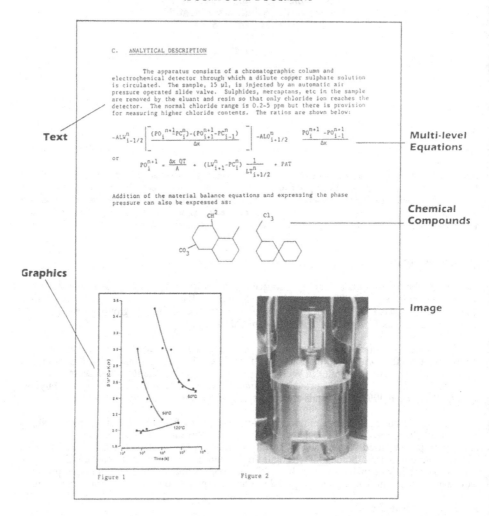

Figure 1

The equivalent of 350,000 A4 pages of technical documentation is produced per annum by ca. 80 secretarial staff who support the technical staff. Of the ca. 80 secretaries, 12 are organised into two small Technical Report Word Processing Units and the remainder are scattered across the length and breadth of the Research Centre. Some 40% of the total pages produced are of the Compound type, as illustrated in Figure 1, with up to 75% of the research staff wishing to produce this type of document at some stage during the working year. Up until mid-1985, technical documentation was produced on stand-alone and shared facility word processing systems from no less than four different vendors, with graphical and imaginal data manually cut and pasted into place for copying on volume photocopiers and small offset-lithographic printing systems in a conventional print room.

3. The Sunbury Integrated Technical Publishing System

Following a major review of the facilities for secretarial, word processing and reprographics support on the Sunbury site, proposals were made for an integrated technical publishing system with the following aims:

- To provide the most efficient and effective in-house, technical document publishing system to the Research Centre, using available technology, systems and standards.

- To establish a Sunbury site standard for technical word processing and document production.

- To provide a modular and flexible architecture for electronic publishing at the Research Centre capable of taking advantage of innovational change in systems and procedures.

The Sunbury Integrated Technical Publishing System has a number of component sub-systems which have been implemented in phases throughout 1985 and 1986. Figure 2 shows the initial phases of the system which are currently in place.

SCHEMATIC OF THE SUNBURY INTEGRATED TECHNICAL PUBLISHING SYSTEM

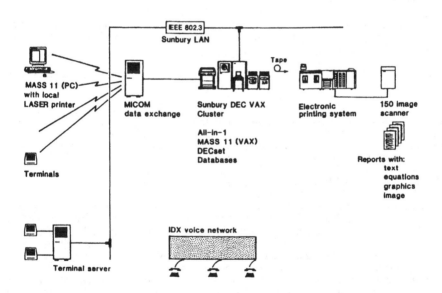

Figure 2

The sub-systems are:

- Personal computers running feature-rich, scientific word processing and communications software (MEC'S MASS 11) with desk-top local laser printers. Currently the PC's are Rainbows with LN03, however, IBM and compatible PC's are also in use. (They are both replacing and augmenting existing stand-alone WP systems);

- Site-wide Local Area Network (LAN) to IEEE 802.3 Standard backed by a Data Exchange providing low speed asynchronous connections;

- Compatible scientific WP software (MASS 11) running on the site central computing facilities (currently a VAX cluster with VAX 8800, 8650, 11/785 and 11/750 processors);

- VAXmail Electronic Mail (EM) software, menuised to run with MASS 11, and used for distributing and circulating technical documents during drafting;

- Modified terminals, capable of displaying the full DEC Technical Character Set, to access the VAX based MASS 11 software for casual users;

- Distributed LN03 laser printers connected to the VAX cluster, to provide low volume, text/equations-only output for casual users;

- Database and job progressing software, built around a number of Battelles BASIS databases running on the VAX cluster, and providing a central document progressing system and indexing facilities for the long term retrieval of technical documents;

- VAX based typesetting software (DECset, from DataLogics of Chicago) menuised and modified to run with MASS 11, allowing Rainbow and VAX produced MASS 11 documents to be easily typeset to a number of BP standard formats (including the capability to call into a document scanned graphics/images at the print stage);

- A high volume 300 x 300 dpi laser printer, a Xerox 8700 centrally sited with the VAX cluster and set up to take output tapes from DECset; an on-line link between VAXs and the laser printer is currently being evaluated;

- A centrally based Xerox 150 IMG (300 x 300 dpi) image scanner etherneted to the Xerox 8700, to capture graphical and imaginal data at the print stage.

The initial phase of the system covers the basic requirements for technical publishing. During the remainder of 1986 the system will be enhanced with links to the Telex network and to a Sunbury based facsimile switch to allow for the transmission of complete compound documents to other parts of the BP Group. The range and number of electronic printing systems will also be increased to improve the spread of quality output devices over the Sunbury site.

4. Links to Records Management Systems

Later phases of implementation during early-mid 1987, include the linkage of the Sunbury Integrated Technical Publishing System to the Site Records Management system. Currently all technical documents produced since 1959 are held in the Sunbury Technical Records Centre in microform (16 mm film at 24X reduction, stripped into jackets and diazo copied) with an index of each record held in the BASIS databases already mentioned above. Production of microimages is a labour intensive manual process. Accessing historical technical records is by database search and the manual retrieval and distribution of microform records. It is intended to partially replace the manual production of microimages with a high facility COM (Computer Output in Microform) unit capable of producing the bulk of compounds documents directly from DECset files.

To complete the system it is hoped to establish a microimage retrieval system, which will allow end-users to undertake a database search to establish the desired records to be retrieved and to be able to trigger a robotic retrieval, digitazation and the encoding (as a CCITT Group III/IV FAX file) of the retrieved microimages which will then be transmitted into the end users VAXmail box to be picked up, decoded and viewed on VT 241´s (or equivalent graphics terminals) using an on-line FAX file decoding utility. These two features are illustrated the the schematic in Figure 3.

SCHEMATIC OF THE SUNBURY INTEGRATED TECHNICAL
PUBLISHING SYSTEM

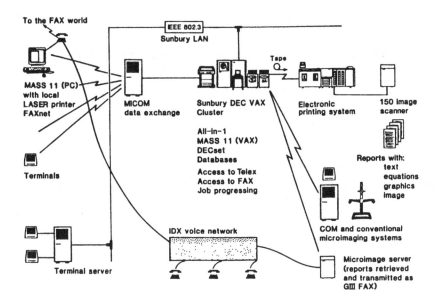

Figure 3

5. Future Systems

Later during 1987, many of the facilities described above will develop into workstation based desktop publishing systems with desktop scanners and laser printers and hopefully, WYSIWYG (What You See Is What You Get) versions of MASS 11 running on PC's and small VAX systems.

Beyond these phases lie tentative plans to add voice annotation to compound document production systems to assist in the speedy editing of draft documents.

Most of the system described above (conceived during mid-1984) is in place or currently being implemented with a target for completion by the end of 1986 or early 1987. Once implemented, the Sunbury Integrated Technical Publishing System will provide a firm foundation of support services for research and administrative staff at Sunbury for the remainder of the decade.

Presenting documents on workstation screens

P.J. Brown

Computing Laboratory, The University, Canterbury, Kent, CT2 7NF.

ABSTRACT

Some documents are best read from paper, while others are best read from computer screens. This paper is concerned with the latter. It describes how the interactive facilities of a graphics workstation can be exploited to allow readers to tailor on-line documents to their own needs.

KEYWORDS: on-line document, interaction, workstation, Guide.

Introduction

There are two likely reasons for displaying documents on a workstation screen. The first is to preview a document that is ultimately to be printed on paper; here the aim, as encapsulated in the term what-you-see-is-what-you-get, is to make the image on the screen resemble as closely as possible the image that will appear on paper. The second is as an end in itself: the document is being presented to the user so that he can read it and extract the information he desires. It is this second application area that is the subject of this paper.

The two application areas place diametrically opposite constraints on the software that presents the document on the screen: the aim in the first case is to imitate paper whereas in the second case — so we will argue — imitating paper is a disastrous policy.

Paper and screen

As we know, modern workstations are much superior to glass-teletype terminals for presenting documents. They offer higher resolution, larger size, the availability of a multitude of possible fonts, graphics, and perhaps colour. Nevertheless the average reader still prefers to read a document from paper rather than a workstation screen. If the presentation software simply tries to imitate a paper document on the workstation screen, we believe that, in spite of future hardware improvements, readers will continue to prefer paper. The reason is simple: the imitation will always be inferior to the real thing.

The aim instead must be for on-line documents (i.e. documents designed to be read on-line) to complement the properties of paper ones. The great advantage of on-line documents is that the user can interact with them. This advantage is magnified by the high degree of interaction that is possible on good graphics workstations: the user can point using a mouse (or its equivalent), he can move objects round the screen, and he can display several windows at once, thus allowing him to compare different pieces of information. The workstation software can help the user by providing continuous feedback, by providing simple and flexible user control (e.g. through dynamic menus), and generally by supporting a good user interface. Thus the possibility is open for the user to interact closely with a document that is displayed on the screen, and tailor it so that the information it provides is just the information he wants. If this possibility is exploited, then on-line documents have a huge potential advantage over static paper ones.

A research programme on exploiting workstations

For the past four years, a group of researchers at the University of Kent has been working on software for graphics workstations. Some of this work has been supported by SERC or ESRC, and some by the University itself. One part of this research has been related to the display of documents, and has led to the construction of the *Guide* software for displaying documents. Guide is aimed specifically at the opportunity identified in the previous Section: the opportunity to allow readers to tailor on-line documents to their own reading needs.

Guide was developed for the ICL PERQ and SUN workstations. More recently, OWL (Office Workstations Ltd. of Edinburgh) have obtained commercial rights to Guide and have developed implementations of Guide that run on cheaper hardware, such as the Apple Macintosh and the IBM PC (running Microsoft Windows software).

Most of the rest of this paper is devoted to describing the Guide system. The Figures are taken from the SUN implementation, but the general principles of Guide apply to all implementations.

The Guide system

The facilities of Guide are best explained by means of an example.

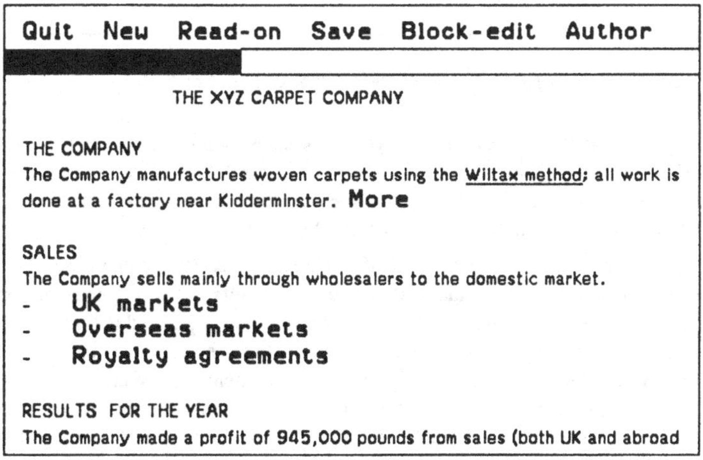

Figure 1: a Guide screen

Figure 1 shows how Guide might initially display a document. Along the top of the Guide display is a menu, and beneath this is a scroll-bar (which we will explain in a minute). The rest of the display is occupied by the document, which in this case is an annual report of the XYZ Carpet Company. The document consists of a mixture of ordinary text and *replace-*

buttons. The latter are in the same bold-faced font as the menu (e.g. **More** is a replace-button). They are selected just like menu-items: the user can point at any replace-button and then click the mouse. When this happens the replace-button is replaced by a body of material associated with the button. For example, assuming that the author of the document is not a perverse soul, if the user selects the **Overseas markets** replace-button, this is replaced by the description of the overseas markets of the company.

In Figure 1 the document is too big to fit on the screen and part of it has scrolled off the end. Guide represents documents as a single scroll, rather than as pages — a technology based on paper. The user can move about the document by pointing at the appropriate place on the scroll-bar. (The black area of the scroll bar represents the part of the document that is in view and the white area represents the part that is out of view.)

```
 Quit   New   Read-on   Save   Block-edit   Author
 ████████████████

               THE XYZ CARPET COMPANY

 THE COMPANY
 The Company manufactures woven carpets using the Wiltax method; all work is
 done at a factory near Kidderminster. More

 SALES
 The Company sells mainly through wholesalers to the domestic market.
 -    UK markets
 -    Overseas sales are mainly in Germany and the USA. According to a
      recent DTI survey, the company is, for its size the largest UK carpet
      exporter, since exports are 56% of sales. More
 -    Royalty agreements
```

Figure 2: result of selecting the **Overseas markets** *replace-button*

Figure 2 shows what happens after the **Overseas markets** replace-button has been selected. The new material itself contains further replace-buttons, and, indeed, Guide allows buttons to be nested to any desired depth. Because of the insertion of the new material some of the material previously displayed has been scrolled off the screen.

The way a user interacts with a Guide document is to select replace-buttons until he has tailored the document to provide exactly the details he wants. Any previous button selection can be 'undone'. Thus if the user subsequently decides that a particular level of detail is too great he can go back to the previous level. Sometimes the user will want to save the resultant document for further use. He can even print this document on paper, thus combining the merits of the interactive workstation in allowing him to generate the document he wants, and the merits of paper in providing a portable and readable medium for representing the document thus generated.

Glossary-buttons

The aim of Guide is to provide a flexible way of viewing a document using as few facilities as possible. The biggest thrills in the development of Guide occurred when a single simple facility was found to replace several complicated ones. To adapt a recent slogan: if a user can point he can use Guide.

There are, however, two further facilities apart from replace-buttons that some readers may choose to use. There are the *glossary-buttons* and the *editing facilities*. The former are like replace-buttons but are used for material that is better displayed in a separate subwindow rather than within the main text. Glossary-buttons can be used for explaining jargon, for citations (to books, to people, etc.) and footnotes. Glossary-buttons are underlined in the document (e.g. Wiltax method and DTI survey are the glossary-buttons in Figure 2). Figure 3 shows the result of selecting Wiltax method in Figure 2.

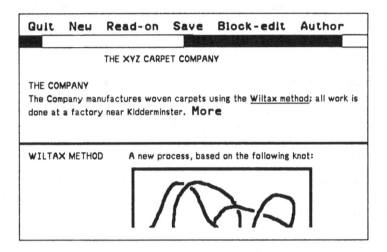

Figure 3: the result of selecting the Wiltax method glossary-button in Figure 2

When the first glossary-button is selected the screen is split into two sub-windows and the definition of the glossary-button is placed in the lower one — the *glossary sub-window*. This can be seen in Figure 3. Subsequent definitions of glossary-buttons are inserted in alphabetical order into this same glossary sub-window, so that this sub-window always represents the reader's personal glossary. Like the main document, the glossary sub-window can subsequently be saved and indeed printed on paper. (However once it is on paper the interactive element is lost: you cannot point at an item on paper and have its definition pop up.)

Figure 3 also shows a further facility of Guide: documents can consist of graphics as well as text. (In fact part of the picture in Figure 3 has been scrolled off the screen, which may be fortunate, since the Company's vital trade secret has not been fully revealed.)

Editing

Readers often want to add their own personal annotations to documents. With an on-line document this can be achieved in a particularly natural way, and Guide therefore provides annotation facilities. Guide is, indeed, a screen editor and the user may point at any position in the document and add new material or delete existing material. Guide does not differentiate between the original document and the user's changes, though the user himself may choose to mark his additions. Thus annotations, such as a remark that compared the XYZ Carpet Company with another company, can be inserted at exactly the appropriate place in the document, rather than being squeezed into margins.

Uses of Guide

Guide can be used for any nature of on-line document. It is especially useful for documentation about computer software, such as a 'help' system.

On a multi-window system Guide is often run in one window while other activities are conducted in further windows. For example Guide could display 'help' information concerning software that is running in a separate window. It is vital that software which runs in a multi-window environment should be able to run in any size of window. Guide thus formats the document to fit the current window size. Indeed, if the user changes the window size while Guide is running — and this is a not uncommon happening — then Guide automatically re-formats the document to fit its new surroundings.

Guide as a front-end

A lot of documents are generated by computer programs. Thus a huge collection of numbers may come out of a FORTRAN program, a report may come out of a COBOL program or a textual document may come out of a retrieval system. Such computer-generated documents typically contain a huge amount of information in a form that is hard to digest. A promising application of Guide is to act as a front-end to programs. Guide then displays the output from the program using its button facilities, so that the user can readily extract the material he really wants. In order to achieve this the appropriate Guide codes for buttons need to be inserted into the output document. This can be done by modifying the underlying software or by a pre-processor. Figure 4 shows the use of Guide to display the results from the *Prism* information-retrieval system. This work was done in collaboration with J.D. Bovey.

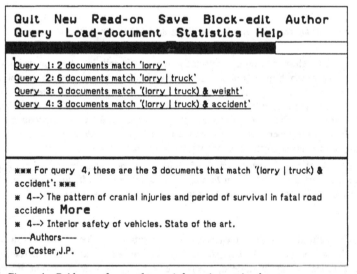

Figure 4: Guide as a front-end to an information-retrieval system

In Figure 4, the results of all the user's queries to the retrieval system are shown in the main sub-window. It was felt that these should be kept together, uninterrupted by other text. They are therefore displayed as glossary-buttons. The definition of each glossary-button gives the documents that match the query. Each document can be viewed at increasing levels of detail, using replace-buttons. In information retrieval the user might only be interested in a small proportion of the documents retrieved, and the Guide method of presentation allows him to reject the irrelevant ones without cluttering up screen space. In Figure 4, the user has expanded the results of the fourth query.

In detail the system works as follows. The Guide menu is augmented by a further set of commands, which allow the user to communicate with the underlying software. In Figure 4, the **Query** command is used to send queries to the retrieval system. The user first selected **Query**, and in answer to its prompt (not shown in the Figure), typed 'lorry'. Guide displayed the result as a glossary-button, which is the first line in Figure 4. The user, at this stage, was not interested in the matching documents, and he tried three more queries. Seeing the result of Query 4, he decided he might now have found some relevant documents, and thus decided to look at them. He therefore selected the Query 4: 3 documents match ... glossary-button. The replacement of the glossary-button first displays, for each matching document, its title followed by a **More** replace-button. (Every title is prefixed with the number of the query that matched it, so that even when he scrolls about a large glossary sub-window, the user can easily relate documents to queries.) In Figure 4 the user has selected the **More** replace-button of the second document in order to find out more details (e.g. Authors, etc.).

The user continues in this manner until he is satisfied that he has found what he needs. He then saves the glossary sub-window, since it lists the relevant documents.

This is just one example of Guide as a pre-processor, but hopefully it gives a flavour of how relatively complex information can be presented in a way that is pleasant to peruse.

Authorship

Guide documents can be created from scratch or they may be created from existing documents. A prime aim of Guide has been to make authorship simple. There is no separate 'author language'; instead the author uses Guide just as a reader does. We have seen that readers can edit documents. This is just how an author creates a document: he starts with a null document or an existing document and edits it. There is a subsidiary menu (invoked by selecting **Author** in the menu) which allows new buttons to be created. The replacement of buttons, like the rest of the document, can be made up of new material or existing material. Pictures may be inserted where desired.

Clearly it would be a long and tedious task to convert a large body of documentation to Guide form. Happily, if the existing documents are marked up in some systematic way, this task can be done automatically. For example Section headings could be converted to button names with the body of the section as the replacement. Such automatic conversion has been performed with the UNIX† *manual pages*, which provide the documentation for the UNIX system. Clearly automatic generation can be improved by subsequent authorship by hand (e.g. adding some glossary-buttons), but even without this the converted form, when displayed by Guide, is much easier to peruse than the original.

Multi-way replacements

Authors can provide different replacements to suit different readers. This is, of course, another facility well-suited to on-line documents rather than paper ones. It is achieved by the Guide *enquiry*, which consists of several buttons with interspersed text. A sample enquiry is:

Are you an **Expert**, a **Casual** user or a **Novice**?

If the user selected, say, the **Novice** button then the complete enquiry would be replaced by the material associated with this button. There are facilities for responses to enquiries to be 'pre-

---

† UNIX is a trademark of AT&T Bell Laboratories in the USA and other countries.

set', so that a user is automatically assumed, for example, to have selected the Novice button for each enquiry that contains this button. As a result the user would see a document tailored for novices. Pre-setting can also be built into Guide itself, so that, for example, only certain people see information that is designated for managers.

Enquiries allow on-line documents to cover a wider spectrum of readers than paper ones. Nevertheless experience shows that enquiries are most valuable when used with restraint. If one attempts to cover too large a spectrum of readers the document becomes tedious for everyone.

Conclusions

For those documents that are best published in paper form, the role of the workstation is to act as a previewer.

Other documents are best published in electronic form so that users can interactively extract the parts of the document that they want. Graphics workstations provide an excellent medium for supporting the necessary interactive environment. In particular they support interactive buttons, 'pop-up' information, multiple windows, windows of changing size, and direct editing — none of which apply to paper documents. It is by exploiting these facilities, rather than by trying to imitate paper, that on-line documents can be made to meet the reader's needs.

Genie-M, A Generator for Multimedia Information Environments

Ian O. Angell
Department of Information Systems
London School of Economics, UK

Yuen Ping Low & Adrian R. Warman
Department of Computer Science
University College London, UK

Abstract.
    This paper gives a methodology for describing and controlling an information environment, and proposes a mechanism for its implementation. Deriving from earlier work on multimedia document architecture, **GENIE-M** (**GEN**erator of **M**ultimedia Information **E**nvironments) will allow the construction of environments for a variety of applications. The environment will enable the mixing, integration and interaction with static media types such as text and graphics, as well as dynamic types such as sound, video, film, text and graphic animation. There is also provision for real-world control and feedback through the screen or digital and analogue switches. The proposed model uses a homogeneous geometric data structure to represent associated data spatially and discretely. This is the theoretical basis for the construction of prototype document preparation and lecturing systems. GENIE-M is of particular benefit for handling document-type material, whether it be text, graphics, images or sound.

Key Words: Information, Environment, Observer, Interpretation, Data, Presentation, Geometric Data Structures, Hub, Modules, Tiles, Windows, Multimedia, Document Structure, Object-Oriented, User Interface.

1. Introduction.

    Advances in computer technology have tremendous effects in the areas of multimedia information acquisition, manipulation and presentation. GENIE-M is constructed around a specialised geometric data structure that facilitates the organisation of such technology for the manipulation of multimedia data. This geometric representation of data and their inter-relationships can be used to describe various computerised scenarios, such as on-line documentation and publication, distributed electronic lecturing and conferencing systems, etc. We propose an electronic multimedia information system that offers the potential of increased availability of information, shared access to up-to-date versions, and alternate presentation (or interpretation). This paper emphasises a geometric document architecture and data structure approach linked to object-oriented methodology for relating and generating information in a multimedia environment, using a window-based graphical editor as a user interface.

2. The Information Environment.

    In order to understand GENIE-M, we introduce a working definition of 'Information' to be the Observer's interpretation of Data presented by the Environment. The term 'Data' refers to the raw material used in all kinds of computation and inference, whether by man or machine, and regardless of source or destination. The term 'Observer' refers to the end-recipient of one or more results, or alternatively to the supplier of data. Typically, this will be a human user, but it could equally refer to a data storage mechanism.

    The observer's interpretation of data is the key to understanding information. Data, no matter how presented, is meaningless until interpreted by an observer. Since the experience of the observer will directly affect how he or she considers the data presented, the interpretation will influence the information derived from the data. For example, most people can interpret pictorial data more easily than numerical tabular data.

The 'Environment' handles the task of accepting data into the system, manipulating and performing computation upon that data, and presenting results obtained. The jobs involved in accepting, manipulating or presenting data can be simple or complex, and it follows that each job within the environment must be considered on an individual basis. The description of the environment involves detailing all jobs or 'Modules'. These modules manipulate data using software tools and object-oriented techniques, as well as by interaction with other modules in the environment. The flow of data and results between modules takes place using 'Module Links'. These links can connect across intra- and inter-machine boundaries, although links between machines will usually be handled by modules dedicated to supporting communication standards between machines.

Module operation consists of the following three stages: firstly, data is presented to the module, with instructions on exactly what task is required; secondly, the module performs the task as efficiently as possible; and lastly, the results are made available in accordance with the instructions or design of the module links.

This description means that environment modules can behave in a similar fashion to the process nodes used in data-flow diagram theory [Yourd78] and Petri Nets [Peter77]. In general, modules may only execute when all data and instructions for manipulating the data and processing the results have been obtained. Some modules will be purely computational; others take results and prepare them for presentation, or else accept data into the environment. The presentation or acceptance of data takes place at the 'Interaction Boundary'. The interaction boundary is delimited by a number of 'Interface Modules', which consist of software on the environment side of the boundary, and (typically) a hardware link on the other side to a data source/sink such as a database or other machines. A human observer is in fact considered to be an interactive data source/sink.

As well as being a passive receiver of data into the environment, GENIE-M can be an active controller by presenting data to the real world across the interaction boundary. If the data passed through an interface module is considered to be the digital equivalent to analogue values, then the interface module can become a controller of a device in the real world, such as a lighting circuit or projection system. Such control of the real world helps in the presentation of data, and allows the GENIE-M user greater flexibility in many applications.

GENIE-M is in fact a <u>generator</u> of information environments because all aspects of the information environment under consideration can be, and indeed, must be modelled within GENIE-M. Having provided the tools to model the information environment, GENIE-M can then be used to monitor and manipulate any or all aspects of the environment via the graphical display and editing of a geometric data structure.

3. Geometric Data Structures.

3.1. Philosophy.

GENIE-M is a generator of a data handler, and the key feature of this concept is the 'Tile'. These tiles will hold the data which can subsequently be manipulated and displayed[1]. GENIE-M data will be presented through user-controlled windows on the display device. The tile can include sound data (as

---

[1] It should be noted that use of the term 'displayed' does not imply a restriction to visual portrayal only.

well as other data types), and this sound - for example, speech - could be represented graphically as icon.

The tiles are 'intelligent' objects, which will interact with their neighbouring tiles depending on their relationship with those tiles. Each of the tiles will behave according to the task it is intended to perform. A tile can examine its relation with other tiles to establish areas of overlap and intersection. If a number of tiles are geometrically positioned relatively to a 'reference' tile, and this reference tile is altered or moved in some fashion, then the relative tiles must be able to adjust themselves appropriately. If one tile is moved to a new location within the tile space, then all the others must move as well.

The tiles can be used for document production by more than one author. There could be many people working on the material, and such interaction leads naturally to the use of GENIE-M in multimedia conferencing. The display device windows will usually be controlled by the user, but could also be coordinated by the conference manager to ensure that the appropriate material is being presented and updated correctly.

3.2. Physical Description.

All modules in GENIE-M use a homogeneous geometric data structure, which is composed of the tiles. A tile can be rectangular in shape and its size can vary relatively or absolutely with other tiles. The tiles are positioned in a stack of two-dimensional planes, called the tile space. Each tile has a 'tile record' which contains information about that tile, such as type of contents (text, graphics, spreadsheets, sound, programs, etc), attributes (character fonts, colour schemes, language used, etc), and most importantly, the relationships with other tiles.

Tiles can contain three main types of object: raw data, formatted data (for display), and executable program code. Depending on the primary use to which they will be put, such tiles are called 'Data Tiles', 'Display Tiles', or 'Program Tiles'. Program tiles would not normally be displayed, display tiles would not normally be used for holding raw data, and data tiles would not normally be executed. However, tiles can always be handled by modules in the same way, regardless of their content.

The data held within a tile is dynamic. For example, a data tile could hold a reference to a current share price for use in a financial report. Each time that the tile is accessed, the latest up-to-date value would be obtained. A program tile could access a data tile holding spreadsheet values, and take the data to produce, say, a pie chart which is held in a display tile. Program tiles will often bind closely to one or more data tiles, although they can also be for general purpose use by the system.

The geometric positioning of display tiles in the tile space reflects their actual location within a particular document or application. The position is represented using the topological relationship between tiles described in the tile record, in a similar fashion to Knuth's [Knuth83] concept of nested boxes connected by stretchable glue in the $T_E X$ system. Tiles cannot overlap on the same plane and are affected by any changes in size of neighbouring tiles. For example, a display tile of graphical data which is located below another display tile of text in the tile space would be placed accordingly in the document presented on the display device.

Tiles holding text data to be formatted for display must also take into account the effect of that formatting on related tiles. For example, if a tile is required to divide its text into a number of columns with a diagram in the centre, then the formatting must allow for the size and position of the diagram.

If the diagram changes size, then the text layout will probably need to be altered as well. Similarly, tiles that hold sound data should be able to detect two or more voices 'speaking' at once.

Tiles may themselves contain sub-tiles. If a tile contains text and it is desired to emphasise certain portions of the text (possibly by italics or underlining), then either the text could be subdivided into more and smaller tiles, or the tile could have sub-tiles which hold the emphasised portions of text.

Tiles which store animation material will bind very closely to each other. Although each is an independent unit, any alteration made to one of the tiles in the group will probably affect other tiles within the same group. The method by which animation is achieved can vary - the simplest technique would be to have a number of "frames" stored, one per tile, and the frames can then be cycled, in a similar fashion to that used in ordinary cinema films. The frames would be stored in a 'stacked' fashion within the tile space, so that by 'descending' through the levels of tiles, each frame can be displayed in turn.

Tiles are not only restricted to holding data. They can also contain references or 'pointers' to information; or for control and command files or programs. A tile could specify how another tile is to be used. Allowing tiles to hold instructional information of this kind makes GENIE-M very flexible.

4.   GENIE-M Architecture.

4.1.   Modules and the Environment.

All modules within a GENIE-M environment have the same structure: executable code, and local data. Their operation is specifically hidden from all other modules or tasks running on that or other machines, allowing modules to be written independently of each other. This means that subsets of GENIE-M environments are easily constructed by omitting those modules not required for a given application. A further advantage of the modular architecture is that GENIE-M is well suited to making use of multi-processor computers, as opposed to running on a time-shared basis on single-processor machines.

One unique module which must be present is the 'Hub'. This module has the same structure as the other modules, but rather than manipulating data, supervises the relationships between modules. The hub does not oversee modules, because each module normally functions independently of any other module. However, the hub does examine the overall running of the system to ensure that no problems or deadlocks occur. It also has the responsibility of creating and removing modules from the environment, and serves all the needs of modules present in the system. The hub maintains a record of which modules are present in the environment by using its own geometric data structure. Any modifications to the environment are reflected by updating this structure.

Several modules present on a system may perform similar or related tasks. They may be grouped together because they have a common type of task; or for physical reasons such as being distributed between one or more other machines in the system. For example, modules that handle keyboard I/O, light-pen and mouse input or VDU output, could all be grouped together as user-interaction modules. Such related modules are said to be grouped together into a 'Sub-Environment'. Just as the main GENIE-M system has a hub to control the environment, so each sub-environment will have its own 'Sub-Hub'. Since the hub is responsible for activating all modules in its environment, a bootstrapping technique can be used in initial construction of a GENIE-M system, and later activations.

4.2. Tile Transfer and Manipulation within GENIE-M.

Each module within the environment only inputs or outputs data in tiles, so that a module can work with any kind of data, regardless of what it actually represents. The exceptions to this are the interface modules which accept raw data for conversion into a tile format, or present results having extracted them from display tiles.

A tile which contains, for example, bit-map information could readily be transferred to another module which manipulates the bit-map, without actually knowing what the data is. In a simple case, the bit-map image would perhaps be 'reversed'; in a more complicated case, the image could be 'skewed' or 'slanted'. Tiles can be read and converted by 'Intermediary Modules' which are used to supply data to programs or machine processes that would not otherwise understand data tiles.

4.3. Module Organisation within the Environment.

The main feature of GENIE-M module organisation is the hierarchy of module invocation. Initial work in preparing a GENIE-M prototype has suggested that a typical system will have a large number of fairly small modules performing elementary tasks. A system which retains modules on a most-recently used basis will allow frequently used modules to float to the top of the priority table, giving faster overall response. Most modules will connect to only a few other modules, and typically two will provide input, while one or two modules accept output.

The organisation of modules is therefore very important in order that data may flow as quickly and as efficiently as possible around the environment. At the 'centre' of the environment will be the hub module, and around it is (conceptually) placed inner service or 'core' modules. These core modules will tend to perform tasks of an administrative nature within the environment. Frequently, they will initiate activity without user interaction. Most sub-environments will be located near to the hub, since they form a natural division of tasks into related areas - they also follow a similar organisation to that being considered. Further from the hub, elementary rather than compound modules or sub-environments will begin to predominate. These perform tasks of a more operational nature.

Finally, nearer the interaction boundary, the modules will become more machine dependent in nature with hardware connections and dependencies. The majority of user interface modules will be located here, because they are closely linked with the interaction boundary.

4.4. The User Interface.

The 'User' is a general term used here for the human user and the display device being utilised to portray GENIE-M data from a display tile. The display device is defined to consist of objects such as vocoders for sound reproduction; VDUs for visual information; keyboards, mice and light-pens for information and command entry, and so on.

At the user interface level, all internal communication tasks are performed in a manner transparent to the user or users by the interface modules of a particular application. Each of these modules within the system has a specific and clearly defined set of tasks to perform in order that GENIE-M data may be edited and presented as desired.

An example is the window administrator module, which is one of the fundamental components in GENIE-M. This module has a full knowledge of the devices under its control. For every display window or viewport, the window administrator will keep an internal record of its structure, current contents, inter-relationship with other windows, ownership, and other details. This module is primarily responsible for presenting display tiles on the display device by creating windows and removing them when not required. It therefore 'knows' about the geometric and implicit topological organisation of data for a specific application, in order to accurately map the data onto one or more display windows.

Another module of importance is the geometric structure editor, which manipulates, creates and organises tiles of data in a tile space. It is capable of grouping tiles into larger structures such as a tile plane. Inter-relationships between tiles, for example, cross-referencing of data within an application, or even among applications, are defined in this way. This type of linking, cross-referencing and ordering of data in some instances resembles that of structure editors [Kimur86] and hierarchy editors such as PEN [Allen81].

The human user 'interacts' with an application via GENIE-M windows which in turn associate with relevant display tiles. The means of user interaction are usually locator devices - a mouse is the most likely choice or a keyboard on a windowing system. Other means such as a vocoder could be easily introduced into the proposed system.

The geometric structure, when regarded as an abstract data structure, provides an implicit indexing scheme[2] which can be used to assist a human user in the search for certain information. Tile attributes are inserted using a generic tile template that is accessible via menus available at that stage of the interaction. Specific tile templates may be maintained for particular applications.

5. Application Examples.

5.1. Mixed Media Documents.

GENIE-M's philosophy is realised by applying interactive multimedia documents for presentation, manipulation, storage, and final hard-copy. The geometric data structure interface allows the human participant to interact with presented data. The participant selects relevant data by traversing the geometric planes using a locator device (a mouse, or cursor keys, etc.). The inter-relationships between different data objects (for example, text or dynamic graphics) within a document are represented by tiles in a tile space. The tiles are associated with processes such as text or graphics editors. At any time, the participant is presented with an accurate portrayal of the portion of data associated with selected tiles. Data hiding can be effected using access rights defined on the tile for data security.

Modification of, or addition to, the currently presented document is performed by editing old or inserting new tiles within the tile space using a geometric editor at the interaction boundary. The tiles are associated with processes created and coordinated by the hub. The tile planes provide a simple mechanism for generating and organising animated graphics, text or images in a dynamic document structure or lecture scripts.

---

[2] An indexing scheme is a technique of organising data for the purpose of accessing it efficiently.

5.2. Newspaper Layout Construction.

Daily Newspapers have many features in common. The majority of the information and news is printed in black ink on white paper, and so in order to present the reader with some variety and also to catch the eye, a number of type-sizes, fonts, styles, and photographs are included. Each of the main news stories has its own "block" somewhere on the page, sometimes with a relevant photograph placed at some location within the block. It is not always the case that such a photo would be in line with the block of text, and indeed photographs to one side of the text (and so forming an "L" shape block) are common.

Given the somewhat haphazard nature of block layout, it is a difficult job to lay out the page in a readable and presentable fashion, while fitting in the maximum amount of information on the page. Furthermore, as news stories are updated or invalidated, the block could be altered by being increased, or reduced, or removed altogether.

There has been considerable discussion recently over the use of "high-technology" in producing newspapers, because such use would enable the layout editor to perform the task more effectively and quickly. However, the techniques being introduced make little attempt to integrate the entire process – if a block is being manipulated on a VDU, it is unlikely that the contents of the block will be considered, and if a block is later re-written then the layout process must be repeated again to ensure that the material still fits.

GENIE-M would allow the concept of "newspaper" to be broken down into smaller and smaller logical units: newspaper to pages to blocks to paragraphs to words, and so on. Each one of these units corresponds to a GENIE-M tile. A high-level tile (for example, the "page" tile) would hold references to lower tiles (the blocks on that page). Block tiles would refer to paragraph tiles holding text, or possibly photographs. Each one of these tiles would be individually edited by the journalist, directly into the GENIE-M newspaper database. As the tiles are entered into the system, the section or feature editors can combine the tiles into tile groups, for example all international news items would be collected together into a local number of pages.

These tile groups can themselves be built up into groups to build the entire paper. The layout of each of the tiles at this stage is comparatively free, although there will naturally have been specification of paragraphs, emphasised text or fonts, position of photos relative to the text (for example, between two text paragraphs, or to one side of a paragraph or another photo). Most importantly, the entire news item is considered to be one unit, and the author never has to consider the possibility of splitting the text over a number of pages.

Once the data tiles have been entered, the GENIE-M system can begin automatically formatting the document. It will know from the tile records which tiles relate to each other, and so it can build up the display tiles knowing the contents and attributes of a tile, and also its relation to other tiles. In the event of a tile being too large for the available space, the GENIE-M system can create a new tile to hold the extra material, and this new tile can then be submitted into the tile space for another convenient page, along with bi-directional cross-referencing of the form "continued on page XX" and "continued from page XX" (possibly including column numbers also).

The author of each item will have already specified information such as type of tile contents, paragraphs, size of font, type-face, and other details. The section or feature editor will have included further information regarding the relation of items to each other – for example major news items would be expected to appear above and/or to the left of minor items. Within these constraints, the GENIE-M system will construct display tiles that reflect the individual layout of blocks, as well as the combined page layout of all the blocks on that page. The display of these tiles allows the overall view of the page to be considered, as well as the layout within each of the blocks. If any one block needs changing, only the relevant tile needs to be altered, and then the reformatting process to re-construct the relevant display tiles can be repeated.

Time-sensitive material can easily be included - for example many newspapers carry information on stock prices or exchange rates, and program tiles can be entered into the document that describe the layout of the information they carry, as well as references to the source of the information, but not the actual information itself. At any time when any display tile is constructed which uses such program tiles, the cross-reference is followed and the most up-to-date value is automatically inserted.

GENIE-M is ideally suited to the high-speed and quickly changing environment of newspaper publishing. Since all contributors to a paper (in whatever context - journalist, editor, and others) all have direct access to the relevant portions of the paper, which can then be combined and manipulated within the same system, the overall effect is of a much higher production rate, at lower costs to both the publisher and the reader. Since GENIE-M is context-sensitive to the display device being used, the material can be formatted appropriately for the device - for example if a publisher wishes to place selected material into micro-film format, the exact same display tile construction process is followed, but using the micro-film device filter. Each of the tiles would be stored in the core module(s) and later archived into a news file, and the very nature of the tiles makes cross-referencing an easy and trivial task (albeit on a large scale).

5.3. Lecture and Presentation Control and Structure.

Better lectures and seminars have a structure to them. After an initial introduction to the topic being discussed, the main body of the presentation consists of a submission of fact, information and views, which may well be discussed among the group. Finally, a summary and conclusion is presented. Throughout, there is often use of diagrams and pictures to help explain ideas or portray facts more clearly. The diagrams could be in the form of slides (and overhead projections), films, and (more recently) television and video. Some presentations may also draw on audio material from tapes or records.

Given that the material and portrayal of material has a structure, it becomes apparent that GENIE-M offers a number of useful capabilities in this application. The entire lecture could be prepared by the lecturer, with each constituent object being allocated a tile. For example, each section of text in the notes could be allocated its own tile. The tiles would be displayed to the lecturer in turn, who can then present the material - alternatively, if the lecturer is running behind schedule, it would be an easy matter to skip onto the next section, knowing that all the cross-referencing of related material will be carried out appropriately.

Other tiles could be used as "channels" for the input of information from outside sources. For example, in a large auditorium, televisions may be used to display camera views of the lecturer or diagrams. A camera could be used to "channel" the image directly into a GENIE-M tile. The lecturer then has real-time control of this image around the auditorium, and as each new diagram is to be displayed, can simply direct the appropriate tile to the televisions. A tile which holds pictorial information for projection on a large cinema-type screen could have an associated attribute file that would automatically dim the hall lights while the tile is active; once finished with the image, the lights could be restored to their normal intensity. Alternatively, the lecturer could have a "control panel" presented on the display device so that personal control of the environment can be obtained as and when desired.

The display device for the lecturer's use would ideally be of the "electronic lectern" device frequently seen today at major conferences and seminars. This device has a transparent display screen in front of the speaker, onto which is projected the text of the speech from a projector underneath. The angles involved in this "head-up-display" mean that the audience does not see any of the speech notes, and further the transparency of the screen means that the speaker is not obscured in any way. A small foot control device could be installed to control the speed of the presentation of material onto the screen, thus leaving the lecturer's arms free.

Setting up such a lecturing system would require that the lecturer arrive early with a technician to connect up the appropriate apparatus and its control mechanisms. As each device is identified and a driver incorporated into the GENIE-M system, the driver can be permanently kept on record for later re-use.

With all the material on hand in this form, the lecturer could display actual copies of the notes in the form of projections, simply by redirecting tile contents to the display device. A mobile pointer (possibly driven by a mouse) could be superimposed on the projected image, in a similar fashion to a multimedia conferencing system. Finally, having all the material stored in this way would allow hard-copy notes for the audience to be produced easily and quickly. It would also be easy to construct a new lecture structure from the information tiles already stored in GENIE-M format.

6. Related Research Areas.

6.1. Information Browsing, Presentation and Preparation.

One of the problems that our proposed model will be addressing is data (or knowledge) exploration in a multimedia environment. The problem of knowledge exploration comes from the fields of computer-aided instruction (CAI) [Osin76] and non-linear text systems, also known as hypertext systems (e.g. [Weyer82]).

In hypertext document systems, text fragments are embedded in a directed graph with labelled edges and instructions allowing the user to traverse the edges. Their user interfaces include state of the art technology such as high resolution graphics, sophisticated pointing devices, and even pictorial simulations. However, these systems lack a content-based query facility. This means that hypertext users must wander through text units trying to find relevant information and must decide on an order in which to read it once they find it. Some database systems, such as the MIT Spatial Data Management System (SDMS), have adopted a hypertext approach to allow users to wander among the information in a database. SDMS [Herot80] provides a user with graphical querying and presentation of the database.

Dennis Shasha [Shash85] suggests a fragment theory for retrieval and knowledge exploration in his data model called NetBook. The knowledge is represented in the forms of text fragments (including a picture, an experimental simulation, or a live performance) with relations defined among them, and queries in a natural language form helps users to access the appropriate fragments. The GENIE-M system provides a tile structure for representing the data of either mixed or single types in the geometric model. This concept resembles in some ways the above text fragments, although the latter system, being text-based, offers very limited user interaction with the message content.

A complex mass of information can be more clearly presented with the aid of colour and dynamic representations which are available on most graphics and engineering workstation technology. The graphics editing system developed by Feiner, Nagy, and Van Dam at Brown University [Fein82] uses this approach in preparing and presenting technical manuals. Their system uses colour, very high resolution graphics, and menu selection to provide flexibility in scanning a document. Brown and Sedgewick of Brown University have demonstrated the ability to see dataflow and control structures of algorithms and software as they execute in their algorithm simulator and animator, BALSA [Brown84]. BALSA uses a dynamic graphic interface as the natural mode of interaction. The GENIE-M user interface adopts the dynamic representation features and software tools discussed above for scanning data within GENIE-M system.

Another important research issue that is relevant to our model is based on document preparation systems. Examples of some existing research systems that allow for interactive document editing and formatting operations are Janus [Chamb82] and Andra [Gutkn84], of which Andra provides additional hardcopy capability on a laser printer. Other document systems like CD-GUIDE [Brown86] allow for interactive viewing, editing and storage using a CD-ROM disk. GENIE-M is capable of handling interactive document editing and formatting operations, and providing hardcopy on any printer, but using modules and a uniform data structure.

A renewed interest in text processing research has resulted in new text editors and document formatters producing integrated programs that format documents dynamically during the editing session [Furut82], [Gutkn85], and [Peels85]. General hierarchy editors for documents, programs, and graphics are in existence. The system that we are proposing encourages the user to organise his own sub-application environment in a novel way. However, our GENIE-M geometric editor has features that are in common with the hierarchy editors.

Hierarchy editors consist of interactive programs which browse through and modify, tree-like structures. Editors such as Walker's Document Editor [Walk81] and PEN are used specifically for document editing and are of related interest to us. Some editors (such as Walker's) include facilities for cross-referencing to show inter-structural linking, though these are not explicitly shown in the hierarchical structure. By way of contrast, GENIE-M's linking capability is portrayed by the geometric structure. Both cross-linking and topological data organisations in GENIE-M become natural products of one uniform structure, like ZOG [McCr84] and Textnet [Trigg86].

6.2. Information Structuring.

The drawback of existing integrated editor/formatters is that the high-level structure of the document is not well-represented [Furut82a]. 'Pagemaker' [Seyb85] on the Apple Macintosh [Vari84] exhibits cut-and-paste operations in preparing mixed-media documents with no proper overall structure. The implicit topological and geometric structure of a GENIE-M document is apparent, rather than obscured as in existing systems. This permits more flexible manipulation of logical document entities.

Hewitt's 'actors' [Hewit77] uses 'message passing' in viewing control structures, and are purely active objects with no recognition of any data structures. We are, however, interested in representing both the control and data structures using a message passing mechanism. The OPAL system [Ahls84] has the same interest in its concept of a 'packet' as the principal data and action structuring mechanism. A related area of research into actors formalism is used in a programming system by Byrd et. al. at IBM Thomas J. Watson Research Center

[Byrd82]. We intend to incorporate a similar message passing technique in our geometric data structure.

6.3. Information Interchange.

The format for interchange of information among remote components in GENIE-M is not a major aspect of our research at present. However, we anticipate ODA (Office Document Architecture), the ISO draft proposal for a logical document structure standard used primarily for information interchange (that is, transmission) as a likely candidate [ISO84].

6.4. Graphical User Interface.

The design of a user interface management tool to improve human-machine interactions is also an important concept in our design of GENIE-M. A discussion of User Interface Management Systems presented by Olsen et. al., identifies some of the major problems UIMS research should be addressing [Olsen84]. Other papers on the UIMS model can be found in [Thom83], [Ender84] and [Ender84a]. Interesting topics covered include: the interface of the UIMS to the application and graphics; and the structure of a UIMS. The design of the GENIE-M user interface is modelled closely upon UIMS features.

Traditional document systems show very little of their internal state to the user. Recent developments in screen editors, spreadsheets, and electronic desktops are making use of graphics to show as much of the state as possible on the computer screen. Examples are Xerox Star [Smith82], Apple's Lisa [Ehard83], Apple's Macintosh, Alis [Appl84], and Framework [Harr84], etc. A concise review of the current approaches to the use of windows in screen dialogues by application systems can be found in [Konsy85].

For GENIE-M we chose to use a menu-driven, windowed user interface that makes use of the 'cluttered desktop' concept of overlapping windows (examples are Xerox Star, Apple Lisa and Macintosh, etc). Nonetheless, our windowing interface has to associate with the underlying geometric model in order to allow users to transfer information between windows in a more structured manner than that provided in earlier systems. For example, a user can work on the text for a document in one window, and draw a figure for the document in another, which can then be transferred to the text window at any selected position in the document.

Commercial document environments like Framework by Ashton-Tate and Symphony by Lotus Development Corporation [Jadrn84], and others, provide extended capabilities, such as spreadsheets, word processing, database management systems, graphics, and communication software. Framework allows users to create documents using an 'outline' function; entries in the outline, such as a graph or a spreadsheet item, can be imported from different component packages. The way these systems integrate different tasks has caused an imbalance in that each package has grown around the success of one subportion of the task activities (for example, spreadsheet or word processing), and the others are only half-heartedly supported. The GENIE-M modular architecture, based on object-oriented programming methodology [Goldb83], [Cox84], and [Cox83], offers high-level integration of applications, and their task activities in a consistent user environment.

The users of GENIE-M will need sophisticated software tools for entering and viewing information. This support is likely to include editors for knowledge networks, composition tools for creating useful video or audio sequences and animation. The GENIE-M infrastructure allows convenient communication with editors and users at remote sites, and more.

7. Conclusion.

The GENIE-M model has the following objectives and advantages over non-integrated systems:

- Providing an integrated framework for handling data from diverse media types in a coherent fashion.
- Specifying and directing the manipulation of objects and relationships stored within a geometric data structure.
- Aiding the user in the processing and presentation of data using simple structure traversing and editing or formatting techniques.
- Monitoring and controlling the movement and modification of objects within an application environment, using access rights associated with parts or the whole of the object.
- Ensuring efficient use of the processing powers of different devices during data preparation and presentation through a modular architecture.
- Providing multiple-process message-passing primitives for intra- and inter-communication between data processing modules.

The model is widely applicable in many areas: a computer conferencing system where the ordered control of information is important; electronic multimedia documents; phototypesetting; distributed and semi-automated lecturing sessions where control of lecture devices (e.g. lectern, slides, projectors) and lecture notes are to be pre-specified within the document structure for interactive presentation; newspaper publication requiring a structured layout of information using current computer technology.

The ideas behind GENIE-M were initially developed using a PERQ 1. A GENIE-M prototype is currently being implemented on the SUN workstation[3] and VAX 11/780 under the UNIX[4] operating system, and written in the C programming language.

Acknowledgements.

This work is supported by grants from the Science and Engineering Research Council, and the Overseas Research Students Award Scheme.

---

[3] SUN Workstation is a registered trademark of SUN Microsystems, Inc.
[4] UNIX is a trademark of AT&T Bell Laboratories.

References.

[Ahls84]   Ahlsen, M.; Bjornerstedt, A.; Britts, S.; Hulten, C.; and Soderlund, L., "An Architecture for Object Management in OIS.", ACM Transactions on Office Information Systems, Vol. 2(3), Jul. 1984.

[Allen81]   Allen, T.; Nix, R.; and Perlis, A., "PEN: A Hierarchical Document Editor.", Proc. ACM SIGPLAN/SIGOA Symposium on Text Manipulation, Oregon, Vol. 2(1 & 2), June 1981.

[Appl84]   Applix, Inc., "Alis - A next-generation office software system from Applix: Application Summary.", , 1984.

[Brown84]   Brown, M.H.; and Sedgewick, R., "A System for Algorithm Animation.", Computer Graphics, Vol. 18(3), Jul. 1984.

[Brown86]   Brown, P., "Viewing Documents on a Screen.", CD-ROM: The New Papyrus; S. Lambert and S. Ropiequet (Eds.), Microsoft Press, 1986.

[Byrd82]   Byrd, R. J.; Smith, S. E.; and de Jong, S. P., "An Actor-Based Programming System.", ACM SIGOA Conference on Office Information System, Vol. 3(1/2), 1982.

[Chamb82]   Chamberlin D. D. et. al., "JANUS: An Interactive Document Formatter based on Declarative Tags.", IBM Systems Journal, Vol. 21(3) pp. 250-271, 1982.

[Cox83]   Cox, B. J., "The Object Oriented Pre-Compiler.", SIGPLAN Notices, Vol. 18(1), January 1983.

[Cox84]   Cox, B. J., "Message/Object Programming: An Evolutionary Change in Programming Technology.", IEEE Software, January 1984.

[Ehard83]   Ehardt, J.L., "Apple's Lisa: A Personal Office System.", The Seybold Report on Office Systems, Vol. 6(2), 24 Jan. 1983.

[Ender84]   Enderle, G., "The Interface of the UIMS to the Application (Working Group Report).", Computer Graphics Forum 3, North Holland, 1984.

[Ender84a]   Enderle, G., "Seeheim Workshop on User Interface Management Systems (First Report).", Computer Graphics Forum 3, North Holland, 1984.

[Fein82]   Feiner, S.; Nagy, S.; and Van Dam, A., "An Experimental System for Creating and Presenting Interactive Graphical Documents.", ACM Transactions of Graphics, Vol. 1(1), Jan. 1982.

[Furut82]   Furuta, R.; Scofield, J.; and Shaw, A., "Document Formatting Systems: Survey, Concepts and Issues.", Document Preparation Systems; J. Nievergelt, G. Coray, J.D. Nicoud and A.C. Shaw (Eds.) North-Holland, 1982.

[Furut82a]   Furuta, R.; Scofield, J.; and Shaw, S., "Document Formatting Systems: Survey, Concepts, and Issues.", Computing Surveys, Vol. 14(3), Sep. 1982.

[Goldb83]   Goldberg, A.; and Robson, D., "Smalltalk-80: The Language and its Implementation.", Reading, MA: Addison-Wesley, 1983.

[Gutkn84]   Gutknecht J.; and Winiger, W., "Andra: The Document Preparation System of the Personal Workstation Lilith.", Software - Practice and Experience, Vol. 14 pp. 73-100, 1984.

[Gutkn85]   Gutknecht, J., "Concepts of the Text Editor Lara.", Communications of the ACM, Vol. 28(9), September 1985.

[Harr84]   Harrison, B., "FRAMEWORK: An Introduction.", Ashton-Tate Publ., 1984.

[Herot80]   Herot, C.F., "Spatial Management of Data.", ACM Transactions on Database Systems, Vol. 5(4), Dec. 1980.

[Hewit77]   Hewitt, C., "Viewing Control Structures as Patterns of Passing Messages.", Artificial Intelligence, Vol. 8, 1977.

[ISO84]   ISO, "Information Processing - Text Preparation and Interchange - Text Structures - Part 2: Office Document Architecture.", ISO/TC 97/SC 18 N 267, Apr. 1984.

[Jadrn84]   Jadrnicek, R., "SYMPHONY: A Full-Orchestra Version of Lotus 1-2-3.", BYTE, Jul. 1984.

[Kimur86]   Kimura, G. D., "A Structure Editor for Abstract Document Objects.", IEEE Transactions on Software Engineering, Vol. SE-12(3), Mar. 1986.

[Knuth83]   Knuth, D. E., "The T_EXbook.", Addison-Wesley Publishing, Reading, MA, 1983.

[Konsy85]   Konsynski, B. R.; Greenfield, A.; and Bracker, W. E., Jr., "A View on Windows: Current Approaches and Neglected Opportunities.", AFIPS Conference Proceedings, 1985 National Computer Conference, Vol. 54, AFIPS Press, 1985.

[McCr84]   McCracken, D. L.; and Akscyn, R. M., "Experience with the ZOG Human-Computer Interface System.", International Journal of Man-Machine Studies, Vol. 21, 1984.

[Olsen84]   Olsen, D. R., Jr.; Buxton, W.; Ehrich, R.; Kasik, D. J.; Rhyne, J. R.; and Siber, "A Context for User Interface Management.", IEEE Computer Graphics and Application, Dec. 1984.

[Osin76]   Osin, L., "SMITH: How to produce CAI Courses without Programming.", International Journal of Man-Machine Studies, Vol. 8, 1976.

[Peels85]   Peels, A. J. H. M. et. al., "Document Architecture and Text Formatting.", ACM Transactions on Office Information Systems, Vol. 3(4), October 1985.

[Peter77]   Peterson, J. L., "Petri Nets.", Computing Surveys, Vol. 9, No. 3, September 1977.

[Seyb85]   Seybold, J., "An Imagesetter for the rest of us: Apple's Laserwriter", The Seybold Report on Publishing Systems, Vol.14(9), January 1985.

[Shash85]   Shasha, D., "NetBook - a Data Model to Support Knowledge Exploration.", Proceedings of VLDB 85, Stockholm, Aug. 1985.

[Smith82]   Smith, D. C.; Irby, C.; Kimball, R.; and Verplank, B., "Designing the Star User Interface.", BYTE, Apr. 1982.

[Thom83]   Thomas, J. J. (Workshop Chairman), "Graphical Input Interaction Technique Workshop Summary.", Computer Graphics, Vol. 17(1), Jan. 1983.

[Trigg86]   Trigg, R. H.; and Weiser, M., "TEXTNET: A Network-Based Approach to Text Handling.", ACM Trans. Office Information Systems, Vol. 4(1), January 1986.

[Vari84]   Various Authors, "The Apple Macintosh Computer.", BYTE, Vol. 9(2), February 1984.

[Walk81]   Walker, J. H., "The Document Editor: A Support Environment for Preparing Technical Documents.", Proc. ACM SIGPLAN/SIGOA Symposium on Text Manipulation, Oregon, Vol. 2(1 & 2), June 1981.

[Weyer82]   Weyer, S. A., "The Design of a Dynamic Book for Information Search.", International Journal of Man-Machine Studies, Vol. 17, 1982.

[Yourd78]   Yourdon, E.; and Constantine, L. L., "Structured Design: Fundamentals of a Discipline of Computer Program and Systems Design.", New York: Yourdon Press, 1978.

A COHERENT SPECIFICATION METHOD FOR THE USER INTERFACE OF DOCUMENTATION SYSTEMS

J. Preece, G Davies, M. Woodman and D.C.Ince

Computing Department, Faculty of Maths, Open University
Milton Keynes, MK76AA

ABSTRACT

There is no coherent methodology for specifying the design of the user interface of documentation systems. Foley and Van Dam [8] have produced a four stage methodology which provides a valuable framework for making design decisions. It is a landmark in interface design methodology; However, it has many weaknesses. For example, it is difficult to map from one stage to the next and the stages need refining into more usable sub-stages. In the first part of our paper we demonstrate the strengths and weaknesses of Foley and Van Dam's methodology by describing its application to a graphics documentation system. In the last part of our paper we describe the prototype of a new methodology.

1. Introduction

There are many variations of the definition of a user interface. Moran [1] takes the global view that 'the user interface consists of those aspects of the system that the user comes in contact with physically, perceptually and conceptually ,whilst those aspects that are hidden from the user are often known as the implementation.' However, he points out, that systems are generally not partitioned cleanly. This is because the designer is usually not aware of what will show through to the user. A typical system compels the user to be aware of some aspects of its implementation. Parnas [2] provides a more tractable definition; he has stated that that the user interface is 'the aspects of the system that the user sees'. Sibert [3] provides the fuller, but equally pragmatic definition. that the user interface is: 'the definition of all inputs from the user to the computer; the definition of all outputs from the computer to the user; and the definition of the sequencing of such inputs and outputs, which are made available to the computer user'.

Our work implies a pragmatic definition but we aspire towards Moran's view since it acknowledges the influence of the user's knowledge on the way he uses the system and hence on the user-orientated design considerations.

There is a need for an overall method of user interface design; much is written about the importance of design principles [4]. Moran [1], for example, has stated that 'the system should help the user without getting in his way (allowing him to concentrate on his task, not on the system); it should be efficient to use and easy to learn; it should be consistent, logical, 'natural'; amen.' There are also guidelines for the use of colour, size of text [5,6], styles of graphical displays and general screen design issues [7]. Unfortunately, a problem exists in utilizing many of these principles and guidelines: they tend to be either so specific that they cannot be generalized, or so general that that it is difficult to know how to apply them in particular examples. In any case there is, unfortunately, a serious shortage of work on embedding design principles and guidelines into a coherent and systematic interface design methodology.

The aim of this paper is to discuss a design methodology for creating the user interface to documentation systems (DMCUDS). The paper will first briefly review Foley and Van Dam's language model of interface design [8] as it provides the basis of our methodology. It will then point out some obvious strengths and weaknesses of their methodology, and in so doing so will refer briefly to other approaches currently in use. This discussion will be used as a basis for demonstrating how Foley and van Dam's language model can be applied to the design of the interface of part of a documentation system to produce Computer Science graphical representations [9] Using this example we shall demonstrate how the methodology can be refined and extended. Finally, we shall summarize the key points in our discussion and then describe our plans for the next stage of this research.

2. Methodologies for Designing the User Interface of Documentation Systems

Foley and van Dam have made one of the first attempts to define a complete methodology for specifying the design of a user interface. Having first described Foley and van Dam's methodology we shall briefly discuss two sets of proposed refinements [10,11]. Then we shall examine some of the weaknesses of the methodology with reference to some currently popular interface design perspectives. In particular, we shall focus on three perspectives. These are: user-orientated design, principle-orientated design, and grammar-orientated design.

2.1 Foley and van Dam's interface design methodology

Foley and Van Dam's language model [8] provides a top-down approach and is broadly based on an analogy between human dialogue and human-computer dialogue. Many of the ideas which are embodied in this methodology are similar to, or adapted from, earlier work on command language grammars (CLG) [1]. These grammars provide a representation for the user interface of interactive computer systems. A CLG is a representation that designers can use to create new systems and not a design methodology. Like Foley and Van Dam's methodology, its main advantage for the designer is that it guides him by ordering the decisions that he has to make; but does not help him to make those decisions.

After task analysis there are four design stages in Foley and Van Dam's methodology. These are: conceptual design, semantic design, syntactic design and lexical design.

Conceptual design defines the key application concepts that must be mastered by the user. It is the 'user' model of the application. This conceptual model is defined in terms of objects or classes of objects and their attributes; relationships between the objects; and the actions on the objects. For example, a simple text editor has objects which are lines and files. The relationship between the objects is that files are sequences of lines. The actions on a line are insert, delete, move and copy, and the actions on a file are create, delete, insert rename, and copy.

Semantic design specifies the detailed functionality of the interface but not its form; that is, what information is needed for each action on an object, the semantic errors that may occur and how they are handled, and the results of each action.

Syntactic design defines the sequence of inputs and outputs. For input, this is the grammar: the rules by which sequences of tokens (i.e. words) in the language are formed. The input tokens are typically commands, positions, quantities, and text; the output tokens are whole units of meaning conveyed graphically as symbols, drawings and text. Foley and van Dam suggest the use of state transition diagrams and a BNF notation for specifying input and screen 'mock-ups' for specifying output. However, they provide little guidance on how to produce this design stage.

Lexical design determines how input and output tokens are formed from the available lexemes of the hardware primitives. The commands available from a mouse and screen and presses of individual keys or function keys are examples of lexical input. Lines and characters and their attributes such as colour and position are examples of output. In practice, it appears that the syntactic and lexical design stages are so closely associated in the design process [3] that they are often dealt with together. As with the lexical design stage, little advice is given on how to produce this stage of the design.

It has become apparent to us that main value of Foley and van Dam's methodology was as a 'thinking tool'. It provides a framework for defining the different parts of the design process so that each can be considered in turn, while, at the same time, keeping the overall design coherent by building upon the previous stages of the design in a top-down fashion. Working in this way the designer starts by focusing on the user and ends with machine. Therefore, implementation issues are postponed until the end.

The obvious weaknesses of the methodology are that it pays little attention to the difficulty of matching the conceptual model used in the design with users' models of the system. The design stages need breaking down into smaller sub-units as there is far too much to consider at each stage. In addition the mapping between the stages is difficult. The syntactic and lexical stages need a lot more development and a formal grammar for specifying these stages should be included. Guidance is needed also on how to embed design guidelines into the design.

After practically applying the methodology to the interface design of a graphics documentation system we reached the same conclusions and also discovered other, less obvious problems.

2.2 Buxton and Nielsen's work

Refinements to the Foley and Van Dam methodology are provided by Buxton [10] and Nielsen [11], who focus on the need for including additional design stages.

Buxton proposes breaking the lexical level down into lexical issues which have to do with the spelling of tokens (i.e. the order and nature of lexemes) and pragmatic issues which are concerned with issues of gesture, space and devices. (This is not a completely new idea; Moran used it in his CLG [1]).

Buxton proposes this refinement as 'the primary level of contact with an interactive system is at the level of pragmatics, this level has one of the strongest effects on the user's perception of the system.' He also claims that there is an important interplay between the syntactic and pragmatic levels concerned with principles of chunking and closure [12].

Closure being concerned with combining actions into a single gesture and chunking being concerned with deciding when an action is complete and remaining in its present state until the user decides to change it again. He suggests that by correctly applying these principles, the cognitive burden of learning and using a system could be reduced.

Nielsen presents a 'virtual protocol model of computer-human interaction' [11], which has so much in common with the Foley and van Dam methodology that it is reasonable to regard it as a refinement. It is based on 'viewing the interaction as a hierarchy of virtual protocol dialogues. Each virtual protocol realizes the dialogue on the level above itself and is in turn supported by a lower-level protocol. The virtual dialogue approach enables the separation of technical features of new devices (e.g. a mouse or a graphical display) from the conceptual features (e.g. menus or windows)'

Nielsen's model has 7 levels:

- The *goal level* is the goal that the user wishes to realize, e.g. deleting the last sentence in a letter.

- The *task level* deals with computer-related concepts that are representations of the real world concepts from level 7. e.g. certain lines of the text are changed.

- The *semantic level* is concerned with the detailed functionality of the system; exactly what each operation does to each object.

- The *syntactic level* deals with the sequence of input and output tokens that are exchanged.

- The *lexical level* is concerned with the information carrying symbols of the interaction, i.e. the interpretation of tokens.

- The *alphabetical level* contains the primitive information carrying units, i.e. the lexemes.

- The *physical level* is where there is an observable interchange of physical information in the form of light, sound, key presses, mouse movements etc.

The addition of the last two stages may provide useful refinements, which are also in line with Buxton's ideas. However, without applying these suggestions to the design of an interface for a real documentation system it is difficult to comment further on their value.

2.3 User-orientated design

A criticism of Foley and van Dam's methodology is that it fails to provide guidance on how designers may obtain suitable conceptual models upon which to base their designs. It is now widely accepted [13,14,15] that performance on any task, whether it is using a documentation system or some other task, is greatly affected by the knowledge and experience the task initiator brings to that task. This ,in turn, influences the model that the user develops; this personal model is often referred to as the *user's mental model* to distinguish it from the designers conceptual model, which represents how the designer expects the user to view the system.

A good design will incorporate a conceptual model which maps well with the mental models of the users. However, in practice, since users often approach a system with widely differing experiences the mapping between the two may not be as close as the designer might wish.

A system which has features that are intuitive and also easy to learn will facilitate users in developing models which match closely with the designer's conceptual model. It is for this reason that there is a trend for designers to seek appropriate and easy to understand metaphors from everyday life as conceptual models for their systems. The best example of this is the desk-top metaphor of the Macintosh.

Moran [1] succinctly expresses the relationship between the design of the user interface and the user's mental model: 'any aspect of the system that enters the user's model is part of the user interface. To design the user interface of a system is to design the user's model.'

The information required for the designer to produce a good conceptual model comes from knowing how users behave when using the system. Consequently, user-orientated designers, usually advocate basing their designs on empirical evidence. Prototyping is one useful technique for collecting this evidence [16]. However, a problem with this approach is that the designer must start with his own best guess as the basis for the design and obviously this considerably influences the design [17].

An extreme version of the empirically based design is the user devised interface of Good et al. [18]. They built an electronic mail facility purely by observing the behavior of users, who were given no instructions, guessing how to use the system.

There are clear advantages and disadvantages to any user-orientated approach to interface design: the end product is likely to 'fit' the users better but it will take a longer time to produce.

2. 3 Principle-orientated design

Researchers at the University of York have devised an interface design methodology based on the use of 'generative user engineering principles', known as 'gueps'. They have tried to facilitate design by bridging the gap between the user and the designer by providing a higher-order consistency on the interface [19]. 'Predictability' is an example of a guep. A predictable system is one that enables you to decide what to do next on the basis of what is displayed on the screen alone, and it can be Formalized as described by Dix et al. [20].

The value of such an approach is that it provides a framework for taking design decisions. For example, if it was discovered that predictibility lead to benefits for the user then it could be embedded with an enhanced version of the Foley and van Dam methodology, and would have desirable affects for both users and designers of documentation systems.

2.4 Grammar-orientated design

We have said already that the syntactic and lexical stages of Foley and van Dam's methodology are ill defined, poorly developed and lack a formal specification methodology. Reisner's work [21] provides an early example of a grammar-orientated interface design approach, which has been used by several authors more recently, for example by Payne [22]. Reisner used an action-grammar based on BNF notation to specify and compare two versions of a user interface for a graphics system. The grammar described the actions that were performed by the user to construct various shapes. Examining the grammar enabled her to compare aspects such as the number of steps required to complete a task and the consistency of the design. Incorporating a technique like this into the Foley and Van Dam methodology would not only help the designer at the syntactic and lexical design stages, but would also facilitate user testing.

3. Applying Foely and Van Dam's Methodology: A Graphics Documentation System for Computer Scientists

In this section we shall show how the Foley and Van Dam methodology is applied in the design of a graphics system for Computer Scientists. This is one of the products from an Alvey funded project which aims to construct an environment for the rapid prototyping of graphical software tools.

The description shown below refers to a system for editing and displaying a graphical notation known as a data flow diagram. Such a diagram consist of a number of boxes (sources and sinks), circles (processes) two parallel lines (databases). These objects being joined by arrowed flow lines. A simple example of a data flow diagram is shown in Figure 1.

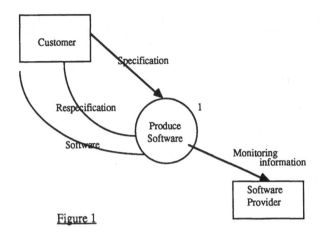

Figure 1

We have concentrated on the first two design stages: conceptual design and semantic design. The reason for this is because it is unclear how to develop the syntactic and lexical stages beyond the general description given in the literature.

We have added comments to the description that follows to show where we have developed the methodology beyond the descriptions given in references [1,3]. *These comments are in italics and enclosed in brackets.*

3.1 Conceptual design

The **objects** in the system are the components of data flow diagrams, namely:

*data flow picture (i.e. the whole diagram)

*refinement of the data flow picture

source (   )

sink (   )

process (   )

dataflow (   )

database/file(   )

(text)

(The star next to data flow picture and refinement of data flow picture indicate that they are different from the other objects; they are made up of the other objects and so can be thought of as meta-objects. This distinction may become more important later, because the actions on these

meta-objects are different from the other objects. Text is in brackets as it may be more useful to regard it as an attribute as we shall see later; the reason for regarding text as an object is that it has its own attributes such as font type, position, size, case type, etc.)

The **relations** between these objects are as follows:

    a dataflow picture contains all the other objects

    refinement of data flow picture decomposes into a more detailed data flow diagram

    data flows connect source with sink via process

    a database is connected to other objects by data flows.

The **attributes** of the objects are:

    source - size, position, text, shading

    sink - size, position, text, shading

    process - size, position, text, shading

    database - size, position, text, shading

    data flow - size, start position, end position, text, curved or straight

    *data flow picture - text

    *refinement of data flow picture - text

    (text) - font type, size, position, character type and size

There are three types of **actions** on the objects are:

    1. Creating or deleting any of the objects listed (basic).

    2. Adding, removing or changing an attribute of an object. (enhancing).

    3. Saving, wiping, shrinking or enlarging the whole picture. (global).

(Foley and Van Dam's description of the methodology does not recognize different kinds of actions, but these distinctions are important in later stages of the design methodology [23].

3.2 Semantic design

    The semantic design is concerned with the functionality of the system: 'what the screen looks like and what the user can do', but not how these things are achieved in the implementation. The link between the semantic design and the conceptual design is through the actions which affect the objects, attributes and relations. Hence, the definitions from the conceptual stage of the design are maintained and the design is functionally developed.

Below is a typical specification for the semantics of a single function. The action on the object is specified as a function with parameters which are the attributes of the object. The description and feedback describe the results of the action. This is the first stage in the design process when feedback and error handling are considered by the designer.

Function
    Create_ object

Parameters
    Symbol_identifier *(i.e. circle, which we do not need to include since we have said that the name and symbol are synonymous)*
    Symbol_position *(e.g. 50,50 i.e. centre of 100 x 100 screen)*
    Symbol_size *(e.g. some default value)*
    (parameters are used in the normal way, but the designer has to think back to her conceptual design - the symbol_identifier is one of the objects defined in the conceptual stage and the symbol_position is an attribute of the object)

Description
    A process symbol of standard default size is created in the centre of the screen. It is now the currently selected object and any further operations apply to it

    (Further actions on this object might result in changing the attributes of the object, or causing some global change to the system but Foley and Van Dam do not distinguish between different kinds of actions)

Feedback
    It appears on the screen highlighted. The feedback which would be needed is:
    1. The result of the last event
    2. Error messages *(see errors mentioned below)*
    3. Selection of commands

Errors
    1. The symbol_identifier is unknown (could be engineered out by use of menu for selecting a symbol).
    2. The symbol_position is outside the viewport (could be engineered out by constraining positioning device to viewport)
    (3. Breaking syntax rules for data flow diagrams such as a sink cannot be attached to another sink etc.
    4. Breaking layout rules such as process cannot over-lap another symbol etc.)

3.3 Some Observations and Conclusions

From our example it can be seen that the Foley and van Dam methodology provides a good framework for decision making; it helps the designer to concentrate on particular types of decisions at certain times. It does not, however, provide much guidance on how to develop the syntactic and lexical levels of the design, nor is it easy to see always how the conceptual level maps onto the semantic level. (A more detailed discussion of some of these points is provided in Preece et al. [23]) In the next section we shall show how we have refined Foley and van Dam's methodology so that mapping between design stages is clearer and the stages themselves are broken down into sub-stages. Again we concentrate on the conceptual and semantic stages, but we also propose some initial ideas to show how the syntactic and lexical stages could be developed along the same lines.

4. A Prototype Methodology for Human Interface Design of Documentation Systems

4.1 Over-view and top level

Our refinement involves a typical system of top-down design, which is generally carried out prior to writing program code. As specified it is, however, rather sequential and takes the form shown below. It is more realistic to consider it is as a model similar to the software life cycle as can be seen by comparing Figures 2a and 2b.

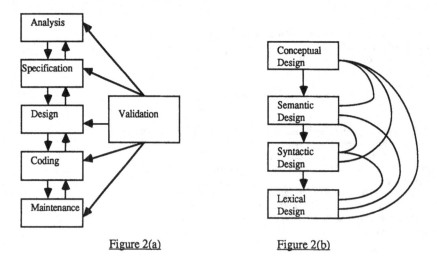

Figure 2(a)

Figure 2(b)

The software life cycle consists of five stages which are undertaken sequentially, but with constant reference from one stage back to previous stages. The end of a stage is accompanied by verification that development from the previous stage to the finished stage accurately produces what is intended. A similar process of reference to previous design stages and verification must take place in interface design.

In the design that follows we have taken the four stages of the Foley and van Dam methodology as the top level of our methodology to produce the interface for a subsystem of our graphics documentation system and then refined them.

We have incorporated the developments that we suggested in the previous section and have also added many new ideas such as how to build in feedback, layout rules and rule for ensuring the correct syntax of the particular category of design being produced by the user.

4.2 Design for methodology

1. Specify conceptual design
   1.1 Specify components (i.e. objects) of diagram
       (e.g. source, sink, process, data flow, file -The symbols are also specified and are synonymous with the names)
       1.1.1 List attributes of objects (e.g. size, position, labeling, shading etc.)

   1.2 Specify relations between objects
       (These will be the rules for creating the diagram - e.g. the syntax of data flow diagrams-e.g. source must be connected to a sink via at least one process, decomposition/refinement rules)
       1.2.1 Specify which objects can be joined by data flows
       1.2.2 Specify rules of refinement.

   1.3 Specify main layout considerations
       (These are layout guidelines which will become rules-e.g. size of display area, proximity of objects, size and position of objects, readability of text-not incorporated by Foley and van Dam)
       1.3.1 Size of display area
       1.3.2 Proximity of objects
       1.3.3 Size and position of objects
       1.3.4 Readability of text

   1.4 Specify main facilities for user. (i.e. actions and facilities provided by system)
       1.4.1 Group actions which affect applications system (e.g. Creating, deleting symbols, refining diagrams, wiping screen)
           *1.4.1.1 Group actions which affect whole or specified part of display-*global action
               (e.g. wiping shrinking, enlarging, refining)
               *1.4.1.1.1 Group actions which affect objects-*basic action (e.g. creating, deleting shading, moving)
               *1..4.1.1.2 Group actions which affect attribute-*enhancing action(e.g. move or change size of an object)
       *1.4.2 Group actions carried out by external system-*external system action(e.g. Saving display, renaming file in which display is saved etc.)

2. Specify semantic design
   2.1 Specify function (i.e. basic action)
      2.1.1 Select type of action (as defined in refinements of 1.4)
      2.1.2.Select object (as defined in refinements of 1.1.1)
         {Comments can be used any where in the design but would be
         particularly helpful here as a reminder of what should happen
         after these refinements}
   2.2 Specify parameters of object { select appropriate attributes from refinement 1.1.1}
   2.3 Specify feedback (i.e. response to user)
      2.3.1 Indicate that requested action has been processed
         2.3.1.1 Show that action has been successfully completed (e.g. show currently created
            object highlighted)
         2.3.1.2. Show what can be done next (e.g. continue, save refine etc.)
      2.3.2 Display error messages
         2.3.2.1 Object not available (e.g. if misspelled)
         2.3.2.2. Attribute not possible (e.g. position off screen, object already shaded etc.)
         2.3.2.3 Relations cannot be maintained (i.e. syntax rules for diagram broken)
         2.3.2.4 Layout rules contravened.
      2.3.3 Display any messages about the state of the external system.

3. Specify syntactic design
   3.1 Write rules for syntax of diagram as a grammar
      3.1.1 Specify how rules are constructed
   3.2 Write rules for layout as a grammar
      3.2.1 Specify how rules are constructed
   3.3 Write rules for sequencing of operations (e.g. you cannot create an attribute before
   creating an object)
      3.3.1 Specify how rules are constructed

4. Specify lexical design {how actions will be realized using the available hardware}
   4.1 Specify style of displayed information.
   4.2 Specify how actions will be achieved (e.g. suppose mouse and keyboard are input
   devices and screen is output device)
      4.2.1 Specify what user will type in full
      4.2.2 Specify what function keys are available
      4.2.3 Specify when mouse will be used
         4.2.3.1 Specify what can be dragged
         4.2.3.1 Specify when click will be used
            4.2.3.2.1 State which states are affected by single click and how.
            4.2.3.2.1 State which states are affected by double click and how

5. Summary and Future Research

We have demonstrated, both through theoretical discussion and practical application, that with further refinement the Foley and Van Dam design methodology has holds great potential for the design of user interfaces for documentation systems. The methodology becomes more useful when broken down into substages using a program design language; this also facilitates mapping between stages, which is problem with the original methodology.

Another advantage is that decisions involving guidelines for screen design and rules for user development of specific kinds of diagrams, such as data flow diagrams, can be built into the methodology. Our design also provides scope for developing a conceptual model which will 'fit' users more accurately than at present. Points at which various stages of the design are tested with users are built in.

Buxton's and Nielsen's suggestions for sub-dividing the syntactic and lexical stages will be addressed in the next stage of the work. The need for providing a formal grammar to define these stages will be given high priority, and the idea of incorporating guiding principles such as predictability will be considered.

References

[1] Moran T. P., The Command Language Grammar: a Representation for the User Interface of Interactive Computer Systems. *Int. J Man-Machine Studies.* **15**, 3-50, 1981.

[2] Parnas D.L., On the Use of Transition Diagrams in the Design of a User Interface for an Interactive Computer System. *Proceedings 24th National ACM Conference.* New York, 1969.

[3] Sibert R., Workstation User Interface Design. Computer Graphics Consultants, Inc. 1982.

[4] Gould J.D. and Lewis C., Designing for Usability: Key Principles and What Designers Think. *Comms. of the ACM,* 28, 300-310, 1985

[5] Sutherland S., PRESTEL and the User: A Survey of Psychological and Ergonomics Research, University of Sussex, 1980.

[6] Reynolds L., The Presentation of Bibliographic Information on Prestel, *Royal College of Art, BL R & D Report 5536,* 1980.

[7] Davis E.G. and Swezey R.W., Human Factors Guidelines in Computer Graphics: a Case Study. *Int. J. Man-Machine Studies,* **18**, 113-133, 1983.

[8] Foley J.D. and van Dam A., *Fundamentals of Interactive Computer Graphics,* Addison-Wesley, 1982.

[9] Ince D.C. Syntactic Description of Graphical Notations and Its Application to the Rapid Construction of Software Tools. S.E.R.C Grant GR/D/60362.

[10] Buxton W., Lexical and Pragmatic Considerations of Input Structures. *Computer Graphics*. 31-37, January 1983.

[11] Nielsen J., A Virtual Model for Computer-human Interaction. *Int. J. Man-Machine Studies*. 24, 301-312, 1986.

[12] Biggs J.B. and Collis K.F., *Evaluating the Quality of Learning: The SOLO Taxonomy (Structure of Observed Learning Outcome)*. Academic Press 1982.

[13] Gentner, D and Stevens, A. L., Mental Models. Lawrence Erlbaum Associates. New Jersey, U.S.A. 1983.

[14] Norman, D.A., Some Observations on Mental Models. In *Mental Models*. (Gentner, D. and Stevens, A. L. Eds.). Lawrence Earlbaum Associates. New Jersey. U.S.A. 1983.

[15] Wason, P. C. and Johnson-Laird, P. N., in *Analogical Processes in Learning* (Rummelhardt, D.E. and Norman, D. A. Eds.). CHIP 97, Centre for Human Information Processing, University of California, San Diego, USA. 1980.

[16] Hekmatpour S and Ince D.C., A Review of Software Prototyping. *Oxford Surveys in Information Technology*. 1987 (To Appear).

[17] Monk A., A Procedure for Identifying Unpredictability, Unnecessary Complexity, Inconsistency and Effects Which are Hard to Reverse. *Proceedings CHI*. York. 1987. (To Appear).

[18] Good M. D., Whiteside J. A,. Wixon D. R., and Jones S. J., Building a User-derived Interface. *Comms. of the ACM*, 27, 1032-1043, 1984.

[19] Thimbleby H., User Interface Design: Generative Engineering Principles. In *Fundamentals of Human-computer Interaction*. (A. Monk. Ed.). Academic Press, 1985.

[20] Dix A. J., Harrison M. D., Runciman C. and Thimbleby H. W., Two Working Papers on Formalizing Interactive System Design. *University of York. Report YCS.75*. 1985.

[21] Reisner, P., Formal Grammar and Human Factors Design of an Interactive Graphics System. *IEEE Transactions on Software Engineering*, 7, No. 2, March, 1981.

[22] Payne S.J., Task-action Grammars. In *Human-Computer Interaction, Interact '84*. (B Shackel (Ed.)). North-Holland 527-532, 1984.

[23] Preece J., Davies G., Ince D., Woodman M. Specifying the User Interface. *CDFM Technical Report 86/6*. Computing Dept, Open University MIlton Keynes. 1986

A Graded Interface for Novice/Expert Interaction

MICHAEL D. BUTCHER

Department of Mathematics and Computer Science, University College of Swansea,
Singleton Park, Swansea SA2 8PP, W. Glam., U.K.

Abstract

As the diversity and number of potential users of interactive computer systems increases, there is a growing awareness that the design of the user-machine interface is crucial for their efficiency and acceptability. Systems designers often talk of the fundamental dilemma in dialogue design being the conflict between making an interface easy to use for novices and quick and sophisticated for expert users. This so-called 'trade-off' has become so well established that one could be forgiven for believing that the form of dialogue either suits novices *or* experts, but cannot cater for both.

This paper describes a model for an Interactive Graphic Interface (IGI) to an Electronic Office System (EOS) which is currently being developed at the Computer Science Department of the University College of Swansea. Attention is focused on utilities available within the system which give a graded, consistent interface across a range of users of varying experiences. That is, both novices and experts interact with the system in the same style but the nature of the interface allows experienced users to proceed more rapidly towards their goals.

Key Words : user classification, screen, location cues, excursion,interactive-deadlock.

User Classification and Interface Design

Since there have been no long-term studies on user classification, it is difficult to evaluate the benefits of such classification on interface design. While some designers ignore user classification entirely, others claim that interface design cannot proceed without it [1].

Based on the assumption that different types of users need different types of interfaces, there are several approaches to design. One method is to have a different interface for each intended user group. This, however, creates problems with users at boundaries between groups and with users graduating from one group to another. In addition, a user may be expert in some areas and inexperienced in others causing inconsistencies in any attempted classification. A possible solution is to have users assess their own abilities and explicitly state at which level they wish to interact with the system. Such a system of self-classification may cause users to resent having labels (eg. 'novice') associated with their individual abilities, resulting in attempts to interact with the system at levels too high for their competency.

Another approach to interface design is a mixed-style interactive dialogue where casual users interact with the system via descriptive menus and experienced users are able to take 'short-cuts' by issuing direct commands. However, this can cause confusion as users have to learn two styles of interaction in parallel (and a greater number of commands) which places a burden on short-term memory. What is apparent is that some sort of graded interface is required which is consistent across a range of users in that the interactive style remains the same, but that the flexibility of the design allows users to interact at the skill level to which they are best suited.

The IGI model incorporates an interface with a single style of interaction for all users and does not explicitly distinguish between the skill level of individuals. However, users familiar with the system are able to proceed more directly towards their goals, while novices can still sequence through the menu hierarchy until they feel more confident about taking short-cuts.

Model Structure

Prior to commencing a session with any interactive system, it is assumed that a user has a specific goal, or set of goals, in mind. Rather than issuing complex command sequences from a keyboard (which are often incorrectly typed) users, especially novices, are tending to prefer to perform a series of sub-tasks where their goal is achieved in stages. Menus and 'pick' devices have become a common and attractive alternative to using a keyboard where, at each in the dialogue, a fresh menu can be generated for that instance which does not contain any redundant keys [2].

The sequence of choices which a user makes on the way to achieving a goal can be represented by paths within a tree, Figure 1. At each of the nodes, a to s, information is presented to the user within the context of a 'screen'. A menu displays options pertinent to the current screen where selection of an option will either achieve the desired goal/sub-goal, or reveal another menu at a greater depth in the hierarchy.

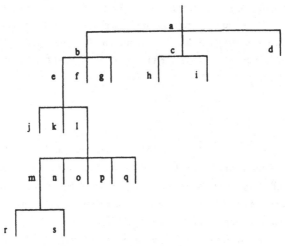

Figure 1

Each screen in the IGI model is divided into two functionally distinct areas. In the 'command area' are displayed all menu options which may be selected at the current screen. The 'display area' displays any information relevant to a particular option selection. Presenting all options pertinent to the current screen means that there is no searching for commands as they are all visible. This contrasts to the 'pull-down' menu approach where a user may have to pull-down several menus before locating the required command.

Depth Vs. Breadth

When designing menus for a hierarchical system careful consideration should be given to menu-selection parameters : 'How many options are appropriate for a single menu ?', and 'Does a deep menu lead to loss of orientation ?' [3].

Menu hierarchies can be arranged with many options in a menu and a minimal number of menus (breadth) or with few options in each menu and a greater number of levels (depth). Trend analysis indicates that search speed and accuracy improve as a function of menu breadth. In addition, the response times for the broadest menu structure are relatively unaffected by practice, whereas response times for the deepest hierarchy become faster with practice [4].

The trade-off between depth and breadth appears to follow a trade-off between two human-performance measures : visual scanning and short-term memory. Asking a user to select one option from many displayed within a single menu places a strain on visual scanning. At the other extreme, with a deeper hierarchy having fewer option choices and more menus, the load on short-term memory increases. As users move through deeper levels of a hierarchy, their ability and the time taken to correctly select an option depends on their memory for previous selections.

In the IGI model, a compromise has been adopted on the depth-breadth trade-off, with the number of options appearing in the command area never exceeding six. This places little burden on the users visual scanning abilities and minimal strain on short-term memory. It has been suggested [3] that 'help' fields of upcoming options would be most beneficial in improving user performance in searching through deep menus. These are incorporated in IGI within the on-line 'help facility' and 'navigational' aids.

Location Cues

It is intended that 'location cues' should serve to remind users of their current position in the system without attracting attention away from the task in hand. These cues comprise a set of screen attributes which collectively identify a screen with a specific location in the menu hierarchy. The attributes consist of a depth indicator, a screen colour and a unique screen title.

The depth indicator, d, appears in the top right-hand corner of the display area and indicates the level at which the current screen lies within the hierarchy. When $d = 0$, the current screen is at the top level and a value of n indicates that the current screen is n levels below the root. So for an m level hierarchy, the range of d is, $\{ d \mid 0 \leq d \leq m - 1 \}$.

Colour also acts as a depth indicator with all screens at the same level having the same colour attribute. Colour can make displays more appealing, helps show logical connections between system states and enhances safety (eg. red can call attention to dangerous situations) [5]. However, all too often computer displays have a tendency to employ too many colours even when only a few are available. To counter this tendancy, an approach using a limited set of well chosen colours creates a system more readily acceptable to the user and maintains consistency across content areas.

In addition to the depth indicator and colour attribute, each screen has a unique screen title which identifies a screen at a given level. As users become more familiar with the system, they will intuitively associate a screen's attributes with a specific location in the hierarchy. These location cues are designed to supplement the more detailed 'navigation aids'.

Navigation

During the earliest stages of learning, user knowledge of a system and its dialogue is likely to be incomplete. Under such circumstances it seems reasonable to assume that users will need to make a number of attempts before succeeding at each task goal [6]. A frequent criticism of menu systems is that users can become disorientated and be forced to ask the question, 'Where am I ?'. It is important that users feel in the control of the system and to make control possible they must know :

i)   Where they have been;
ii)   Where they are;
iii) Where they can go from their current location.

To incorporate such knowledge, IGI provides a 'navigation facility' which may be summoned at any screen. A 'conceptual map' of the system is then displayed showing the menu hierarchy, the users current location and the decision path which lead there, Figure 2.

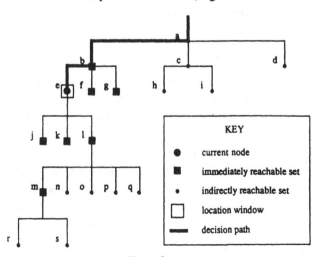

Figure 2

The map gives a preview of where additional steps down the tree would lead and by providing a lateral view of adjacent nodes, users are assisted in establishing their current position [7].

Novice and Expert Interaction

While well suited to the novice, menus can be too verbose and tedious for experienced users, constantly requiring them to sequence through many levels before achieving the required goal. A related problem concerns the activity of 'retreating' after the user has either made a mistake or changed goal. The IGI model achieves flexibility by allowing users to 'jump' about within the tree without being constrained to follow the usual menu sequences.

In Figure 2, node e is the users current location in the tree structure and is termed the 'current node'. The set of nodes $R = \{b,e,f,g,j,k,l,m\}$ are 'immediately reachable' from the current node. This means that a user may jump directly to any node in R without having to sequence through the usual menus. The current node may be altered by simply moving the 'location window' to any node in R which then becomes current. All other nodes not in R form the set of nodes which are 'indirectly reachable' from the current node and is denoted by $R' = \{a,c,d,h,i,n,o,p,q,r,s\}$. This means that at least one intermediate node must be visited to reach any node in R' from the current node. Should a user move the location window to select a node in R', a message is displayed indicating that the target node is not directly reachable from the current node. The location window then returns to its initial location. For each node in the tree, a unique R and R' exist. Thus, for two distinct nodes N_i and N_j $(i \neq j)$, $R_i \neq R_j$ and $R'_i \neq R'_j$. From this, it follows that $R_i \cap R'_i = \{\}$, for all i.

It is anticipated that, although this facility is available to all users, advanced users will benefit most by being able to proceed more rapidly towards their goals. Novices, on the other hand, can initially follow the menu hierarchy and, as they become familiar with the system and gain confidence, can gradually make greater use of the 'jump' facility.

Help Facility

Studies have shown that one of the most significant factors affecting user-perceived quality in an interactive system is that it be self-descriptive [8] . That is, for any menu, a 'help-facility' should be available pertinent to the current dialogue situation. The design of user-orientated systems is complicated by the fact that novices and experienced users have differing preferences regarding system characteristics. Novices may find that qualities of self-descriptiveness and fault tolerance are important while more experienced users emphasise the need for greater user-control. It is recommended that man-machine dialogue systems be designed so as to make them more self-explanatory, and hence, more user-friendly, by the inclusion of a dialogue form called an 'excursion tour' [9]. Essentially an excursion is an extended tutorial which is available to the user on-line at any point in the dialogue.

Within a hierarchical menu system a user selects an option at each menu on the path to completing a goal. However, if on coming to a specific location in the hierarchy a user finds that either no command exists that will further an essential sub-goal, or if it does exist but the user has no way of discovering the command within the system, then 'interactive deadlock' results [8]. Such a situation precludes any further progress until the appropriate command can become known.

The worst situation occurs when the user does not know a command required to perform an essential step in the task, and the system provides no help to the user at this point in the dialogue. Using Petri net notation [10], where features of a system are described in terms of 'states' and 'transitions' between states, Figure 3 illustrates a situation in which interactive deadlock can occur. P_1 and P_2 are 'places' in the marked Petri net of Figure 3 which correspond to adjacent nodes in a tree.

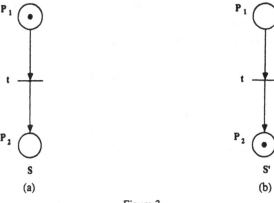

Figure 3

In Figure 3(a), S is the current system state and the current location is P_1. Transition, t, causes the system state to change to S' and the current location to P_2, Figure 3(b). A situation of interactive deadlock occurs if the user does not know one of the following :

i)   the command , c, corresponding to t, which maps the system from S to S';

ii)   the effect, e, of c on the resulting system state S'.

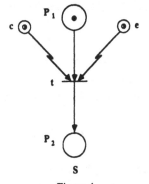

Figure 4

Thus, even if t is 'enabled', ie. ready to be executed ('fired'), interactive deadlock may occur if either c or e are unknown. Figure 4 represents a situation where t is enabled but can only be fired if c and e are also known. Two types of token are used :

- system token - governs the execution of the Petri net;
- user token - denotes that both c and e must be known to enable t.

The enabling conditions for such a transition, t, in a dialogue system now include the existence of a command, c, and an effect, e, corresponding to t such that :

i)   c and e are 'knowable' in S, that is, the user knows or is able to learn c and e in S;
ii)   c is 'applicable' in S, that is, the system will accept c in S;
iii) c is 'processible' in S, that is, the system has the means for processing c in S.

Interactive deadlock therefore arises through the occurrence of one of the following conditions :

C1.   There is no command, c, applicable in S, leading to the enabling of t;
C2.   Such a command, c, exists but the user does not know c and cannot learn c in S;
C3.   c exists and is known in S but the effect, e, of command c is unknown and cannot be learnt in S.

Interactive deadlocks resulting from a violation of C1 are caused by design deficiencies and would usually be found in incomplete or experimental systems. When an interactive deadlock caused by a violation of C2 or C3 occurs, the user almost always has some way of finding the appropriate command and effect by consulting system manuals/user-guides etc., but this would go against the user-perceived quality of self-descriptiveness. That is, a user should not have to go outside the system in order to learn what commands are applicable in a particular state [7].

In the IGI model, all commands applicable at a given location are displayed in the menu for that specific screen. Thus, a situation in which a command is unknown can never arise as all command options are presented at each stage in the dialogue. However, a related type of interactive deadlock occurs when either :

i)   Users are unsure which of the commands presented will further their sub-task;
ii)   Users know which command to use but are reluctant to proceed further as they are uncertain of the effect of the command on the system status.

IGI offers a 'help-facility' in the form of an excursion tour detailing each command, c, and its effect, e, on the system state. An excursion, E, on a dialogue state, S, may be defined as a sequence of transitions, starting and ending in S, where each transition is the execution of an excursion command. Thus, in state S, a sufficient condition for a transition, t, to fire taking the system state to S', is that c and e are 'knowable' in S. That is, c and e can be displayed in S or in some excursion on S.

Summary

The proliferation of systems where man interacts with machines has highlighted the significance of 'good' interface design. What constitutes a 'good' interface is, however, not clearly understood and is the subject of much of the current research in the field of human-computer interaction. A major problem hindering the progress of such research is the general lack of communication between the system-designer and the end-user or, if there is communication, users are often unable to be precise about their requirements. This situation has frequently lead to the design of a system where the interface has been 'tacked' on in the final stages instead of being included in the development phase.

One way to facilitate design is to actively employ a 'user-model' to try to bridge the conceptual gap between the user and designer. However, this pre-supposes the existence of a model which can accurately represent the user. Matters are made more complex as users are non-homogeneous, with differing preferences and attitudes. As a consequence, many key design issues remain unresolved : should a designer be more sensitive to the needs of the novice, or of the advanced user ? ; are all users able to grasp system concepts and learn at the same rate ?

It is important that a rigid framework is not imposed upon users, forcing them to modify their behaviour patterns to conform to the system structure. A pragmatic approach to interface design is required, with the development of a more general user-model so that a systems' behaviour can be constrained to be compatible with it.

References

[1]   Moderator : Potosnak K., Panelists : Hayes P.J., Rosson M.B., Schneider M.L., 'Panel : Classifying Users : A Hard Look at Some Controversial Issues', Human Factors in Computing Systems, CHI '86 Conference Proceedings, April 13-17, 1986, Boston, U.S.A.

[2]   Edmonds E., 'The man-computer interface : a note on concepts and design,' Int. J. Man-machine studies (1982) 16, pp. 231-236.

[3]   Snowberry K., Parkinson S.R., Sisson N., Computer Display Menus, Ergonomics, 1983, Vol. 26, No. 7, pp 699-712.

[4]   Miller D.P, 1981, 'The depth-breadth trade-off in hierarchical computer menus,' Proc. of the 25th Annual Meeting of the Human Factors Society, pp. 296-299.

[5]   Marcus A., 'User Interface Screen Design and Colour', Human Factors in Computing Systems, CHI '86 Conference Proceedings, April 13-17, 1986, Boston, U.S.A.

[6]   Wilson M.D., Barnard P.J., MacLean A., 'Analysing the Learning of Command Sequences in a Menu System', People and Computers : Designing the Interface, Proc. of the Conference of the British Computer Soc. HCI Specialist Group, University of East Anglia, 17-20 September 1985, Ed. Johnson P., Cook S., Cambridge University Press.

[7]   Heppe D.L., Edmonson W.H., Spence R., 'Helping both the novice and advanced user in menu-driven information retrieval systems', People and Computers : Designing the Interface, Proc. of the Conference of the British Computer Soc. HCI Specialist Group, University of East Anglia, 17-20 September 1985, Ed. Johnson P., Cook S., Cambridge University Press.

[8]   Dzida W., Herda S., Itzeldt W.D., 'User Perceived Quality of Interactive Systems', IEEE Trans. on Software Engineering, Vol. SE-4, No. 4, July 1978.

[9]   Darlington J., Dzida W., Herda S., 'The role of excursions in interactive systems', Int. J. Man-machine studies (1983) 18, pp. 101-112.

[10]   Peterson J.L., Petri Net Theory and the Modelling of Systems (1981), Prentice-Hall.

The Storage and Retrieval of Documents in an Electronic Document Delivery/Exchange Service for Academic Institutions

L.A. Beddie and P.E. Napier

Napier College
Edinburgh, Scotland

Abstract

In 1985, the authors undertook to conduct a study to investigate the feasibility of setting up a wide area network to provide an electronic document delivery/exchange service between certain Scottish academic institutions. A central database would hold data on research papers, conference papers, monographs, student projects and distance learning packages, all of which would be held in full text for transmission across the network.

Documents of this nature have a varied format, length, presentation and standard, which ensure that their storage and entry on to the database is not straightforward. The software to effect document delivery has to be capable of much more flexibility than that used with traditional bibliographic database, and must provide student/tutor dialogue for the teaching packages.

Keywords: electronic document delivery, distance learning, document structure, software, grey area, Scotland.

1. Introduction

In 1982, the authors completed a SEFI funded project which laid the groundwork for further investigation. At that time, the CURSEFI bibliographic database, dedicated to European engineering education, was accessible in pilot form, when most data held by online retrieval services was also of a bibliographic nature.

Between 1982 and 1985, two major developments took place which radically affected such services. Firstly, as a result of the tremendous advances made in computing technology, full text databases, in which whole journal articles are transmitted, became available. Secondly, the academic world woke up to the need of people in full time employment for continuing education, but not through the traditional means of attendance at colleges.

The Open University was the pioneer of modular, distance learning courses. In addition, new teaching methods using such media as audio-visual packs, training packages, and learning-by-appointment, became more popular.

In 1985, the authors, taking the University of Milan network as their model (Canzii et al, 1984), undertook to carry out a study to investigate the feasibility of setting up a wide area network to provide an Electronic document Delivery/Exchange Service (EDDS) between certain Scottish academic institutions. It was envisaged that the service would hold data on research papers and reports, training and distance learning packages, conference papers, theses, and ultimately, selected journal articles.

This paper looks at why the service has been proposed, the market for the service, the varied kinds of information held on the central database, and the software problems and solutions in making the material available for delivery and exchange.

2. Document Delivery Projects

Of late, the information world has been much occupied with the challenge of electronic publishing on the grand scale, particularly in relation to journals and the articles contained within their covers. (The major projects are outlined in Appendix 1.)

This pioneering work naturally encountered problems, some of which have imposed major delays in the introduction of the proposed services. For our proposed service, it therefore seemed timely to look at existing technology from the starting point of a small scale project and work outwards.

3. The Market

At first, both new and existing networks were investigated as suitable carriers for the service. The JANET network served the academic communities, but many colleges were not eligible to join. It seemed sensible therefore to create a JANET-compatible network so that any changeover could take place if and when circumstances altered. Events have moved on quickly, and membership is now possible. Because the proposed service was to be small scale in comparison to the international projects, the network was envisaged as serving the Scottish Central Institutions; but before making any plans, it was necessary to establish that they would be willing and enthusiastic partners. Responses from the two organisations approached early in the study were very encouraging. Investigation also shows that there is absolutely no demand for yet another network, and, with the advent of JANET membership, the need has completely disappeared.

The concept of a "grey area" full text database specializing in education, however, is a very different matter. As the study progressed suggestions for material for inclusion on the database were made by all those interviewed. Not only is the service capable of expanding well beyond the boundaries of Scotland, but the user community can grow beyond the academic world. Inclusion of teaching packages would attract industrial organisations to participate by providing their training packs for inclusion on the database.

Turning to the commercial world of journal publishing, research has identified that the concept of EDDS has been given close attention over the last four years. Many very large international projects have begun, each with varying degrees of success. All have had governmental or intergovernmental funding (see Appendix 1). The Commission of the European Communities (CEC) identified in 1982 a European market of 28 million requests for scientific, technical and medical documents, a substantial part of which could be fulfilled by EDD. This has led to some ten major experiments (Vernimb, 1983). This certainly indicates that there is a market for this type of enterprise because commercial publishers would not invest money on projects with little or no prospect of profit.

4. Database Information Content

The proposed information content of the database will be drawn initially from material held in the participating institutions and beginning with works from the host college. The subject areas which will be covered are engineering education and computing. A deliberate decision to start with "grey area" literature was made because

- this material is very hard to find,
- interlibrary loans have a disquietingly low rate of successful fulfilment,
- the main thrust of demand comes from the academic communicty (White, 1986).

However, there are problems with this type of material in that all aspects have very different printed formats, presentations differ, lengths vary, and quality of presentation varies from the published scholarly text to the rough and ready report. In addition, there are diagrams and tables embedded in the documents.

The complexity of the problems will become more apparent when the types of material are related to the points outlined above. It is proposed to include research papers and reports (both published and semi-published), conference papers, postgraduate student projects, monographs, certain highly-selected journal articles, and teaching packages (no particular chronological order inferred).

5. Documents and Document Structures

When looking at document structures and layouts, it is important to remember that the printed form has been evolving for centuries and that its presentation to the reader is the culmination of many inter-related choices made by both author and printer with the specific purpose of navigating the reader through the document in the clearest and easiest way. In addition to indexes, chapter titles, headings, etc., the use of typographic and other design effects on the page gives rise to a very rich structure with a complex syntax of its own (Tuck and Kirstein, 1985). Even the colour of the paper can be a powerful navigational aid. FAX transmission, which can handle tonal differences reasonably well, is not yet capable of transmitting colour. For the electronic document, there is, as yet, no comparable system. Not only will the electronic document have to carry its abstract, but it will also have to provide some way of revealing its structure and navigational channels, alongside the channels between related documents.

Varying document lengths and presentation reveal other fundamental aspects of bibliographic control and access. It is not the norm to find documents which carry abstracts and keywords for retrieval purposes. This means that considerable in-house editing will be needed to supply these, and also to give essential descriptive synopses to longer documents such as monographs and theses.

A further less serious consideration has to be addressed in relation to document length. Research has shown that long journal articles are less likely to be published and that there appears to be an optimum length (Palmer, 1986). Many documents in this database will be very long indeed. A possible solution might be for synopses to be provided by suitable referees or by the host site. This will, in effect, provide a synoptic publishing facility similar to that of the Netherlands Agricultural Report Depository (NARD) set up in 1984 (Van der Heij, 1985). The difference will be that back up material will be delivered on line if required.

Distance learning packages too have their differences. Formats range from the Open University style of written text with self-assessment questions to varied bundles of leaflets containing the expected student work, usually with a high degree of practicality. Document lengths again vary, as does the level of scholastic writing, which is in turn related to the academic standard of the course.

6. Software

The software needed for the service must be sufficiently flexible to incorporate a wide variety of functions in support of the database. There appear to be no software packages on the market, as yet, which are able to fulfil all the requirements (Kimberley) 1986). It is not unrealistic to assume that this gap will be plugged in the near future, though, of necessity, the software will be large and consequently expensive. At present, the only solution is for it to be developed in-house.

The functions to support the database include those which are well known and used in bibliographic information retrieval, and some additional operations in respect of full text retrieval and of the interactive nature of distance-learning material.

The major functions are as follows:

i) Handling of a mixture of text and graphics embedded in a document.

This is common to most papers, articles, monographs and is an essential part of distance-learning material (scan any text book for evidence of the vital role of pictures and diagrams in teaching and learning). The graphics element of a paper cannot be separated from the words, nor dismissed, and this poses problems for the input and output media. Documents will need to be input to the database through FAX or a book scanner in order that the diagrams remain an integral part of the work and to save storage space (storing diagrams in ASCII format is very wasteful of disc space). This in turn means that the full text document can only be output in hard copy form through a FAX device. This could prove awkward for some institutions where no such device exists and is expensive to purchase.

As regards the actual make-up of the documents, very often the split between narrative and diagram or table is well defined, but learning material can have a very mixed format. In addition, it is likely that exercises or assessment questions will be included.

ii) Keyword searching of documents.

This is a standard bibliographic operation, whereby documents are selected by meeting some criteria and otherwise eliminated as being irrelevant. This function is unlikely to be needed for the distance-learning material as this will almost certainly be selected by name, but is vital for other papers and articles. In the context of this particular service, keyword searching does post some further questions.

Firstly, how are the keywords to be selected? Some documents do have keywords already defined, others, particularly the monographs, do not. Selection of keywords therefore becomes the task of an information scientist at the control site, or a relevant referee. Even if the keywords are already defined, they will still need to be input separately from the document itself, as FAX will not analyse a document.

Secondly, what will be the search dialogue? Should it emulate one of the well used command languages? Should it conform to the Common Command Language (Mahon, 1986)? Should it be a new dialogue entirely and use natural language processing?

iii) Full text retrieval and transmission.

There is nothing particularly new or problematic here, except that the software must retrieve the documents by search/selection or directly by reference, and they must be transmitted to a VDU screen or FAX type device or to a printer for distribution by post.

iv) Insertion and deletion of material.

Again, not a new field, except that, for the purposes of managing and controlling the database, a decision must be taken on WHO can add and subtract material. Should it be by centralized control, or by any user?

v) Updating and amendment of material.

Normally, the documents and abstracts on the bibliographic databases are not of a volatile nature. Material is added, but rarely deleted and certainly not altered. In the case of the distance-learning packages however, update and amendment is to be expected.

Many of these packages contain assignments or exercises, and these will need to be amended or changed each time the course is run, or at regular intervals. The actual text of the learning modules may need to be enhanced or updated according to changes in syllabus or technology. Again, the question of just who can be given the control of amendment is to be addressed.

vi) Electronic mailing.

This will be used principally to enable student-tutor interaction in the distance learning environment. Here, a course tutor mailbox will be created for each course in order that a student need only address it, rather than the mailbox of a named individual. (The actual tutor may change during the course.) A tutor can then reply to a particular student. It is not envisaged that student-student mailing is essential.

vii) Management of assignments.

A useful feature would be to hold a number of different question/answer pairs for any one assignment, and for the software to select one in sequence to effect the principles in (v) above.

Before any software can be designed, it is clear that the decision on hardware and communications must be taken. If FAX is to be used for input/output, then the documents will retain their original appearance and meaning, but some manual effort is needed for keywords and abstracting. If FAX is dismissed as being too expensive as an input device at the control site, then OCR or the VDU/keyboard must be used and therefore text and graphics can no longer be integrated in the documents. The solution is then either to delete all graphics from the documents (wherein much of the value of the document would be lost), or to input and store the diagrams separately which would entail more software functions. On the other hand, if FAX were used for input, but some user sites were without the corresponding FAX equipment for output, then they would simply have to use the VDU and the postal service for looking at the full text.

7. Costs

It has been a matter of some concern that perhaps the service will be too expensive and have little or no advantage over interlibrary loans and photocopies sent by post. For an EDDS we are entering into uncharted territory, and even the best researched prediction may prove to be little better than guesswork (Line, 1983). However, such "guesstimates" should be hazarded and even Line's costing for interlibrary loans at that time were averaged out. His national benchmark figures were given as $2.30 (photocopy) and $4.00 for a book loan. Compare this with a rough costing (excluding initial capital costs) of approximately $0.20 for a 5 page document transmitted electronically at 1200 baud (Bull, 1983). Subsequent studies bear out Bull's prognosis, though the BLEND evaluations remain the only constructive cost proposals (Singleton & Pullinger, 1984). The most encouraging pointer for the authors is the success of the EDDS experiment of Reintjes using a home made digital facsimile scanner/printer (Bennet, 1986).

8. Conclusions

When this study was undertaken in 1985, the need for a database devoted to engineering education, identified in 1979, was still strong. It is possible to find such data for retrieval but it is scattered over many databases and consists in the main of bibliographic references to journal articles. As a result of recent advances in computing, full text databases can now be developed. In the academic world, data on engineering and computing education is still contained in many other less traditional forms of publication.

The interest of commercial publishers in EDDS has increased steadily over the last few years as the profitability factors of such services become more manifest. This is demonstrated in the projects started over since 1983. In most cases, success has faltered due to problems such as international standards, compatibility or transmission media. Despite the drawbacks, these projects are going ahead.

It was therefore decided that it might be fruitful to create a full text database specifically for the academic community which would contain papers drawn from the "grey area" of literature on two specific areas of education: engineering and computing. Various considerations regarding the documents emerged during the study - varying length, format and quality, and indexing. It soon became clear that distance learning packages would be desirable additions to the database. The addition of electronic mail would give a very constructive interactive dimension and allow remote dialogue facilities between teacher and student.

Initially the user community would be restricted to Scotland. However, the data would be attractive to the wider academic world. Industrial participation, achieved through the inclusion of their own training packages, would enable employees and students to work at a time and place convenient for themselves. The learning rate could be monitored, problems dealt with through electronic mail, and assignments allocated.

The software needed for the service must be flexible enough to cope with a variety of user functions. It must include the facilities to allow:

- handling mixed text and graphics in a document,
- keyword searching,
- full text retrieval and transmission,
- insertion, deletion, amendment (update) of material,
- electronic mailing,
- assignment management.

This software will be developed in-house as no single package exists to support all these facilities.

None of the problems concerning the documents or the software are insurmountable, they simply require further analysis and investigation and highlight the innovative nature of EDDS.

Appendix 1

Back in 1980, the Adonis project, set up by a group of publishers, began work to modernize document delivery services by storing journals on high capacity digital/optical discs (Somerfield, 1983). ADONIS will not provide the user with search facilities but will supply quick retrieval of the appropriate journal article through existing channels, e.g., the British Library (Oakeshott, 1983). This work has encountered high costs, but goes ahead steadily.

In 1981, the National Physical Laboratory and Pira undertook a study to demonstrate the use of Teletex for document delivery which would stimulate product development and provide a foundation for a subsequent public service (Yates, 1983). Project HERMES failed in its attempt to develop an experimental electronic mail/document delivery service based on Teletex.

The EuroDocDel and APOLLO projects require international cooperation in their goals to provide document delivery services. EuroDocDel, launched in 1984 and implemented in 1985, uses videotex for finding and ordering European Commission documents which are then printed on demand (Yeates, 1986; I'M no 39, 1985). The APOLLO project will provide a high speed digital information transfer system suitable for long data messages, in particular for document facsimiles using EUTELSAT communication satellites (I'M no 41, 1985).

ARTEMIS is one of the CEC experiments involving a consortium of publishers providing journal articles online using Group 3 FAX to effect fast digital transfer (Katzen, 1983).

Project UNIVERSE is another major experiment in satellite communications which has been set up by a consortium involving the British government, industry and the universities. This will develop the Universities Extended Ring and Satellite Experiment which will transmit multi-media documents using a mixture of network components (Winfield, 1984).

BLEND aimed to explore and evaluate alternative forms of user communication through an electronic journal and information network, and to assess the cost, efficiency and subjective impact of such a system (Shackel, 1982).

Most recently, the Quartet project has been announced, which follows on from BLEND and experiments at University College, London. Four British institutions will collaborate over the next 4 years to produce a single integrated information system (Santinelli, 1986).

References

1. Bennet, R.J., Interlending and document supply: a review of recent literature, IX Interlending and Document Supply, 1986, vol 14, no 1, ppl. 15-21.

2. Bull, G.E., Document delivery services and copyright, Aslib Proceedings, 1983, vol 35, no 4, ppl. 83-204.

3. Canzii, G., et.al., A scientific document delivery system, Electronic Publishing Review, 1984, vol 4, no 2, ppl. 35-143.

4. I'M Information Market, no 39, April-June 1985, p. 8.

5. I'M Information Market, no 41, Oct-Nov 1985, ppl.-2.

6. Katzen, M., editor, Multi-Media Communications, Pinter, London, 1982.

7. Kimberley, R., et.al., Text Retrieval - a directory of software, Institute of Information Scientists, 1986.

8. Line, M.B., Document Delivery, now and in the future, Aslib Proceedings, 1983, vol 35, no 4, ppl. 67-176.

9. Mahon, B., Common Command Language - common or uncommon, Conference of Institute of Information Scientists, 1986.

10. Oakeshott, P., The impact of new technology on the publication chain, British National Bibliographic Research Fund Report, 1983.

11. Palmer, T., Length of journal articles: implications for document delivers, Interlending and Document Supply, 1986, vol 14, no 2, pp. 50-54.

12. Santinelli, P., Quartet's Key Change, Times Higher Educational Supplement, 1986, 11 April, p. 11.

13. Singleton, A., & Pullinger, D.J., Ways of viewing costs of journals: cost evaluation of the BLEND experiment, Electronic Publishing Review, 1984, vol 4, no 1, pp. 59-71.

14. Somerfield, G.A., Selective article delivery, Proceedings of 10th meeting of IATUL, 1983, pp. 83-97.

15. Tuck, W.R., & Kirstein, P.T., Research into the Electronic Document, British Library R & D Report, July 1985, no 5864.

16. Van der Heij, D.G., Synopsis publishing for improving the accessibility of "grey" scholarly information, Journal of Information Science, 1985, vol 11, no 3, pp. 95-107.

17. Vernimb, C. & Mastroddi, F., The CEC experiments on EDD and electronic publishing, Proceedings of the 7th International Online Information Meeting, 1983, pp. 119-130.

18. White, B., Interlending in the UK 1985, Interlending and Document Supply, 1985, vol 14, no 1, pp. 3-9.

19. Winfield, B., Document transfer by satellite, Aslib Proceedings, 1984, vol 36, no 4, pp. 77-185.

20. Yates, D.M., Project HERMES, Aslib Proceedings, vol 35, no 4, pp. 77-182.

21. Yeates, R., Videotext in libraries and information centres, The Electronic Library, 1986, vol 4, no 1, pp. 56-63.

The Standard Generalized Markup Language

Robert Stutely, BSc MIOP

Her Majesty´s Stationery Office
Norwich, UK

Abstract

The Standard Generalized Markup Language (SGML) has reached the final stages in its preparation as an international standard and it is expected that it will be published shortly. The standard describes a methodology for creating tagging schemes for marking-up documents in a generalized manner.

The elements of an SGML-coded document are tagged according to their role and not their style of presentation. The hierarchical structure of a document is recognized and specified in the document type definition which precede a marked-up SGML document. The document type definition also shows the names of tags used in the document, what the shorthand references are in their expanded form and the character coding scheme used.

A document may be fully marked-up with generic tags, or specific tags may be omitted where no ambiguity would arise. Further economies of mark-up may be achieved by using control codes or short strings of codes to imply tags. Tags may contain attributes which further describe some function of the marked-up element. Methods are provided for extending the character set in a machine-independent manner beyond the repertoire of the equipment used for data entry and for allowing words, phrases and unkeyable strings to be expressed in a shorthand manner. References to non-SGML data such as graphics may be included in the marked-up text.

A number of standards and technical reports are being developed to support the main standard. The standards bodies of fifteen countries have participated in some way in the development of the Standard Generalized Markup Language.

International interest in the standard is being shown by the adoption of SGML by a number of leading printers and publishers, by the holding of conferences and by the number of support services being offered by industry research bodies and consultants.

Keywords: CLPT, Computer Language for Processing Text, document, generalized, generic, markup, SGML, Standard Generalized Markup Language.

1. History and Background of SGML

The Standard Generalized Markup Language (SGML) is a method developed by the International Organization for Standards (ISO) for marking-up the characteristics of text in a standardized manner. The structure of documents may be defined using SGML techniques allowing meaningful markup which in turn maximizes the potential use of the documents. The concept of SGML encourages the identification of various documents types; the standard is not a tagging scheme in itself but a methodology for creating tagging schemes for individual document types. The idea is borrowed from a basis principle of database management theory that data should be separated from the application.

SGML is based on the Document Composition Facility Generalized Markup Language (DCF GML) developed within IBM by Dr. Charles F. Goldfarb and two colleagues. Dr. Goldfarb was awarded one of the coveted IBM awards in 1985 for his work on DCF GML.

The idea of generic coding, that is the marking up of the elements of a document to indicate their logical structure independently of the way in which they are to be presented, was conceived by William W. Tunnicliffe some twenty years ago. William Tunnicliffe recognized in GML the implementation of similar concepts to his own and he persuaded Charles Goldfarb to put GML into the standards arena so that more people would be able to benefit.

Within ISO, SGML became part of a larger project known as the Computer Language for the Processing of Text (CLPT) and was developed initially by TC 97/SC 5, the subcommittee responsible for computer languages. The major part of the development work was done in the United States of America, principally at the American National Standards Institute (ANSI) meetings.

Because the emphasis was on a computer language rather than a text processing language, printers and publishers in the United Kingdom did not generally realize that a standard of potential interest to them was being developed within the standards bodies. There was some awakening of interest at the end of 1982 when Charles Goldfarb spoke on the subject at a conference in Amsterdam sponsored by the Graphics Communications Association (GCA) of America.

However, in 1983 BSI withdrew from active participation in the project because of the lack of interest within the computer languages subcommittee dealing with CLPT. This meant the UK then had no say in the development of the evolving standard.

In January, 1984, a meeting was called at the National Computing Centre (NCC) in Manchester to discuss the need for further action in the UK as a result of which various organization and individuals lobbied BSI to change its status back to that of a participating member but this was initially resisted by BSI.

Fortunately for the printing and publishing industry, the main technical committee for this work within ISO was restructured and the CLPT project was transferred to the subcommittee responsible for Text and Office Systems, TC 97/SC 18. The Computer Language for Processing Text project was then allocated to working group 8 which deals with Text Processing and Markup.

Because the national standards bodies usually mirror the structure of ISO, the British Standards Institution (BSI) and ANSI restructured their groups in a similar manner. Mrs. Joan M. Smith of the NCC chaired an ad hoc meeting at BSI to discuss CLPT and to report back to the parent subcommittee, OIS/18 (now IST/18). The report recommended that the UK become involved in the project again and in due course, a working group known as panel 8 of OIS/18 was set up under the chairmanship of Mrs. Smith. There were ad hoc meetings until this UK working group was regularized in January 1985 and regular meetings have been held since.

The first international meeting since the restructuring was held in Rotterdam in October 1984, chaired by William Tunnicliffe. It was attended by a large contingent from the United States and experts from Holland, Germany, Belgium and Luxemborg. Because BSI was not officially involved at that time, Mrs. Smith was invited to attend as an individual expert.

Subsequently, international meetings have taken place at about six-month intervals in Germany, London, the USA and Luxembourg.

The proposed CLPT standard was to be composed of 10 parts, of which SGML was to be part 6. The SGML part was registered first as a draft proposal. The plenary meeting in April 1985 of the ISO subcommittee SC 18, parent of working group 8, approved the elevation of SGML to a draft international standard, ISO/DIS 8879, but asked that it be separated from the remainder of CLPT.

The UK voted against the issue of the draft international standard on technical grounds and asked for a number of changes to be made. These were considered at the May 1985 meeting of the ISO working group in Bad Soden, Frankfurt.

One of the UK proposals in particular concerned with character sets and code extension techniques, occupied several long days (and nights) of fierce, but good natured, battle. Another topic which has lead to changes is that of conformance to the SGML standard which in turn is related to validation procedures. With the aim of making the International Standard one which could be dual-numbered and issued also as a British Standard a large number of editing points were also raised. The result is a standard that should be much more acceptable to UK and other European publishers.

The final draft of ISO/DIS 8879, Information processing - Text and Office Systems - Standard Generalized Markup Language (SGML) was presented to those attending the next working group meeting held in London in September 1985 and also sent to ISO Central Secretariat. It was published shortly afterwards for a period of six months for public comment.

The public comments from each country were collected by that country's member body and discussed at the next ISO working group meeting held in San Jose in April 1986. The editor of ISO/DIS 8879, Dr. Charles Goldfarb took these comments into account to produce a revised version for review and final checking at the September 1986 meeting of the working group in Luxembourg. The final draft was also submitted to the ISO Central Secretariat for Council Vote at about the same time. If disapproval is not registered within a six-week period, tacit approval is assumed and at that stage, SGML may be referred to as an International Standard.

While work on developing the international standard was going on, interest in SGML has been growing in the printing and publishing community. A second conference on SGML, called Markup '84, was held in Oxford in April 1984. It was during that conference that Mrs. Joan Smith proposed the setting up of an SGML Users' Group for the sharing of information.

Several informal meetings were held in the UK prior to the formal inauguration of the Users' Group at the Markup '85 conference in Heidelberg in June 1985. Markup '86 took place in July this year in Luxembourg and the fifth such conference is being planned by GCA to take place in, perhaps, Holland, Spain or Yugoslavia in 1987. The European Chapter of the SGML Users' Group has since held a number of meetings in the UK and one in Luxembourg and a special interest group for FORMEX ((the Formalized Exchange of Electronic Documents) has been formed as part of the Users' Group. The first edition of the Users' Group Bulletin was published recently; further editions are planned at the rate of about three a year

The Standard Generalized Markup Language is now being discussed at electronic publishing conferences other than at the Markup series. So the momentum is beginning to build up.

2. Basic Concepts of SGML

2.1 Definitions

The Standard Generalized Markup Language is based on the concept of marking-up elements of a document in a generalized but meaningful way.

There does seem to be some confusion and disagreement over the exact meaning and terms used to describe methods of marking-up documents. The following definitions are taken from the forthcoming ISO Technical Report on Vocabulary for Computer-Assisted Publishing:

- Process-specific markup/specific markup/procedural markup

    Markup that specifies the way in which the date content should be formatted or otherwise processed.

- Generic markup

    Markup that is system-independent, but that may nevertheless be specific to a particular type of process or application.

- Generalized markup

    Markup that describes the structure and attributes of a document in a rigorous and system-independent manner, so that it can be processed for a number of different applications.

2.2 Tagged elements

The elements of an SGML document are tagged according to their role and not their style of presentation. SGML markup recognizes the hierarchical structure of a document. For example, a book may be considered to have front matter, a main body and back matter. The main body may be composed of chapters; each chapter may be sub-divided into a number of topics each with a heading, paragraphs, sub-paragraphs and so on. This may be illustrated by the following diagram:

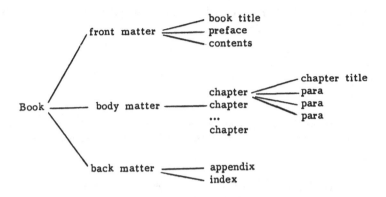

In a fully marked-up SGML document, each of these elements would be tagged at the start and end. An example of a tag is <p>indicating the start of a paragraph. The corresponding tag at the end of the paragraph would be </p>. The start-tag <para> and end-tag </para> are equally valid - the user is free to choose meaningful or easy-to-key tags. Similarly, the "<" called start-tag open, "</" called end-tag open and ">", the tag close, may be chosen to suit the user.

This demonstrates some of the flexibility of the language. The standard specifies an abstract syntax which says how things are to be done, and a concrete reference syntax which allocates certain characters to specified roles - the "<" to start-tag open, for example. If different delimiters are preferred, perhaps the open square bracket instead of the less-than symbol, there is a means of specifying the alternative concrete syntax.

2.3 Shorthand coding omitting some tags

It is not always necessary to include all end-tags or, indeed, it may not be necessary to include all start-tags.

The OMITTAG feature allows an end-tag to be omitted for an element if the element content is followed either by an end-tag of another open element or by an element that is not allowed in its content. For example, provided a list item is declared as not containing another list item, a list could be marked-up as follows:

```
<list>
<item>Here is the first item
<item>Here is the second item
<item>Here is the last item
</list>
```

A start-tag can generally be omitted if the element is a contextually required element and any other elements that could occur are contextually optional. This means that the start tag of the first item in the example of a list can be omitted if the list must always contain at least one item but the start-tag of subsequent items must be present because the subsequent items are contextually optional. There are some exceptions: a start-tag cannot be omitted if the element type has an attribute which is required or the containing element has declared content or the content of the element is empty. For example, the element "list" cannot contain some introductory text to the list items if the first item start-tag is to be omitted.

It is possible to omit the start-tag of the list items by mapping the newline code within a list to the item start-tag using the SHORTREF feature. This assumes that the text is being prepared and displayed in lines on a device such as a word processor where a newline code would be present in the text string.

By enabling both the OMITTAG and SHORTREF features, it is possible to omit both the start-tags and the end-tags so that a list may be keyed as follows:

```
<list>
Here is the first item
Here is the second item
Here is the last item
</list>
```

Features such as these can thus simplify the keying of documents on existing word processors where the mark-up of the documents is to conform with the SGML international standard.

2.4 Attributes

There are basically two types of list: ordered and unordered. An ordered list may be "numbered" with Arabic or Roman numerals or letters of the alphabet in capitals or lower case. The actual form of the numbering need not be decided at the document preparation stage. By tagging an item as a list item, the processing system can generate the number at a later stage to the predetermined style. Another advantage is that no re-numbering is necessary if items are added to or removed from lists.

It matters not that an item may be referred to from elsewhere in the document by an as yet unspecified number or identification letter. An element may be named uniquely to distinguish it from all other elements by the use of an attribute. An attribute is part of the start-tag and appears after the generic identifier. For example:

```
<para>The following countries actively participated:
<list ident=active>
<item>USA
<item>UK
<item>Germany
</list><para>
```

Here, the list has been given the name "active", which must be a unique identifier within the document; the list may be referred to by this name from elsewhere in the document. This is a particular use of the attribute where it is declared as having a unique identifier but attributes may be used in a variety of other ways. A simple example might be as follows:

```
<memo status=draft>
```

Here the tag "memo" includes an attribute called "status". The declared status of the memo is "draft".

More than one attribute is permitted. In the following example, the title element is identified as "HMSO" and the short title, which could be used as a running head in a printed document, is "SGML at HMSO":

```
<title id=HMSO st="SGML at HMSO">The Use of the Standard Generalized Markup
Language within Her Majesty's Stationery Office</title>
```

2.5 Context sensitive code

In an SGML document, quotations are identified as such rather than treating quotation marks as ordinary characters. For example:

```
<para>This paragraph contains <quote>a quotation</quote> within it.<para>
```

If other items are to appear in quotation marks, an unusual use of a word, for example, they should be tagged according to their role.

This method has the following advantages:

- single or double quotation marks can be selected at the output stage to suit the edition or house style;

- if the output is to a typesetter or other device with a comprehensive character set, the 6 and 9 or 66 and 99 style of quotation marks can be output;

- quotations can be retrieved as elements separate from any other item that might appear in quotation marks.

Although this example uses explicit tags to identify the quoted material, SGML does provide a means of using the more familiar double-prime marks on a word processor which may be interpreted as start- and end-tags.

The technique is to specify that character mappings, otherwise known as character look-up or conversion tables, are different for a particular element. This may be declared at the start of the document as follows:

```
<!ENTITY qtag     "<quote>" >
<!ENTITY qendtag  "</quote>">
<!SHORTREF paramap `"´qtag>
<!USEMAP paramap para>
<!SHORTREF quotemap `"´ qendtag>
<!USEMAP quotemap quote>
<!ELEMENT para (quote #CDATA)*>
<!ELEMENT quote (#CDATA)>
```

The ELEMENT declarations state that a para element may contain a quotation element or characters (specified by CDATA) or a mixture of the two and that the quote element may contain only characters but no nested elements.

The SHORTREF declarations state that in the case of paramap, the quotation mark is to be converted to the entity called "qtag" whereas in the quotemap it is to be converted to the entity "quendtag".

The USEMAP declarations say that for para elements, the character mapping is amended by paramap and, for quote elements, the character mapping is amended by quotemap.

Finally, the ENTITY declarations say that the entity "qtag" is really the string "(quote)" and the entity "qendtag" is the corresponding end-tag.

The markup:

<para>Here is "a quotation" in the paragraph.</para>

is the equivalent of:

<para>Here is <quote>a quotation</quote> in the paragraph.</para>

At the beginning of the para element, the paramap is active and when a quotation mark is found, the SGML processor will convert it to the quote start-tag. Once the quote element has been started, the "quotemap" becomes active and the next quotation mark is interpreted as the quote end-tag, whereupon the paramap becomes active again as a move is made up the hierarchy back to the para element.

In practice, because other elements in addition to the para element may contain quote elements, the mapping of the quotation mark role to qtag would probably take place at a higher level in the document structure.

When using a word processor for entering SGML coded text, it is possible to adopt a similar technique for using certain features of a word processor as short references. For example, book titles might be underlined and author's names shown in bold on the word processor but, depending upon the way in which the word processor handles these, it is often possible to arrange for the SGML processor to convert these to explicit tags.

In the right circumstances, the markup:

<para>Here is a paragraph that contains "a quotation" followed by *the name of a book* and **the author's name**</para>

could be the equivalent of:

<para>Here is a paragraph that contains <quote>a quotation</quote>followed by <title>the name of a book</title> and <author>the author's name</author><para>

The former is almost certainly a lot easier to key and check.

2.6 Extended character set and unambiguous expansion of abbreviations

The SGML makes provision for obtaining characters additional to those directly available on the machine used for data-entry. One method is to use a mnemonic enclosed in delimiters. The reference concrete syntax uses an ampersand before the mnemonic and a semi-colon after but other delimiters may be chosen if preferred. There is a comprehensive list of suggested character entity names in Appendix E to the international standard; a few examples are reproduced here:

&alpha;	small Greek alpha
&Gamma;	capital Greek Gamma
&aacute;	lower case a with acute accent
&lt;	less than sign
&dagger;	dagger

This method is known within SGML as character references and is a simple and effective method of dealing with infrequently occurring characters but it is rather tedious if a document contains, say, a lot of accented characters or several sentences in Greek. A more satisfactory method in these circumstances is to use the code extension techniques of ISO 2022 in combination with the character sets of ISO 4873, 8-bit Coded Character Set for Information Interchange and ISO 6937, Coded Character Sets for Text Communication. In practice, a document may contain both SGML character references and characters to be obtained by code extension techniques.

The SGML syntax allows for the word processor equivalent of global exchange or search and replace. A short name, called an entity reference in the SGML standard, may be used to refer to a lengthy or unkeyable string. This looks very much like a character reference in use. The declaration:

<!ENTITY HMSO "Her Majesty's Stationery Office">

means that a reference to HMSO in the form "&HMSO;" would be replaced at processing stage by the full form "Her Majesty's Stationery Office". Where an entity reference is followed by a space, the semi-colon delimiter may be omitted.

2.7 Non-text data

Although SGML is based on the coding of textual data, diagrams, photographs and other graphics may be included in the document. They are regarded as non-SGML data and may be stored in separate entities coded in accordance with other standards. A generic tag would be included with the text in the appropriate place but the tag would probably refer to an external entity. At processing stage, the SGML processor would pass control to other software to process the graphic, if this was required, and then resume with the text which followed.

2.8 Definition of document types

All the rules for a document are contained in a document type definition. The two most important declarations that can occur in a document type definition include:

element declarations which define the generic identifiers that can occur in each element and in what order; they also declare the omitted tag minimization allowed;

attribute declarations which define the attributes which are associated with particular element types;

entity declarations which define the entities that can be referred to in a document;

short reference mapping declarations which define the short reference delimiters that are mapped to general entities for each map;

short reference use declarations which link maps to element types.

The document type definition also indicates the document character set and concrete syntax used, and, where required, contains the link type definition.

The document type definition may either precede the marked-up document in the same entity or the document type definition may be passed to the SGML processing system in advance. In an author-publisher relationship using existing types of word processors, it is likely that most authors will never see or know of the existence of a document type definition. The document type definition will probably be set-up and retained by the publisher and the author will just be instructed about the tags to be used and their meanings.

3. Support for SGML

The above is a brief overview of SGML. The key document is obviously the SGML international standard document ISO 8879. The ISO working group dealing with SGML is also preparing a number of supporting standards or technical reports.

Techniques for using SGML with non-SGML text entry systems is to be the subject of an ISO Technical Report. This is intended to give some guidance to those implementing SGML on the current generation of word processors or on computers running word processing packages.

One company is already marketing an SGML-sensitive text entry system and other companies in the USA and UK are known to be developing or have shown interest in developing systems on similar principles. Requirements for SGML-sensitive text entry systems is a subject under development by ISO with the intention to publish an international standard

Technical reports on a vocabulary for computer-assisted publishing and on the techniques for using SGML have been drafted. The latter is designed to help users get started in using SGML: a starter document type definition has been designed with an accompanying starter set of tags.

Draft International Standards on an SGML document interchange format (SDIF) and on registration procedures for public constructs are likely to be published shortly. The latter is to allow for document type definitions or alternative concrete syntaxes to be registered so that they may be consulted or referred to in a unique manner. By reference to the register of public constructs, it might be possible to avoid "re-inventing the wheel".

Work is also being undertaken with some urgency on the description and identification of character fonts. With the convergence of office systems and traditional typesetting systems, this is of interest to both communities.

Full details of the current project of the working group ISO/TC 97/SC 18/WG 8 are given towards the end of this paper.

The ISO work of SGML and related subjects is supported by the following countries:

Australia	Finland	Netherlands
Belgium	France	Norway
Canada	Germany	Sweden
Czechosolvakia	Italy	UK
Denmark	Japan	USA

In the USA, the GCA who have been active in supporting SGML since its inception, published their implementation in 1983 based on the sixth working draft of SGML. This standard also had the title "GCA Standard 101-1983-Document Markup Metalanguage" because US Department of Defense wanted to adopt SGML but were required to refer to an existing standard to do so.

The American Association of Publishers (AAP) sponsored a project, which was undertaken by Aspen Systems Corporation, to develop a standard set of Author Guidelines specifically aimed at the book publishing industry. The project was completed this year with the publishing of a number of reports. Coding in the guides conforms to the Standard Generalized Markup Language.

In the UK, PIRA - the Printing Industry Research Association - is actively supporting the work of BSI and ISO committees on SGML. PIRA is closely associated with the IEPRC - International Electronic Publishing Research Centre. The IEPRC and STM - an international group of Scientific, Technical and Medical publishers - have set up a group called the European Publishers Markup User Group, or EPMARKUP for short. This group is a broadly-based European forum for discussion of SGML and other markup applications.

A number of Government bodies have adopted SGML for some of their work. Examples include Her Majesty's Stationery Office in the UK, Department of Defense and Internal Revenue Service in the USA, the CEC in Luxembourg and the European Patent Office in The Netherlands and Munich.

Not a great deal has yet been published commercially on SGML in the UK. A number of articles have appeared in some trade magazines and Mrs. Joan M. Smith has produced guidelines for authors, guidelines for editors and publishers and a state-of-the-art report for the British Library.

4. Benefits of SGML

Some of the potential benefits of using SGML are:

Benefits to an Author

- any text editor can be used for SGML text entry
- text can be marked-up electronically with a command language which is meaningful to the author
- text can be prepared in a standard way independent of the publisher, printer or page layout
- the author concentrates on the content and structure, not appearance
- greater control because of fewer opportunities for accidental alterations later in the production process
- greater acceptability by publishers because of potentially lower production costs
- potential to use text for more than one purpose
- purpose-designed text-entry systems may eventually offer error checking
- computer-assistance for repetitive tasks such as indexing and numbering

Benefits to a Publisher

- text received from authors in a standard form reducing data conversion cost
- improvements in editing processes
- savings in typesetting costs
- speed of production
- possibility of multi-media output, eg laser printer, phototypesetter, magnetic tape or disc, CD-ROM
- possibility of selecting material from different sources to produce new publications

Benefits to a Typesetting House

- text received from authors or publishers in standard form allowing more systematic working
- larger number of potential customers
- faster and more economic service to customers
- opportunity to offer additional services to customers, e.g., automatic production of indexes, contents and references sections

Benefits to General Public

- cheaper publications
- increased access to information
- more timely information

5. Conclusions

There is a growing awareness of the existence of SGML and the benefits it can bring to the printing and publishing industry if widely adopted. Suppliers have been quick to see the opportunities and have begun development of purpose-designed editors (of the electronic type) to simplify the entry of text marked-up with SGML coding. The publishing of the definitive version of the standard should accelerate the taking-up of the Standard Generalized Markup Language by printers and publishers world-wide.

Current projects of the working group ISO/TC 97/SC 18/WG 8

Computer languages for Processing Text

ISO/DIS 8879   Standard Generalized Markup Language (SGML)
Editor: Dr. Charles F. Goldfarb

ISO/TR xxxx   Reference Model for Text Description and Processing
Languages
Editor: John Oberholzer

ISO/TR xxxx   Computer-Assisted Publishing - Vocabulary
Editor: John Trevitt

SGML and Text Entry Systems

ISO xxxx   Requirements for SGML-Sensitive Text Entry Systems
Editor: Lawrence A. Beck

ISO/TR xxxx   Using SGML with Non-SGML Text Entry Systems
Editor: Robert Stutely

Text Composition

| ISO xxxx | Text Composition Semantics and Syntax |
| Editor: | Francis J. Cave |

| ISO xxxx | Text Presentation Metafile |
| Editor: | Robert Cymbalski |

SGML Support Facilities

| ISO/DP 9069 | SGML Document Interchange Format (SDIF) |
| Editor: | Dr. Charles F. Goldfarb |

| ISO/TR xxxx | Techniques for Using SGML |
| Editor: | Joan M. Smith |

| ISO/DP 9070 | Registration Procedures for Public Constructs |
| Editor: | Francis J. Cave |

Description and Identification of Character Fonts

General editor: Edwin J. Smura

ISO xxxx/1	Introduction
Editor:	English text: F. Christopher Holland, Archie Provan
	French text: Jacques Henry

| ISOxxxx/2 | Registration and Naming Procedures |
| Editor: | to be appointed |

| ISO xxxx/3 | Character Identification Method |
| Editor: | to be appointed |

| ISO xxxx/4 | Character Collections |
| Editor: | to be appointed |

| ISO xxxx/5 | Font and Character Attribute |
| Editor: | Ronald Pellar |

| ISO xxxx/6 | Description and Identification of Character Fonts |
| Editor: | Allen Griffee |

| ISO xxxx/7 | Font File Interchange Format |
| Editor: | Paul Gloger |

References

1. ISO 8879 *Information Processing - Text and Office Systems - Standard Generalized Markup Language (SGML)* (Geneva:ISO) (forthcoming).

2. ISO 646 *Information Processing -7-bit Coded Character Set for Information Interchange* (Geneva:ISO) (1983).

3. ISO 6937 *Information Processing - Coded Character Sets for Text Communication* (Geneva:ISO) (1983).

4. ISO 4873 *Information Processing - 8-bit Coded Character Set for Information Interchange* (Geneva:ISO).

5. ISO 2022 *Information Processing - ISO 7-bit and 8-bit Coded Character Sets - Code Extension Techniques* (Geneva: ISO) (Forthcoming).

6. ISO TR xxxx *Computer-Assisted Publishing - Vocabulary* (Geneva: ISO) (Forthcoming).

7. Smith, Joan M., *The Standard Generalized Markup Language and Related Issues,* British National Bibliography Research Fund Report 22, (London: The British Library)(1986).

8. Smith, Joan M., *The Standard Generalized Markup Language (SGML): Guidelines for Authors.* British National Bibliography Research Fund Report, (London: The British Library)(1986).

9. Smith, Joan M., *The Standard Generalized Markup Language (SGML): Guidelines for Editors and Publishers,* British National Bibliography Research Fund Report, (London: The British Library)(1986).

10. *Standard for Electronic Manuscript Preparation and Markup,* (Massachusetts: Association of American Publishers)(1986).

11. *Author's Guide to Electronic Manuscript Preparation and Markup,* (Massachusetts: Association of American Publishers)(1986).

12. *Reference Manual on Electronic Manuscript Preparation and Markup,* (Massachusetts: Association of American Publishers)(1986).

13. *Markup of Mathematical Formulas* (Massachusetts: Association of American Publishers)(1986).

14. *Markup of Tabular Material* (Massachusetts: Association of American Publishers)(1986).

15. *GenCode and the Standard Generalized Markup Language* (USA: Graphic Communications Association)(1983).

16. FORMEX, *Format for the Exchange of Electronic Publications* (Brussels and Luxembourg: Office for Official Publications of the European Communities).

17. Smith, Joan M., and Stutely, Robert, *Readers' Aids to ISO 8879 Standard Generalized Markup Language (SGML)*(Forthcoming).

Organizations and Contacts

Aspen Systems Corporation
1600 Research Boulevard
Rockville, Maryland 20850, USA
Telephone (301) 251-5000
Sperlin Martin, Vice-President
Ms. Joan E. Knoerdel, Consultant

Association of American Publishers, Inc.
2005 Massachusetts Avenue, N.W.
Washington D.C. 20036
Telephone (202) 232-3335

British Library Publications Sales Unit
Boston Spa, Wetherby, West Yorkshire
LS23 7BQ, UK
Telephone 0937 843434
Telex 557381 BLLD G

BSI Sales Department
Linford Wood, Milton Keynes, MK14 6LE, UK
Telephone 0908 320033
Telex 825777 BSIMK G

Graphic Communications Association
1730 North Lynn Street/Suite 604
Arlington, Virginia 22209 USA
Telephone (703) 841-8160
Telex 510 600 0889
Norman W. Scharpf, Executive Director
Marion L. Ellidge, Program Manager, Information Technologies

IEPRC - see PIRA

IBM Corporation
Almaden Research Center
K 84/803, 650 Harry Road
San Jose, California 95120 USA
Dr. Charles F. Goldfarb, Senior Analyst

ISO
Case postale 56
CH-1211 Geneve 20
Switzerland
Telephone 022 34 12 40
or contact local standards body (BSI in UK)

The National Computing Centre Limited
Oxford Road, Manchester M1 7ED
Telephone 061-228 6333
Telex 668962 NCCMAN G
Mrs. Joan M. Smith, Senior Consultant

Office for Official Publications of the European Communities
"New Technologies" Department
2, rue Mercier
L-2985 Luxembourg
Telephone 352 499281
Telex 1324 PUBOF LU
Christian Guittet

Printing Industry Research Association
Pira House, Randalls Road, Leatherhead
Surrey KT22 7RU, UK
Telephone 0372 376161
Telex 929810
Francis Cave, Senior Research Officer

SGML Users´ Group
c/o Information Services Division
BPCC Graphics Limited
Slack Lane, Derby DE3 3FL, UK
Telephone 0332 47123
Telex 377017 BPCCOX G

Peter Howgate, Secretary
Mrs. Joan M. Smith. President
William W. Davis, Vice President
Francis Cave, Treasurer

STM
Keizersgracht 462
1016GE Amsterdam
The Netherlands
Telephone 020 225214

The Chelgraph SGML Structured Editor

Peter H. Cadogan

Chelgraph Ltd., Oriel House
Oriel Road, Cheltenham GL50 1XP, UK

Abstract

Standard Generalized Markup Language (SGML) is an ISO Draft International Standard for text processing which is designed to enable authors to mark up their documents on the basis of their logical structure rather than their final typeset appearance.

The rich and variable syntax of SGML makes it a somewhat difficult language to understand and its verbosity is a possible hindrance to its more widespread acceptance. To assist in the creation of SGML coded documents, Chelgraph is therefore developing software tools for document design and creation in the IBM-PC environment.

Keywords: SGML, Editor, IBM-PC, Markup, Typesetting.

1. Introduction

The primary purpose of SGML as a language is to separate the logical structure of a document from its final typeset appearance. By using abstract names, such as "section", "heading", and "paragraph", rather than concrete formatting commands, such as point size, font and measure, a single document can be output to a range of devices (eg., laser printers for proofing, typesetters for final output) and/or in a variety of formats (eg., single/double column) without having to modify the source text extensively. Within an SGML coded document, individual elements are not numbered explicitly (eg., Chapter 4, Figure 3.1.6); instead, all numbering and cross-referencing is delayed until the document is finally output, making the maintenance of complex documents an easier task than it otherwise would be. Furthermore, the widespread adoption of a standard generic markup language by the international community should facilitate the transfer of structured documents between one system and another, independent of hardware supplier. SGML files may also be suitable for full text databases, to produce documents such as dictionaries and encyclopedia.

It is not the purpose of this paper to describe the full capabilities of the SGML language, as these are described elsewhere (1,2), but some of the basic concepts must be introduced. Firstly, it should be noted that SGML is both a document definition language and a text markup language. In other words, the names that are used to identify parts of a document (called elements) must themselves first be defined in terms of other elements.

Furthermore, the very symbols (tags) that are used to enclose the elements (eg., "<" and "!") are themselves configurable. It is hardly surprising then, that a reference concrete syntax has been defined and that there is also a strong demand from potential users for a "starter document type definition". The very abstractness of SGML as a language is certainly a potential threat to its more widespread adoption by the publishing community. It is almost equivalent to asking computer programmers to design a computer language in a foreign tongue before they can write their first program!

Another potential disadvantage of SGML as a markup language is its verbosity. The elements of a document must be enclosed by start and end tags, each of which must be embedded within tag delimiters. There is a very real danger, in fact, that a complex document may contain more markup than text.

In order to alleviate this potential problem, the designers of SGML have introduced what is known as markup minimization, by which certain tags may be omitted if such omissions do not introduce ambiguities. Furthermore, certain commonly used tags may be represented within documents as single keystrokes (eg., carriage return = end paragraph, tab = start next tabulation column). Such extensions to the language certainly reduce the number of keystrokes that are necessary to create a document, but it remains to be seen whether they make it any easier to create syntactically correct SGML files.

In view of the potential problems facing the prospective user of the SGML language, Chelgraph Limited is developing an IBM PC-based software package that should greatly facilitate the creation of document types and their subsequent use to create SGML-coded documents. The central idea behind the Chelgraph SGML Structured Editor is that all document markup should be totally invisible, effectively avoiding the issues of reference concrete syntax and markup minimization. Likewise, the names of elements may be descriptive rather than terse (eg., "chapter" rather than "ch"), because these names will never be shown as such within the body of the text being edited. Furthermore, by making the text editor cognizant of the logical structure of the document being edited, the author may make direct references to particular elements, such as paragraphs and sections (eg., exchange chapters 6 and 7). The SGML Structured Editor does **not** generate data files that are ready for typesetting, but it **does** ensure that documents that are syntactically correct can be produced quickly, easily and in accordance with recommended house styles.

2. Document Type Definition (DTD) Editor

Before any SGML-coded document can be generated, the names of the elements to be used in it (eg., "section", "header", etc.) must first be defined, typically as a separate Document Type Definition (DTD) file. DTD files can range in complexity from ones that can encompass practically all possible document types (like the proposed starter document type definition), to those that are highly specific to a particular application (eg., legal contract, memo, proposal). The specification of a DTD, particularly an all-encompassing one, is a complex task, not least because the implied document structure is difficult to visualize solely on the basis of a sequence of element definitions (Figure 1). It would normally be created by the graphic designer or editor rather than by the author. The Chelgraph SGML Structured Editor is actually two separate programs, the first of which greatly facilitates the production of consistent DTD files. The second is essentially a word processor that is cognizant of the logical structure of the document being edited.

The DTD Editor is capable of modifying existing DTD files as well as creating new ones from scratch. A DTD file is little more than a list of all element types that may occur within the document, describing the elements that it may contain. To be internally consistent, all elements subordinate to the parent element must be defined, together with their subordinate elements and so on. Structures can be defined as being recursive (eg., sections may consist of paragraphs which may themselves consist of sections) but ultimately there must be subordinate elements that can accommodate text or graphic elements, the "leaves" of the structure. Without such leaves, no real document could ever be produced.

In order to represent subordinate elements on the computer screen, a graphical "tree structure" is displayed (Figure 2). Each element is represented as an open rectangular box containing its name (up to 8 characters), the parent element centred at the top of the screen and its subordinates below, each connected to the parent by horizontal and vertical lines. All graphics can be generated using the IBM PC extended character set and therefore a graphics display adapter is **not** required. Subordinate elements can occur in one of three ways. They may be mutually exclusive, such that one and only one subordinate element may occur, in which case the subordinate element boxes will be separated from one another by the "?" symbol. Alternatively, they may have to occur in a well defined order, in which case the sequence will be shown on the screen in left-to-right order, with adjacent boxes separated from one another by a single headed arrow. Finally, a double headed arrow between the boxes indicates that the subordinate elements may occur in any order. Having established the relationship that exists between subordinate elements, the occurrences of the elements themselves must also be represented. A particular element may be optional or compulsory and it may occur once only or more than once. If its occurrence is optional, a "?" is shown in the top left corner of the box. If it is repeatable, a "*" is shown in the top right corner. If both symbols are shown, the element may occur once, many times or not at all, thus only two flags are required to represent the four possibilities that are available in SGML.

Subordinate elements are either "nodes" or "leaves". Leaf elements are shown as boxes drawn with double lines and are of various types. Some may contain text (ie., CDATA)) while others may exist solely to define reference points within text or to mark where graphics are to be incorporated. The type of leaf is shown within the box (eg., HREF). Nodes may be named structures or unnamed "groups", the latter represented in SGML by the use of parenthesis within an element definition. The screen display for a group is a box containing (. . . .).

The width of the screen display (80 columns) is sufficient to accommodate a maximum of seven subordinate elements. If there are more than seven, the display must be scrolled horizontally by moving the cursor to the left or right in order to reveal them all. When the display first appears, the parent box is highlighted (ie., shown in reverse video). Keying return causes the highlight (in effect, the cursor) to move to the first of the subordinate elements. It may then be moved to the right, and then to the left, by using the cursor right and left keys respectively. If there are more than seven subordinate elements, the horizontal line connecting them will extend to the right of the screen, terminated by a right pointing arrow, to indicate that there are more elements. When the cursor is moved beyond the right-most element, the seven existing elements will move one space to the left to reveal the next one and the first is effectively scrolled off the left edge of the screen. If there are more than eight subordinate elements, the horizontal connection will now extend the full width of the screen.

With the parent box highlighted, a number of facilities are available through function keys. The relationships between subordinate elements (eg., CHOICE, RANDOM or SEQUENCE) may be defined, the name of the parent may be changed and it may be defined, the name of the parent may be changed and it may be made optional and/or repeatable. The attributes that are to be associated with a particular element may also be defined, together with possible values for each attribute.

Attributes are extensions to the basic concept of generic coding that enable specific elements, or groups of elements, within a document to be identified. The DTD file defines the identities of the attributes, if any, for each element definition; for each attribute, a list of possible values must also be supplied.

These values may be literal (eg., red, green, blue for the attribute colour) or generic (eg., NUMERIC for issue, STRING for author). In order to assign attributes to elements, and possible values to attributes, use is made of two drop-down menus. The first is displayed at the top left of the screen when the ATTRIBUTES function key is pressed, and shows a list of all the attributes that are currently defined for the parent element, with the top one highlighted. New attributes may then be added to this list, or existing ones deleted, using the appropriate cursor and function keys. Values may be specified for a particular attribute by first selecting it and then pressing the return key. A second drop-down menu will then appear, adjacent to the first, listing the currently available values for the selected attribute. New values may then be added or existing ones deleted (Figure 3).

When an existing DTD file is being modified, or a new one created, the parent element in the initial display is the one that encompasses the complete document (eg., book, doc). The structures of subordinate elements are accessed by selecting them using the return and cursor keys. Whenever a subordinate element is highlighted and the return key is pressed, this element becomes the parent and its subordinate elements are displayed and so on. The entire document structure may thus be readily traversed, with the escape key being used to move back upwards to the parent's parent.

In order to modify the current list of subordinate elements a number of functions are available. New elements may be inserted before or after existing ones, existing ones may be deleted and their occurrence indicators (ie., "?" and "*") may be modified. Facilities are also available to create leaves and groups as well as named elements.

In summary, the DTD Editor enables the document designer to specify the potential structures of documents, in terms of their constituent elements, without having to be concerned with the complex element definition language of SGML. By using a graphical display, the relationships between elements can be appreciated much more readily than is possible by inspection of the SGML source text alone, however carefully formatted this may be. The program can be readily extended to support features such as inclusions/exclusions, entities, marked sections, etc.

3. The Text Editor

Having defined a new document type definition, this may now be used to create a structured document that conforms to its rules. The SGML Text Editor can create a new file from scratch or else modify an existing file, either one that already contains SGML codes or one that consists solely of "raw" text. Output from the SGML Text Editor is in the form of a syntactically correct SGML text file that conforms to the specified DTD. This file is thus ready for translation into typesetter output codes in the normal way, by reference to a matching "electronic style sheet".

The input file either contains its own DTD or else a reference to the appropriate DTD file. The Editor parses the file and presents the author with a representation of the top level structure of the document that bears a superficial resemblance to the "box tree" structure displayed by the DTD Editor, is a parent box with subordinate boxes below (Figure 4). The essential difference is that, in the case of the DTD Editor, the tree represents the **possible** structure of the document, whereas here it shows the **actual** structure. For example, if the possible subordinates to a particular element are FRONT, MAIN and BACK, but only MAIN and BACK currently have text attached to them, then the box containing FRONT will not be shown. Similarly, where the DTD Editor display shows that there is a CHOICE of subordinate elements, the text editor display can only ever show one (ie., the **actual** element selected). Likewise, where there is a connection indicator in the DTD display to indicate that certain elements **must** occur in a particular sequence, there are no connection indicators in the editor display; the elements are ordered exactly as shown on the screen, ie., left to right. Furthermore, if there are two elements of the same type that follow one another immediately (eg., a sequence of paragraphs), the corresponding box will show the **actual** number of such elements (eg., 5) rather than the "*" symbol that, in the DTD display, indicates simply that more than one instance of that element is possible.

The actual document may, however, be traversed in much the same manner as the DTD. Subordinate and parent elements may be selected easily using the return, escape and cursor movement keys. Where the highlighted element represents two or more consecutive elements (eg., 6 consecutive paragraphs), keying return alone will be insufficient to select an element. Instead, one of the elements must first be identified, either by number or by attribute. Selection by number is the default and, by default again, the first element will be selected. If, however, selection by attribute is specified, a drop-down menu showing the possible attributes will appear, from which one may be selected. Again, although superficially similar to the attribute menu shown by the DTD Editor, this menu will only show those attributes which have **actually** been assigned to the selected element, not all of those that **could** be thus assigned. Similarly, when a particular attribute has been selected from the first drop-down menu, the second menu will only show those values that have **actually** been given for the selected attribute. This second menu will therefore show only literal values (eg., red, draft) and never generic ones (eg., NUMBER, STRING). Once the desired subordinate element has been selected, and assuming it is not a terminal element, it will in turn become the parent element, with its subordinate elements below. Where, as described above, the element is one of a sequence of the same type, the sequence number will be shown in the top right corner of the parent box.

Ultimately, as a descent is made through the document structure, a leaf will be reached. Again, there is a subtle difference here between the Text Editor and the DTD Editor. Where a structure has been defined as being recursive, a path can be chosen through the DTD that will never reach a node. This is not the case with the Text Editor, because the only boxes depicted are those to which text has already been attached. When a leaf is reached, the graphical display is replaced by a text display, with the cursor resting at the beginning of the selected element. Unlike a typical word processor, then, where the display initially begins at the start of the file, the author in this system may jump immediately to, say, the start of Chapter 7.

Once in text mode, all the usual word processor/text editor features are provided. These include full screen editing (ie., cursor up/down/left/right, delete, backspace, insert, scroll, etc.), block definition, search and replace, and so on. There are some notable features, however, which characterize this editor and distinguish it from others. In particular, there is no concept of output line length, as this has yet to be defined in generic markup. Instead, words are "wrapped" when the width of the screen is exceeded.

There are essentially two types of text elements that may occur within a document, namely those that are terminated by line end codes (eg., paragraph), and those that are not (eg., short quotation). The first type may contain the second as the subordinate element, but the second cannot contain the first. As the text display does not show any of the tags that will ultimately delimit the elements in the SGML file, ways must be found to distinguish one element from another. There are basically two approaches here, namely line indentation and character emphasis. Line indentation is clearly only appropriate for elements that are terminated by line and codes, and the indentation effectively defines the "depth of nesting" of the element within the document. If a chapter contains sections which in turn contain paragraphs, the paragraphs will be indented more than the sections and the sections more than the chapters. We thus have yet another visual representation of document structure. In the case of elements that are not terminated by line and codes, these can only be distinguished from one another by differences in screen emphasis (eg., colour, brightness, underline, etc.).

In order to clarify further the current position within the document (ie., the element containing the cursor), the top line of the screen shows the logical number of the lowest level elements (eg., Chapter = 3, Section = 2, Para = 1). These numeric values are continuously updated as the author moves the cursor through the document. If, at any time, the ESCAPE key is pressed, the text display will be replaced by the logical document structure tree, where the highlighted element will be the one currently occupied by the cursor. (NOTE that this may not be the one through which the editor was first entered).

One feature of this editor that is common to any WYSIWYG (What You See Is What You Get) editor is that, without markup, an ambiguity can arise when inserting new text. This occurs if the insert point is at the start of an element in mid-line. Is the new text to be appended after the text of the preceding element, or is it to be inserted before the text of the current element? The ambiguity is resolved by having two insert modes (ie., INSERT and APPEND) in addition to the alternative OVERSTRIKE mode. The current mode is shown in the top right corner of the screen.

Where a new element is to be created, its name may be selected from a drop-down menu of elements that are currently available for use at that particular point within the document. This effectively prevents an element from being created where it should not occur (eg., a new chapter in the bibliography).

In some cases, it may not be necessary to select the next element explicitly at all. If the return key is pressed within a paragraph, for example, this will be taken as a command to start a new paragraph; there is no need here to select paragraph from the available elements menu.

Any document produced by this system will always be syntactically correct, although it may not yet be complete (eg., the main body may be defined in the DTD as being compulsory, but the file may be stored without it if other parts of the document are being created first). As much as possible, the author is provided with the assistance necessary to create an SGML document without having to understand the syntactical complexities of the SGML language.

In summary, the SGML Text Editor is essentially a full function word processor that has an integrated "knowledge" of the structure of the document being edited, well beyond the normal level of column/line/page. Whereas a highly skilled operator is likely to be required in order to produce a syntactically correct SGML document on a normal word processor, the Chelgraph SGML Text

Editor requires a much lower level of understanding and will produce files that are guaranteed to be syntactically correct, thus greatly reducing proof reading overheads. Moreover, its availability on a low cost computer makes it a suitable solution for authors who may be physically far removed from the production site, or where terminal resources on a mainframe system are restricted and/or expensive.

References

1. Information Processing - Text and Office Systems - Standard Generalized Markup Language (SGML). Draft International Standard, (ISO/DIS 8879 TC/97).

2. SGML Users´ Group Bulletin, Vol. 1, No. 1, 1986. (contains a full bibliography on page 8).

Components of Personal Publishing

Dr. R. Whitaker and Mrs. L. Robertson

University of Leeds, UK

ABSTRACT

A brief history of personal publishing leading to the current microcomputer based systems. Present systems are discussed with comparisons where alternatives exist and include the use of mainframe computers, microcomputers, and dedicated phototypesetting systems. Production methods are analysed as Front End systems, Page Description languages and Back End systems. A description of a computer communication link to a professional printer's typesetter is given.

KEYWORDS

Personal Publishing; Microcomputers; Printing

Introduction

Personal publishing is to be taken to mean the production of paper text by the use of electronic aids. Although there are connections with other electronic based publication methods such as laser discs and computer based databases these are not considered for the purpose of this paper.

Traditional Methods

It seems sensible to consider all the possible systems first of all, then move on to see what is available at the moment, and finally take a look to the future.

First a quick look at the history of printed publications, which started long ago with 'pen and paper' and humans acting as duplicators, each person producing a hand written copy of someones original. Many years later the influence of mechanisms lead to a uniform way of personal production of writing, the typewriter. The typewriter and printing systems together lead people to expect a quality of printing which is not possible with handwriting and the added economics of mechanical systems resulted in their widespread use and acceptance.

Mechanical typing and printing lead to certain restrictions on material written for mechanical output, machines are not yet as flexible as human hands. Similar restrictions are also characteristic of the more modern Electronic Printing systems, though the problems are gradually being overcome.

The newer Electronic Methods include wordprocessors and printers which produce text which looks very much like the typing from an electric typewriter. The ideas of wordprocessors and electric printing have lead to the many cheap, portable electric typewriters which we can see in shops today.

The next step seems to be to remove some of the restrictions on how and where text is placed on paper, and to allow pictures, graphs and diagrams to be placed in the text as easily as words are at present. Technology progresses and the means to achieve flexibility is becoming available. Prices have dropped and this now makes possible the microcomputer (or computer) based personal publishing system. Today we may well use a microcomputer to take in and store typed text, preview pages of text on its screen, then print it on a laserprinter, and finally send it to a very high quality typesetter for bromides ready to send to a printer.

It is relatively easy to achieve high quality output of text today, though there is less intervention by the printer or publisher which can lead to printed works looking a little like duplicated, typed sheets. The aspects of printing design are very important if the quality of books and journals are to be preserved. The promise of the future is that computer programs will allow design and style to be used automatically as you set up pages of output. This has some way to go before convincing systems are possible. Some measures of quality, such as reading age can be automated as can some grammar analyses and some page layout information can be forced on the text, though a printers design constraints cannot.

Available Systems

Current wordprocessors and some typesetting systems tend to be set up to be used with one printer or output device. The mechanical parts of the system naturally fall into a typewriter-like device to input text with commands, and some kind of separate printer for output. Input devices and systems are usually called Front End Systems and the corresponding output devices are called Back End Systems. This separation of the parts is more noticeable today with various companies working on one area or the other, and sometimes both.

Front End Systems

There are many ways to get text into a system. The traditional approach is to have the text retyped and to have formatting commands added at the same time. Increasingly printers are arranging to have text, which is already in a computer readable form, sent directly to their typesetting systems. In order to show where headings, or other features occur we must insert some commands into the raw text called Mark Up. Other systems for Front End input of text can include:

Optical Character Reading
> (Available from bureaus and as desk top machines connected to microcomputers)

Floppy Disc Readers
> (Several printers have equipment to read a number of different discs - companies can be found to read any disc, but charges can be high.)

Mainframe Links
> (Public packet switched data networks can extend this to any computer connected to a network throughout the world)

Microcomputers
> (These can often be linked directly to printing equipment or use file transfer software such as KERMIT, or have their disc read)

Where the text comes in a machine readable form, the coding for commands has been developed at an international level in recent years. Standardised Generalised Mark up Language (SGML) is to be accepted later this year and printers and publishers are indicating adoption of the standard.

The typesetter and printer will have one kind of Front End System but there are now a range of other programs which can achieve the same thing but with varying degrees of compatibility. These include:

SCRIPT
> (This is a markup language which has developed for computer printers, and has recently been enhanced to provide some typesetter facilities - it is best with typewriter like output devices.)

TEX
> (This was designed for Mathematical typesetting using mainframe computers and is now available on microcomputers eg Macintosh, IBM PCs)

NROFF, TROFF
> (These are for UNIX systems - NROFF is for typewriter like output, TROFF for typsetters.)

Pagemaker
> (One of the best examples of the new programs which make professional typesetting possible on a microcomputer, in this case the Macintosh.)

Wordprocessors
> (Many different wordprocessors are used. They can be used to prepare marked up text.)

Image Scanners
> (Pictures can be included with the text if the image can be digitised.)

Graphics
> (The more general printers can output high quality graphs which may now be integrated into documents.)

It is worth noting that the older programs such as SCRIPT, TEX, TROFF and NROFF are really 'batch' systems where you cannot see the output page until the program has run through the whole of the text file. The new systems aim to show something on the screen which is very nearly the same as what you will get on the paper. This speeds up production and is easier to use, eliminating the need for complicated commands. You don't have to learn to program to use them.

Some of these alternate Front Ends can drive output devices
directly, but the trend is towards some kind of intermediate
description of a page which is then understood by a range of
output devices.

Intermediate Descriptions

For many Front End Systems, to use a new printer requires a change
in the way that the program is set up, which can involve a lot of
work. A solution to this inflexibility has been proposed by
several companies. It is that if some standard way of connecting
a new device is used then it should be easy to print output on a
range of devices, perhaps including a laserprinter and a
typesetter. This would allow cheap proof copies on a laserprinter
and minimal differences with the final typeset version. Device
independant systems include:

> PostScript
> > (This is a Page Description language which allows
> > all kinds of text and images to be mixed on a
> > page. Currently it is available for the Apple
> > Laserwriter and Linotype typesetters. It can be
> > used with any raster output device. It is
> > currently the most flexible system.)
>
> Interpress
> > (This is the Xerox version which is used within
> > their publishing system. Its manuals are freely
> > available but is not so widely used.)
>
> ACE
> > (This is by a British company ,CHELGRAPH.)
>
> CoraV
> > (This is used by Linotype typesetters and is
> > representative of the equivalent manufacturer's
> > specific codes.)

PostScript by Adobe Systems is the most promising Page Description
System. A small PostScript program in a Postscript printer can
simulate a device such as a Diablo daisy wheel printer, or some
other simple printer. The inclusion of Graphics is also very
simple with this language. It is worth remembering that most
people would not see the intermediate Page Description code, since
its programs would be written by the Front End System.

Back End Systems

A printer of some kind is required to show the results of the
composition. The highest quality output is from a typesetter.
The The next best output is that from a laserprinter. These can
vary in quality but the Hewlett Packard and Cannon devices give
good, clear, black images. At a slightly lower resolution a
Versatec plotter gives reasonable results. At lower quality come
the matrix printers and ink jet printers. The common daisy wheel
printer gives quite good quality but will not give graphics or a
wide range of fonts.

It is worth being aware that having a compatible series of Back
Ends would allow text to be prepared for the visually disabled, in

Braille or Moon, probably including graphics, so that disabled people may make full use of publications.

Various specialised printers provide typesetting services as a separate back end for other peoples prepared and formatted text.

The Future

As microcomputers become faster and memory becomes cheaper it will be easy to have a high resolution graphics display which will allow us to see the pages of a book as we type them in. Including pictures and graphics will be easy and output will be on a laserprinter for proof copies and to a typesetter for the final pages.

Laserprinters will have a higher resolution, moving from 300 dots per inch to perhaps 1000 dots per inch. At the same time typesetters will have higher resolutions from 1000 dots per inch towards 5000 dots per inch. This will result in better quality printing, but we will still have to be careful about style and design.

Present Costs

A typical microcomputer based publishing system may be made up of:

Macintosh	£1400
Pagemaker software	£ 520
Laserwriter	£6400
total	£8320

An IBM PC based system would probably cost the same.

A typesetter would cost between £26,000 and £37,000. The cost per copy from a laserprinter is about 10p if we include the cost of the machine as well as its consumable parts. A typesetter costs about £2 per metre of output paper.

A Printer's experience

The term personal publishing suggests that an author has control of all aspects involved in the preparation of a document from initial keying through design and page layout to printed output. However where an author requires high quality output he will need to seek the services of a commercial printer. This section of the paper looks at the experience of the University Printing Service at the University of Leeds in processing text prepared remotely on campus by authors working at word processors, microcomputers or terminals linked to the mainframe.

Background

Eight years ago initial experiments were carried out to see if text could be taken from a computer and passed successfully to the typesetter. Punched tape was fed in to the Compugraphic system and some output obtained. Further investigations were therefore encouraged.

In 1983 a Konnect 2 milking machine was purchased from Inter-Set. Text could be taken from word processor or the mainframe and passed through the Konnect 2 to a Linotype 7000 edit station, code conversion being done in the box. Text could then be justified and paged on the edit station before being passed to the typesetter. Several textfiles were succesfully processed using this system but a number of drawbacks were found. Some corruption of characters occurred, some small amounts of text were lost and the code conversion capability of the Konnect 2 was not sufficient to deal with the degree of markup contained in many of the documents being processed. The preparation of the conversion tapes was also time consuming. Efforts were made to keep up with new developments and to endeavour to find equipment which could overcome some of the problems experienced. In November 1985 'Book Machine' software was purchased from Prefis Ltd. This is a page make up programme running on an Apricot microcomputer.

The System

Textfiles are passed to the Apricot using Kermit communications software. The operator prepares a conversion file and layout file on the Apricot, the layout having been discussed previously with the author, or provided by the publisher. A simple search and replace programme removes the authors tags from the document and replaces them with processing instructions required by the Book Machine. An advantage of the system is the excellent WYSIWIG facility which allows page layout to be proofed on the screen. Pages can be output on a matrix printer for proofing before being passed to the typesetter.

Markup

Markup comprises additional information inserted in a document to facilitate formatting. Documents passed through this system are marked up using generic tags based on SGML. Authors are required to identify the various elements within their documents - paragraphs, quoted matter - but are not required to enter specific processing instructions. The processing instructions are inserted at the code conversion stage by Printing Service staff. This means an author is not required to have an understanding of the CORA coding system used by the typesetter.

Work undertaken

The system is ideally suited to the production of academic books with short print runs, journals, and catalogues. A number of books have already been typeset for such publishers as Butterworths and Gowers, and monthly Oncology Bulletins are produced - the bulletins catalogue developments in cancer research. The publication comprises an average of 250 pages and is delivered, printed and ringbound, to the customer within one week of the text being received from the mainframe.

Costs

Authors using this computer-linked phototypesetting service achieve savings of over 50% against the cost of conventional typesetting. When it is considered that 75% of the cost of publishing an academic book with a short print run comprises typesetting, this represents a significant saving. As time is initially invested by the Printing Service in the compilation of a conversion file and layout file documents require to be a minimum of eight A4 pages in length before the service is economic. It is hoped that investment in new equipment will enable costs to be reduced still further.

The Future

The Printing Service is currently looking at the new generation of computer typesetting systems with a view to increasing the flexibility of the system. It is hoped to provide a facility to deal with files prepared using PostScript and Troff, and eventually a means of integrating text and graphics.

Conclusions

Personal Publishing is set to increase by several hundred percent over the next 10 years. The impact will be cheaper publications and therefore more specialist publications with short print runs. I suppose paper is not dead yet.

References

PostScript Language and Reference Manual, published by Addison-Wesley, ISBN 0-201-10174-2
PostScript Language Tutorial and Cookbook, published by Addison-Wesley, ISBN 0-201-10179-3
Hart's Rules for Compositors and Readers, published by Oxford University Press, ISBN 0-19-212983-X
The Oxford Dictionary for Writers and Editors, published by Oxford University Press, ISBN 0-19-212970-8 S

Back to Basics
Simple But High-Quality Text Pagination Systems

Mike Clarke

Bradley Computing
United Kingdom

1. Introduction

This paper considers the characteristics which are desirable for a publication system which is to be used for one specialised task -- that is the production of camera-ready copy for books that are made up largely of text. For the purposes of this paper such books will be referred to as text books, although of course this term is not intended to limit us to academic volumes.

The typical application of this system will be to paginate text files which have been prepared by their author on a word-processing package, before submission to a high-resolution photo-typesetter. The design of the book will have been decided in advance and so there will be no need to make choices about fonts, point-sizes and so on during the pagination process. However there will be a emphasis on the quality of the typography, meaning that the detailed page layout and the general appearance of the book should be of as high a standard as possible.

It is a matter of debate who is likely to be the responsible for the pagination process. Certainly, in the academic field many publishers are asking authors to supply their own camera-ready copy, and authors of particularly complex volumes (for example those in exotic languages) are likely to want to retain control of the typesetting themselves. Other publishers, on the other hand, prefer to keep typesetting under their own control, perhaps so as to maintain a consistent house style. For the purposes of this paper this question is left unresolved and so the system should be designed to be suitable for a variety of users, and should be able to run on the type of hardware which is likely to be available to all such users.

A large number of packages have been developed over the last year or so under the general heading of desk-top publication systems. It is by no means clear whether such systems are necessarily appropriate for the production of copy for text books. They are often designed to be very flexible in their ability to create page images which combine text and graphical images. This very flexibility may make them unnecessarily complex, and yet they may not provide some particular facilities which are highly desirable for the production of well-set text. Lastly, not all such systems will run on the computers which are most likely to be available to potential users. It is the contention of this paper that a system designed specifically to cater for this one task is likely to be more appropriate than a generalized page make-up system.

The paper therefore starts from first principles and aims to develop the specifications of a system which provides, in as simple a manner as possible, the facilities necessary for pagination text books to a high typographic standard. The system will be suitable for a range of users from authors to typographers, and will run on personal computers.

In what follows the general principles of the design of the system are discussed, and specific examples of their application are given by referring to a pagination system called MICROSET [Clarke86], the development of which has prompted the ideas set down in this paper.

2. A Specification for the System

The potential user of the system could range from a specialist typographer to a non-technical author. This means that the system should be suitable for use by people of varying backgrounds and abilities. The key concept to be applied in achieving this aim is flexibility both in terms of the facilities offered, the interface with the user and the level of help given by the system.

So, for example, authors of books with only simple typographic layout may wish pagination to take place largely automatically, with only those cases of poor layout which cannot be handled by the system being logged for user action. When action is required on the part of these users they will probably need to be told in non-technical language what is wrong and what options are open to them. A professional typographer working on a complex layout, on the other hand, may prefer to have hands-on control over the setting of each page, with the ability to tune the layout as required. This user's requirements for help from the system will be limited to brief reminders about how to use the less commonly used functions.

All types of user, however will have some requirements in common. These include:

- standard typesetting procedures for hyphenation, justification and pagination.

- more complex typesetting facilities such as the incorporation of footnotes, multi-column setting and so on.

- some help from the system in recognising aspects of poor typographic layout.

- the ability to view the appearance of each page and adjust it as necessary.

- an interface between the pagination system and the typesetting hardware which allows the correction of minor errors in the final output.

The specification for the system is discussed below in terms of the above topics.

3. Interfaces to the System

3.1 The input interface

Consideration of the input and output interface is to some extent secondary to the design of the core of the system itself, because it is a comparatively simple matter to write different front- and back-ends to provide alternative interfaces. Nevertheless, the discussion of the design of the system commences with consideration of these interfaces because once the principles behind these have been established the role of the remainder of the system becomes more obvious.

The input files for the system will consist of the text to be set, interspersed with layout commands which tell the system how the text is to be formated.

The files may have originated from a variety of sources. They might have been prepared in isolation on an author's word-processor, or may be typed-in with the knowledge that they will be used for this system. In order to maintain flexiblity it is important that the system can accept any character file, with no special requirements so far as the format of layout commands is concerned.

The internal working-level of layout commands will be those which directly drive typesetter functions, such as "change font", "insert em-space", "quad left" and so on. But for many applications it will be convenient to build macro commands at the level of "start new paragraph", "use A-heading style" etc. These macro commands would normally be character codes typed within the text file, but could also, at least in some cases, be driven directly from word-processor control codes. The system will therefore need user-definable conversions between these different levels of layout commands.

It is not intended that the system should normally be used for text input and editing of the text file. It would be better for each user to use their preferred editing utility for this purpose. Nevertheless, a simple editor should be provided within the system so that minor corrections may be made to the input file, for example if errors are noticed during pagination, and for the keyboard input of supplementary text (for example it may be necessary to add an entry name with the word "continued" at the start of a new page in an index).

3.2 The output interface

The output file from the system must drive, either directly or indirectly, the typesetting hardware. In order to provide compatibility with different types of hardware it would be sensible to use some form of generalized page description language [Reid86]. But whatever language is used, the overriding requirement of the output interface is that users should be able to view and understand the contents of the system's output file. This will enable them to edit that file should it be necessary to correct minor errors in the final output. If the system output file was written in binary code, for example, then sections of the text would have to be re-paginated to correct even the most trivial errors.

4. The Screen Display

In aiming at a high-quality end-product the system must provide some sort of preview facility whereby the user may see in advance what each page will look like, and change its appearance if necessary. The facility which can be provided is limited by the resolution of the display screens on the computers on which the system will run. Ideally, we would like to provide a faithful reproduction of the page on the computer display, but it was a requirement of the initial specification for the system that it should run on commonly available hardware. This rules out the use of expensive bit-mapped displays, and while some personal computers do provide high resolution displays which would enable the use of high-quality page displays, it must be accepted that a large number of potential users will be using IBM-PC hardware.

The best resolution achievable by machines in the IBM PC range when using "standard" graphics cards is only 720 x 350 pixels, and this is not sufficient to give a representation of a typical typeset page with characters displayed in their correct shapes. The choice therefore is:

a) show only part of the page in an exact representation, or

b) show the complete page in some other representation.

The latter option is considered to be the correct one, since the visual balance of the whole page is a particularly important aspect of the typograhic style of the finished product. The solution is therefore to represent the whole page on the computer screen by drawing a horizontal line to represent the position and length of each word (see figure 1).

This type of representation is perfectly adequate to provide the user with an indication of how the finished page will look. Inter-word and inter-line spaces are indicated (approximately) to scale, and the placement of headings and the existence of widows or orphans is immediately apparent. The content of the text is not so important at this stage since it will have been proof-read before the pagination commences. Nevertheless it is possible to provide facilities which allow the contents of each line on the page to be inspected. The fact that it is not possible to view characters in their correct fonts is not crucial because the styles to be used will have been decided in advance of the actual pagination. Given a colour display, changes of font could be indicated by plotting the word lines in different colours; this would provide a check that the various font changes specified by the design had in fact been followed in the text input.

Even this simplified display is limited by the resolution of the computer display -- particularly in the vertical dimension. When using the standard IBM graphics adaptor the maximum number of text lines which can be displayed on the screen turns out to be about 80 (the greater resolution of the Hercules graphics card allows it to display 140 lines) and so pages with more than this number of lines will have to be displayed in sections with provision for scrolling from one section to another. The limits of the screen resolution also mean that the screen representation cannot be exactly to scale. The plotting of text lines gives an adequate representation of their vertical separation for most purposes, but if exact measurements are required then the values will have to be displayed in numeric form.

In the MICROSET system the (monochrome) screen display (figure 1) distinguishes between fonts by plotting the word-line for fonts other than the standard one as dotted lines. A cursor ("A") may be moved to point at any line, whereupon the words which make up the line are displayed on the screen ("B"), and a block of statistics about the line is also shown ("C").

5. Hyphenation and Justification

The operation of the system so far as justification is concerned is fairly straightforward. Character widths are determined from width tables and lines are built up using a user-defined minimum inter-word space. Unit adds and subtracts, and kerning are supported. The actual

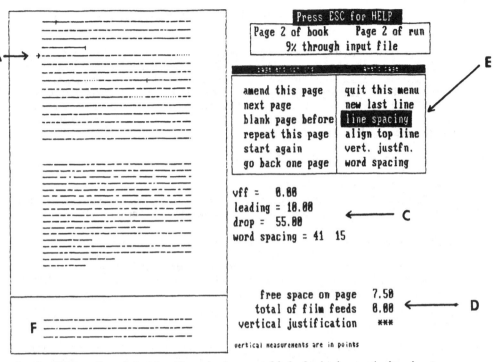

In the thirteenth and fourteenth centuries, any kind of mission sent abroad wat

FIGURE 1 - The screen display of the MICROSET system.

inter-word space for the line is calculated when the line end is reached, and is stored for future use.

Hyphenation is invoked if the actual word-space exceeds a user- definable maximum value. A standard automatic hyphenation routine could be incorporated, but currently only manual hyphenation is provided -- the justification procedure halts and the user is invited to choose where to split the offending word (or he may force the word onto the current or succeeding line). Manual hyphenation conforms to the policy of providing user control where possible, and indeed is a requirement when exotic languages are being set, but automatic hyphenation may be more suitable for some applications.

6. Pagination and Vertical Justification

Once a page has been filled with text lines then it may be that the last line is not exactly at the foot of the page. In this case vertical justification is required, involving increasing the inter-line spacing within the body of the page to force the last line down onto the true end of the page.

In the present system this may be achieved either manually, or automatically by proportionately increasing the current inter-line spacing until all free space at the foot of the page is eliminated. This automatic vertical justification may be applied either to the leadings of the text lines ('feathering'), or may be limited to changing the values of any explicit white space on the page (for example space above and below headings).

7. Footnotes

The ability to handle footnotes is an important requirement for academic texts. This is achieved by supplying a secondary input file which contains only the notes, and marking the points at which they are referenced within the main text. When one of these references is encountered the system reads the next footnote from the secondary input file and notionally sets it at the foot of the page. A check is made to ensure that the footnote reference number at the start of the note itself matches that referenced in the main text. The actual placement of the footnote on the page then depends on how much space is available. When the page is almost full an algorithm is invoked which is similar to that which controls line justification. The implied space which would appear between the foot of the main text and the start of the footnotes is calculated, and is compared with user-defined minimum and maximum values. According to the result of this comparison the footnote may be included on the current page, or be split between two pages, or the whole footnote and the text line which references it may be held over until the next page.

8. Page Layout

Very flexible page layout is not so important for a package limited to producing text books as it is for a more general page make-up system. The requirements for this system will normally consist of the setting of a linear stream of text according to a fairly constant page design. Allowance must be made for leaving space for plates, either across the whole measure or as cut-ins with the text flowing around the space. Text should be capable of being set in more than one column (for example for indexes and dictionaries), and simple tabular layout should be supported.

More general aspects of page layout such as running heads or foots and page numbering are of course required.

9. Aspects of Typographic Style

There are three ways in which the system is designed to help the user achieve a respectable standard of typographic design:

   a) the displays should present users with sufficient information so that they can judge in advance what the page will look like.

   b) the system itself makes some basic checks on style and reports contraventions to the user.

   c) the user is able to change the layout to improve poor design.

9.1 The displays

As has been discussed above, the aim is to display a whole page of text in such a way that the visual balance of the page can readily be assessed. In addition, the first three lines of the next page are displayed so that a check may be made for orphans and other undesirable aspects of layout (see "F" in figure 1).

If the visual representation is not considered to be sufficiently accurate use can be made of the following statistics which are displayed by the system:

   - the actual inter-word spacing on each line ("C" in figure 1).

   - the inter-word spacing which would be necessary to pull an extra word from the next line onto the current line ("C").

   - the inter-line spacing between any pair of lines ("C").

   - the 'free-space' between the last line and the actual foot of the page ("D").

These statistics provide a very precise view of how the page has been set and how it might be altered.

9.2 System checks on style

The system may be asked to check on various aspects of typographic style. It is important to note that the definition of "good style" is not imposed by the system. Users may select whether or not to have these problems reported, and may even make their own decision about their definition; for example a short line at the top of a page will only be considered to be an "orphan" if it is shorter than a user-defined proportion of the total measure. The checks made are:

   - short lines at top or bottom of the page ("orphans" and "widows"). (As shown here.)

- incorrect vertical placement of top or bottom lines.

- the last line ending with a hyphenated word.

- objects such as sub-headings appearing within a specified distance from the foot of the page.

Other potential problems, such as very short lines at the end of a paragraph, could easily be added to the list.

9.3 Dealing with problems

After a page has been set by the system the user may alter it in a wide variety of ways. Vertical space may be inserted (or removed) between any pair of lines, either to open up space for a plate, or to make subtle adjustments to the balance of the page. Portions of the text may be reset with altered margins (to produce cut-ins) or with non-standard inter-word spacing (to alter the arrangement of words in each line and thereby remove awkward short lines).

Lastly, vertical justification may be imposed before setting of the next page is initiated. In the MICROSET system these options are selected from a menu window ("E" in Figure 1).

10. Automatic (Batch) Running

In order to have complete manual control over the pagination process the system is run in an interactive mode, in which case the system pauses at the end of each page for possible user intervention. In some cases, however, such close control will not be necessary and so various levels of batch running are supported. The batch process is controlled by the choice of system action on encountering any of the above problems. In each case the action may be set to "ignore", "fix" or "pause".

In "fix" mode the system makes its own attempt to overcome the perceived problem, and records what it has done in a log file, while in "pause" mode the system halts for the user to impose a solution. "Ignore" just switches off action for this particular problem (although its occurence is still recorded in the log file).

This arrangement provides users with the ability to decide the exact balance between their own, and the system's, control of the pagination process.

11. Conclusions - An Implementation of the System

The implementation of these principles in the MICROSET system was developed for use with the Oxford University Computing Service's Monotype LASERCOMP typesetter. The system is currently specific to that environment since it uses the OUCS LASERCHECK [OUCS82] language for layout commands in both input and output interfaces. In all other respects, however, the implementation is entirely standard and follows the above specification in most details.

MICROSET has been running on BBC micro-computers for some 18 months, and a version for IBM-PC compatible machines is about to be released; figure 1 is a screen-dump taken from the PC version. A number of books have been produced with the system and the experience gained thus far confirms that it contains the facilities which are needed to help users to produce high-quality typography for a range of different kinds of book design.

It is not suggested that the system specification drawn up here is necessarily original, nor does it claim to provide the last word in pagination systems. But it has been a useful exercise to attempt to provide all the essential facilities for this particular application in as simple a package as possible. The exercise might be seen as an example of an attempt to balance the needs of the application against the limitations imposed by the hardware we wish to use.

Acknowledgements

Thanks are due to those who have supported and contributed ideas to this work, but the views expressed in this paper are entirely the responsibility of the author.

References

[Clarke86] M.I. Clarke, MICROSET User Manual, Bradley Computing, 1986.

[Reid86] B.K. Reid, "Procedural Page Description Languages", in: Text Processing and Document Manipulation , J.C. vanVliet (ed), CUP, 1986.

[OUCS82] Oxford University Computing Service, LASERCHECK User Manual, OUCS, 1986.

Videotex - Current Achievements & Future Prospects

Barry Ashdown

Langton Videotex Ltd.
133 Oxford Street
London, W1R

Abstract

This paper describes the characteristics that differentiate videotex from other technologies and the considerations for its use. It goes on to discuss the application areas identified for videotex. Contrary to popular opinion these are not constrained by industry boundaries but fall into four categories: sales communication, point of sale, management information systems and consumer applications.

Keywords: videotex, viewdata, communications

Videotex is the linking together of an inexpensive terminal to a host computer through a communications network. Nothing clever you might say, so why is this apparently simple technology transforming business operations in so many companies around the world.

First, it permits the connection of a standard terminal to host systems running on almost any make or model of computer. This of course has been achieved before by both Teletype terminals in the 1960´s and ASCII Terminals in the 1970´s. What they failed to achieve however, was one simple, standardized user interface with a command language that could be mastered in a few minutes. Videotex truely gives online interactive computing to remote users with no computing experience.

The term videotex of course encompasses much more than just easy interactive computing. There is information retrieval from a videotex database of frames normally edited with colour and simple graphics, data collection frames which are used for user input of variables to an application program, there is session control and the collection of usage and performance statistics, and there is system management with the ability to control user registration and privileges. Security is an important component. Lastly, there is a sophisticated electronic mail system integrated within most videotex products.

All of this can be delivered to a variety of terminal types across the many videotex networks available.

Videotex, like any new technology, will only be adopted if it benefits an organization - usually by increasing revenue or reducing costs. Videotex is shown by many organizations to achieve both of these goals.

Income is increased through competitive advantage and being able to quickly and accurately locate and price stock. Cost savings come in the form of faster stock turnover and removal of data processing intermediaries for data preparation and error handling. Year one payback on investment is quite normal while some companies have increased their market share by up to 10% through the introduction of Videotex. What is more, staff productivity is often improved through increased job satisfaction.

Many people refer to videotex as being industry specific and point to the travel, motor and insurance industries as early adopters of this technology. However, a review of current application shows that videotex has much broader appeal spanning four generic application areas: sales communication, point of sale (retail outlets), management information systems and consumer applications.

Sales Communications

Salesmen are equipped with a videotex adaptor for their domestic TV, a dedicated videotex terminal or perhaps a PC. Each morning they dial the company videotex system, send and receive electronic mail and look up order history, payment record and other pertinent information on the clients to be visited. Some may be printed out for reference during the day.

At the end of the working day the salesman will once again log onto videotex and use the mail system. Orders can be entered online (instead of filling in and posting forms) and validated immediately.

The salesman benefits by improved communications with the company and his peers, and by having access on demand, from his home, to the information he needs to maximise sales with fewer time consuming visits to the branch office.

The company gains in many ways. Orders are processed perhaps days before they would have been using the post. Stock is turned over faster and warehousing costs reduced. Stationery costs are another savings. There is no need for data preparation staff or a department to sort out erroneous orders.

Combine these savings with the increased revenue generated by an efficient and highly motivated sales team and you really start to appreciate the benefits of videotex. Many companies in the pharmaceutical, cosmetic, chemical, agricultural, confectionery, tobacco and other fast moving consumer goods industries have already realized these benefits.

Point of Sale

Whether installing terminals for use by your retail sales staff or providing a service to third parties, videotex has much to offer.

Stock locator applications pioneered by the motor industry have increased turnover dramatically. No longer does the salesman have to say "I´m sorry Sir, we will have to order that from the factory; it will be here in three months". Using the videotex system the salesman can locate the appropriate vehicle in stock at other dealers, arrange a trade and go back to the client with "We can have it delivered here tomorrow sir; how would you like to pay?" This, of course, is equally applicable to many other businesses.

Many organizations with their own retail outlets employ Videotex as a direct alternative to EPOS. It is particularly well suited to stores selling white and brown electrical goods including gas and electricity showrooms. Here there is a requirement to carry a wide range of goods with only demonstration models in the shop. Using Videotex the salesman can place orders online and confirm price and delivery to the client. The sale is made, the order placed and no paperwork or intermediaries were involved.

In the fiercely competitive world of package holidays videotex has long been the key to major growth among the leading tour operators. It is now standard practice for the High Street travel agent to book holidays through a videotex terminal. The client is serviced more quickly than is possible with telephone calls and can steer the conversation when alternatives are offered. The travel agent closes the sale quickly and is relieved of form filling. The tour operator can handle many more concurrent bookings at less cost than was possible when working through VDU operators at the head office.

Insurance companies and finance houses need to communicate with sales outlets whether it be broker, agent, High Street building society office or car showroom. Increasingly these outlets are going to place business with the company that provides easy online access for quotation and policy look up. Gone forever are the days of the quill pen!

Management Information Systems

Maximum business efficiency can only be achieved if managers at all levels have timely and accurate information to work with. Printing out great reports is a sure way to miss that goal. Putting it online using regular VDU´s may benefit the computer literate but will baffle the rest. Videotex is the solution.

Videotex is simple enough for children and chief executives to use (both have terrible trouble with VDU´s). Information can be displayed in colour with bar charts and histograms. Accessing the system is as easy for the remote branch manager as it is for head office staff. With a terminal at home the busy manager can have access to the latest data 24 hours a day, seven days a week.

Consumer Applications

It has been said that applications for the population at large have been slow to take off. This is hardly surprising when you consider the enormous social impact which they herald. As a consumer you can now do from the comfort of your armchair many things which previously required letter writing, form filling, phone calls or trips to the High Street. For businesses wishing to reach the consumer the potential is enormous.

There is a wealth of information services particularly on public videotex systems; from weather forecasts to timetables, from company marketing through to share prices. However, it is the interactive applications which are of more consequence.

Shopping is easy. Order the goods online and they are delivered to your door. Whole mail order catalogues are available and some supermarkets are providing a grocery service.

For the financially astute, telebanking and share dealing services are providing online access to customer accounts. For those who prefer to trust to luck, there are betting services. Online voting and opinion polls are used in association with TV talent shows and current affairs programs. How long will it be before we have online referenda on local government and national issues.

Videotex is slowly but surely changing our lives!

Authors' Biographies

Rae A. Earnshaw

Dr. Earnshaw was born in York, England and educated at Roundhay School and the University of Leeds. He holds the BSc and PhD degrees and has been a faculty staff member for 18 years. He heads the graphics team responsible for campus-wide provision of computer graphics hardware and software. His PhD in computer graphics was the first to be awarded by the University.

He is a member of the British Computer Society, Chairman of the Computer Graphics and Displays Group, and Vice-Chairman of the Technical Committee on Computers in Graphics, Design, and Manufacture. He has been a Visiting Professor at Illinois Institute of Technology, Chicago; Northwestern Polytechnical University, Xian, China; and George Washington University, Washington D.C. He has acted as a consultant to US companies and the College CAD/CAM Consortium and given seminars at a variety of UK and US institutions and research laboratories. He is the author and editor of many papers, monographs and proceedings, including "Fundamental Algorithms for Computer Graphics" published by Springer-Verlag in 1985, and also co-editor (with David F. Rogers) of "Techniques in Computer Graphics", also published by Springer-Verlag in 1987. He has been a Panel Chair at SIGGRAPH 84 and SIGGRAPH 85.

His current interests are graphics algorithms, integrated graphics and text, display technology, CAD/CAM, and human-computer interface issues. He is a member of SIGGRAPH, ACM, IEEE, IEEE Computer Society, an Associate Fellow of the Institute of Mathematics and its Applications, and a Fellow of the British Computer Society.

Ian O. Angell

Ian O. Angell is Professor of Information Systems at London School of Economics and Political Science. A member of BCS, he is researching into information systems, geometric modelling, statistical and computational geometry, applications of computer graphics and multimedia document architectures.

Barry Ashdown

Barry Ashdown is a Director of Langton Videotex, Ltd. He has been responsible for Videotex products at Langton since the launch of the PREVIEW formatting package in 1978. He conceived and specified PIII, the Videotex software package for both IBM and Burroughs mainframes. PIII was launched early 1984 and now has an impressive customer list across several countries. He is also a regular speaker at Videotex conferences worldwide. Some of his most recent papers have covered: "Videotex - the New Communications Option" at the Pan Pacific Conference in Australia, "Through the Gateway" at Videotex International, Amsterdam, "Another Distribution Channel for Electronic Publishers" at the Electronic Publishing show at Wembley and "The Way Forward" at the Videotex User Show at the Barbican.

Lesley Beddie

Lesley Beddie is a Senior Lecturer in the Department of Computer Studies at Napier College, Edinburgh. She spent some time in industry before joining the college and now concentrates on the areas of databases and information retrieval.

Bruno Borghi

Bruno Borghi is a research engineer at TANGRAM (France), and has been in the SmScript project since 1984. He formerly worked in the medical imaging team of Thomson-CGR. His current interests are computer typography and software engineering. He received the diploma from Ecole Polytechnique in 1980 and the diploma from Ecole Nationale Superieure des Telecommunications in 1982.

P. J. Brown

Dr. Brown is Professor of Computer Science at the University of Kent at Canterbury. He has worked at IBM (UK) Laboratories, and, as Visiting Professor, at Stanford University. He is a software engineer who, for the past five years, has been working on on-line documentation, and during this time has worked with industry, academia and an Alvey project.

Manfred Burger

Manfred Burger graduated in mathematics from the University of Bayreuth, Federal Republic of Germany, in 1984. Since 1984 he has been working in the Software Technology Laboratories of the Corporate Research and Technology Division of SIEMENS AG in Munich. His current main research interests are methods and tools for software engineering, especially editors. Mr. Burger is a member of the GI (Gesellschaft für Informatik).

Michael Butcher

Michael Butcher obtained his degree in computer science in 1984 from the University College of Swansea. Now in his 3rd year of Phd research, his interests center on Electronic Office Systems (EOS), information/document retrieval and interface design. He is currently working on the development of an Interactive Graphical Interface to an EOS with the emphasis on designing to assist users of mixed ability to file, search and retrieve electronic office documents efficiently.

Peter Cadogan

Originally a chemist, with a research degree in lunar science, Peter Cadogan spent 6 years with Linotype Paul, Ltd., in software development. In 1983, he left with others to found Chelgraph, Ltd., a small research and development company specializing in hardware and software production for the graphic arts industry, where he is currently Software Manager.

Mike Clarke

Mike Clarke has a B.A. in physics from Oxford University and until recently was engaged in transport research with the Department of Transport, British Rail, and Oxford University. He has been associated with computer typesetting for some four years, and is now an independent computer consultant specializing in the development of software for transport analysis and typesetting applications.

Gordon Davies

Gordon Davies is a Senior Lecturer in Computer Science at the Open University. His research interests are software metrics and human factors in computing. He is currently Director of the SERC funded Industrial Applications of Computer Program.

Daniel de Rauglaudre

Daniel de Rauglaudre is an engineer at DIGILOG (France). He has been working for the GIPSI-SM90 since 1985 and has been in the SmScript project since 1986. His interests are compilers and interpreters. He received the Diploma from Ecole Nationale Supericure des Telecommunications in 1979.

W. P. Dodd

W. P. Dodd is a Senior Lecturer and Deputy Director of the Centre and site coordinator for QUARTET project and holds the following degrees: B.Sc. PhD. B'ham. FBCS.

Ruppert Gall

Dr. Ruppert Gall graduated in computer science from the University of Erlangen-Nürnberg, Germany. Since 1983 he has been development engineer at SIEMENS AG in Erlangen. His current main research interests are document editors and exchange of documents. Dr. Gall is a member of the GI (Gesellschaft für Informatik) and ACM (Association for Computing Machinery).

N. S. Hall

N. S. Hall is a Research Associate for BLEND Graphics Project and holds the following degrees: B.Sc. M.Sc. B'ham.

Ulrike Harke

Ulrike Harke graduated in computer science from the Technical University of Munich, Germany in 1984. Since 1984 she has been working in the Software Technology Laboratories of the Corporate Research and Technology Division of SIEMENS AG in Munich. Her current main research interests are methods and tools for software engineering, especially editors. Ms. Harke is a member of the GI (Gesellschaft für Informatik).

John Honeywell

John Honeywell is Assistant Editor of TODAY, which he joined in April, six weeks after launch. He has worked in journalism for more than 20 years, and was a senior production journalist on the (uncomputerised!) Daily Express for almost 10 years.

Darrel Ince

Darrel Ince is Professor of Computer Science at the Open University. His research interests are: software prototyping, software metrics and formal methods of software development. He is currently director of a SERC funded project concerned with software engineering training.

S. Laflin

Lecturer in Computer Science with special interest in computer graphics and associated with BLEND Graphics Project. S. Laflin holds the following degrees: B.Sc., M.Phil Lond., MBCS AFIMA.

Yuen Ping Low

Yuen Ping Low is a research student at University College London. She is also a student member of the BCS Human Computer Interaction Specialist Group. Her research interests are multimedia documents, human factors, object-oriented techniques, software engineering and graphical user interfaces.

Nenad Marovac

Nenad Marovac was born in Yugoslavia. He obtained his Dipl. Ing. in Control Engineering from Electrotechnical Facultet, University of Belgrade, and his PhD in Computer Science (computer graphics) at Imperial College, London University. In his teaching career he was Visiting Professor in the Department of Computer Science in SUNY at Buffalo, and regular faculty in the School of Computer Science at McGill University in Montreal, Massachusetts State at Framingham, and now at San Diego State University. He is a Research Fellow at CSS-Xerox in San Diego.

Pat Napier

Pat Napier is the Serials Librarian at Napier College. She has worked in music and industrial libraries and is a member of the Institute of Information Scientists.

Jenny Preece

Jenny Preece is a Lecturer at the Open University. Her research interests are concerned with interface design methodology, principles, evaluation and user modelling.

Stephane Querel

Stephane Querel has been with the GIPSI-SM90 research and development group at Rocquencourt since 1984. His research interests include graphics editors, document production, and computer typography. He received the Diploma from Ecole Polytechnique in 1982 and the Diploma from Ecole Nationale Supericure des Telecommunications in 1984.

L. Robertson

Mrs. L. Robertson is working in computer typesetting with a printer. She holds an MA (hons) in History from Aberdeen University.

Bruce Spicer

Bruce Spicer is Senior Information Systems Planner at the British Petroleum Research Centre. He has been with the BP Group for five years working on office systems and their integration with DP and telecommunications. Previous experience includes a spell in the civil service, life assurance and management consultancy for both the public and private sectors.

Robert Stutely

Robert Stutely is Deputy Head of Technical Services at Her Majesty's Stationery Office, a position he has held since 1976. Prior to that he was a programmer and systems analyst at HMSO working on computer typesetting systems. He is responsible for text processing in Technical Services and is a member of several committees of the British Standards Institution and the International Organization for Standardization. Robert Stutely has an honours degree in printing technology and is a member of the Institute of Printing.

Adrian R. Warman

Adrian R. Warman is a research student at University College London. He is a student member of BCS and BCS Human Computer Interaction Specialist Group. His research interests include communication, information theory, multimedia documents, operating system, software engineering and human factors.

R. Whitaker

Dr. R. Whitaker has been closely involved in text to typesetting problems for the last two years. He holds a BSc in Electronic Engineering, an MSc in Material Science and a PhD in Control Engineering. Current interests are in robotics.

Mark Woodman

Mark Woodman is a Lecturer in Computing at the Open University where he has written a number of units for computer science courses. He is currently writing material for the new undergraduate course in software engineering. His primary research area is software engineering in which he has published a number of papers on syntax directed documents formatting systems. His background in document systems comes from his work on the Open University prestigeous graphics and audio workstation, Cyclops, whose commercial successor won a BCS innovation award in 1984.

INDEX